COLLEGE MATTERS GUIDE TO GETTING INTO THE ELITE COLLEGE OF YOUR DREAMS

COLLEGE MATTERS GUIDE TO GETTING INTO THE ELITE COLLEGE OF YOUR DREAMS

Editors

Jacquelyn Kung (Executive Editor, Harvard)
Melissa Dell (Executive Editor, Harvard)
Joanna Chan (Content Editor, Harvard)

Contributing Authors

Katherine Jane Bacuyag (Brown)
Angelique Dousis (MIT)
Jane Feng (Stanford)
Otis Gaddis (Harvard)
Mitch Ginsburgh (Northwestern)
Kiran Gupta (Harvard)
Evelyn Huang (Stanford)
Kelly Perry (Harvard)
Rachelle Seibolt (Brown)
Erin Sprague (Harvard)
Manik Suri (Harvard)
Alicia Tam (Yale)

M c G R A W - H I L L

NEW YORK   CHICAGO   SAN FRANCISCO   LISBON   LONDON
MADRID   MEXICO CITY   MILAN   NEW DELHI   SAN JUAN   SEOUL
SINGAPORE   SYDNEY   TORONTO

The McGraw·Hill Companies

1 2 3 4 5 6 7 8 9 0   DOC/DOC   0 9 8 7 6 5 4

ISBN 0-07-144532-3

This publication is designed to provide accurate and authoritative information in regard to the subject matter covered. It is sold with the understanding that neither the author nor the publisher is engaged in rendering legal, accounting, or other professional service. If legal advice or other expert assistance is required, the services of a competent professional person should be sought.—From a declaration of principles jointly adopted by a committee of the American Bar Association and a committee of publishers

McGraw-Hill books are available at special discounts to use as premiums and sales promotions, or for use in corporate training programs. For more information, please write to the Director of Special Sales, Professional Publishing, McGraw-Hill, Two Penn Plaza, New York, NY 10121-2298. Or contact your local bookstore.

 This book is printed on recycled, acid-free paper containing a minimum of 50% recycled de-inked paper.

Library of Congress Cataloging-in-Publication Data

College Matters guide to getting into the elite college of your dreams / editors, Jacquelyn Kung, co-managing editor, Melissa Dell, co-managing editor, Joanna Chan, content editor ; contributing authors, Katherine Bacuyag ... [et al.].
    p. cm.
  Includes index.
  ISBN 0-07-144532-3 (alk. paper)
  1. College choice—United States. 2. Universities and colleges—United States—Admission.
I. Title: Guide to getting in to the elite college of your dreams. II. Kung, Jacquelyn. III. Dell, Melissa. IV. Chan, Joanna. V. Bacuyag, Katherine. VI. College Matters (Organization)

LB2350.5.C6474 2004
378.1'61'0973—dc22   2004012710

This book is dedicated to our loving parents, who have put up with our nutty ways for more years than they care to count. We couldn't have done it without their support. Thank you, Mom and Dad!

(Oh, by the way, sorry for the sky-high phone bills. It wasn't us...uh, really!)

CONTENTS

FOREWORD

Having just recently hung up my "Sorting Hat" after thirty-five years as dean of admission at Swarthmore, Stanford, and Princeton, if anyone had asked me if I'd be picking up a "how-to" book for students approaching college admissions, I'd have said "no way!"

But this book fell into my lap as a result of Harvard's dean of admission, a longtime colleague in the field who suggested to the book's authors that they ask me to get off my duff in retirement, read the book, and consider writing a foreword.

Well, I've done just that and admit to having enjoyed the book a great deal. For one thing, it is written by college students who themselves are not far removed from the college admission process. They have managed to look back on their own and their friends' still fresh experiences and gleaned from those experiences a lot of wise, objective, and very useful advice. As someone who sat on the other side of the desk for many years, I not only found myself nodding my head in agreement with 99 percent of the advice being offered; I was impressed with how comprehensive that advice is.

These authors have obviously learned the art of how to treat a subject seriously without taking themselves too seriously. The tone is nicely informal without being distracting.

My hunch is that while you may already have or will hear bits of the advice presented here from others, for example, your teachers, guidance counselors, or college admissions officers, you'll welcome and be reassured by hearing it directly from these fifteen savvy and sensible young men and women.

I confess I also like this book because unlike just about every other "how-to" book on college admissions, this one was not written for commercial gain by the authors, but rather for the benefit of College Matters and the students it works with.

If I have one concern about the book it's that if lots of students and their families read it and make use of the advice being offered (which I hope happens), college admission officers will find it harder than ever to make decisions among those who have prepared well, applied thoughtfully, and presented excellent applications.

Finally, I think everything in the pages that follow supports well two of my own favorite admonitions to prospective students and their families: (A) Always read the instructions first; and, (B) Keep in mind that wherever you attend college, "batteries are not included" and "some assembly is required."

Enjoy the book. More importantly, benefit from it. And don't forget to thank the authors when the time comes.

Fred A. Hargadon
Former Dean of Admission at Swarthmore, Stanford, and Princeton

ACKNOWLEDGMENTS

Perhaps more than other books, this one has benefited from the help of many, many incredibly giving people. In particular, we would like to thank the following individuals for their support:

All the chapter authors, who have spent long hours on their chapters in lieu of coursework, paid-work, and/or weekend parties. Fred Hargadon, recently-retired Dean of Princeton, Stanford, and Swarthmore Admissions, for penning the foreword. Bill Fitzsimmons, Dean of Harvard Admissions, for introducing us to Dean Hargadon. Jeannie Lang of Let's Get Ready! for her steadfast vigilance for College Matters and our book initiative. Sally Levy and Jennifer Geetter of the law firm McDermott Will & Emery for helping us set up the scholarship fund and for keeping College Matters out of any potential trouble. Greg Skidmore of Harvard Law School (HLS) for his work on the scholarship fund and other legal knick-knacks. Lisa Dealy and Lee Branson of HLS's Pro Bono Service Program for putting us in contact with Sally, Jenn, and Greg. Roger Ediger and Bill Shaw of the law firm Mitchell & Declerck for drafting our author contracts. Dean Whitla of the Harvard Graduate School of Education for his support of the College Matters research to make sure that our book would reach minority and first generation college students and for his contribution to our Special Report on the Application. C. Darryl Uy, Assistant Director of Admissions at Brown University, for his contribution to the Special Report. Heidi Metcalf and Kim Dean of Partnership for the Future for their input to the Parents and Minorities chapters. Coach Mike Barber for his savvy tips on the Student Athletes chapter. Judith Kidd, Meg Brooks, and Mike Bishop from Harvard's Phillips Brooks House, for offering help every step of the way. Melissa's brother Chris Dell for his 15-year-old perspective of what's "cool" and what's "lame." Nilanj Desai for creating the College Matters Web site, and Alex Payson for taking over after Nilanj. Ryan Levesque, Jesse Warren, Frances Brooks, Ramey Ko, Amber Ludwig, Tiffany Chang, Michael Cover, Ryan Stewart, and Amy Achor for their involvement in College Matters.

Ross Cohen for his early help in keeping us out of trouble. Yiting Liu, Riki Helbling, Robert Gee, and Liliya Ostafiychuk for their insight and comments on the book. Clay Pell for his sympathetic ear. Barbara Gilson and Adrinda Kelly of McGraw-Hill for being so great to work with. And last but certainly not least, Jim Perry for introducing us to McGraw-Hill in the first place.

Jacquelyn, Melissa, and Joanna
College Matters Editors

INTRODUCTION

Let's start this book with a confession. None of us on the editing team usually reads the Introductions of books. However, we love to read advice columns, so in that same spirit and to make this intro user-friendly, we decided to lay it out as a Q&A session:

What Is College Matters?

Started in 1999, College Matters is an educational nonprofit run by students. We have given seminars across the world about the ins and outs of applying to selective colleges and winning scholarships. During our seminars, we share aspects of the admissions process that we learned the hard way and only wish we could have known when applying ourselves. It was during these seminars that people started asking us for a book, so we put our heads together and wrote one. Here it is, by popular request.

College Matters has set up a scholarship fund using the proceeds from the sales of this book. Flip to the back of this book to find an application. For more information about College Matters visit our Web site at www.college matters.org.

What Are the Overarching Principles behind This Book?

As a wise person once said, "Learn from the mistakes of others because you don't have time to make them all yourself." Sure, there are plenty of books out there, written by former admissions officers and college counselors that claim to help you work through the college application process. However, what they lack is the insight of someone from your side, someone who has recently gone through the application process. What we offer you is the collective experience of more than fifteen students from the top colleges in the United States who have successfully navigated through the college admissions maze, gathering more than half a million dollars in independent scholarships in the process.

Along with information from admissions officers at prestigious colleges, this book packs tips from sage cohorts who will tell you what led to their success, and what they would do if they could do it again.

Who Is This Book Intended For?

This book was written for students who are aiming for admission to selective universities (admissions rates of under 50 percent) or targeting scholarships to their university of choice (whatever the selectivity rating). It shares with you, and all hopeful students, the secrets of students who have learned to beat the admissions game. Parents, high school counselors, teachers, and college advisors—in addition to students—have found our seminars to be useful, so they too should find this book to be chock full of good nuggets of advice.

What about International Students?

This book is also full of useful information for international students. But applying as an international student takes a few extra steps. Please contact us directly through our Web site to be put in touch with an international student who can help guide you.

How Should I Use This Book— Where Should I Start?

Although all of the advice contained in this book should be helpful, we realize that students who read this book will be at different stages in the college application process. Skim through the table of contents and start with what you find most relevant. If it all seems relevant, then start at the beginning.

When Is the Best Time to Use This Book?

Students should read this book during their sophomore, junior, and senior years of high school. Whether you're a motivated sophomore or a senior about to apply (or the parent of one), this book is packed full of tips for you. If you're really on the ball you can start earlier, but the bulk of what you can do to prepare for the college application process lies between your sophomore and senior years.

Aren't You Just Adding to the Admissions Frenzy?

Critics of this book might say that we are just adding to the college admissions brouhaha, putting even more pressure on already-overworked high school students to succeed. We would reply that we actually wrote this book with the opposite in mind; we aim to cut through the noise and separate the good advice from the bad, equipping you with the information you need in order to make your application process as smooth as possible.

   Furthermore, we don't get paid to conduct our seminars or write this book. Instead, we volunteer our time and efforts because we want to help. Through feedback from students, we've found that the best way to help lay out the admissions game is to tell you about our experiences and the lessons we've learned. That's what we do in our seminars, and that's what we do in this book.

What If I Feel Overwhelmed by What I Read in This Book?

As you read, you might panic and think that you will never get in to the top college of your choice. Don't be scared! Have confidence in yourself. While we can't guarantee that you'll get into your dream college or win big scholarship bucks (nobody can give you this 100 percent guarantee), we can guarantee that you won't achieve any of your dreams if you don't try! Remember that this book represents the compilation of the advice and experiences of many high-achieving students. No one has utilized every trick-of-the-trade that this book reveals, so seniors especially, don't get discouraged if you haven't followed many of our suggestions to date. Utilize the short-term strategies, and you still may be in good shape.

Now that Q&A is done, we want to thank you for picking up this book. We hope you find it useful and would love to hear your feedback once you finish. Simply email us at feedback@collegematters.org. If you are a student, we also hope that you can join the College Matters team when you get to college. There is an application form at the back of this book for all of you who are interested.

We hope to hear from you soon!

Jacquelyn, Melissa, and Joanna
College Matters Editors

CHAPTER ONE

HIGH SCHOOL COURSES

Joanna Chan, Harvard

When you consider your life at high school, you may conjure images ranging from the exciting to the ho-hum. Your pulse might rise with thoughts of your current love interest sitting across from you in class. Or maybe you think of rushing off to an after-school activity, an athletic practice, or a music lesson. Or maybe you're in a bad mood because you have a five-page lit paper due tomorrow and you just can't seem to think of a good topic sentence. (Blank computer screens and fresh sheets of paper have this certain way of staring back at you without being very encouraging.) Maybe it's not a five-page lit paper that's causing the consternation. Imagine instead that it's your *entire high school career.* "Oh, but I've already figured out this high school thing," you think. "The whole reason I'm reading this book in the first place is to get into college, not to learn how to survive high school—that's already a piece of cake. Anyone can do it."

Newsflash: Anyone can "get through" high school, but can anyone also get into those top universities, lovely and almost mythical to the mind? And is your university of choice just going to give away scholarships to anyone who happens to apply for them? Okay, maybe I'm being a bit melodramatic, but you should consider the facts. Of all the students in your high school—better yet, of all the students in your city, state, and country—not everyone will be able to attend a selective university or win a big scholarship. What was it that Darwin said about "survival of the fittest"? You get the point.

Now, instead of thinking about your life in high school, consider where you might want to be at this time next year, or a few years from now. It is a good idea to consider how you're going to get yourself to that place, even if the farthest ahead you usually plan is what to eat for lunch the next day.

Got a Plan?

The first step on the road to getting into your dream college and winning big bucks in scholarships is, surprisingly enough, planning your high school courses. This course plan will serve as your roadmap through four years of high school; later on, your official transcript of courses will provide the academic basis for your college applications. Your course plan is a living document that you can alter to suit your needs and wants. Live it. Love it. It will take you places! (Literally—think college.)

Creating the Roadmap: May the Brown-Nosing Begin!

When planning which high school classes to take, a good place to start is your high school guidance counselor. This person is actually important—really, really important! Why, you ask? By meeting with your counselor, you'll at least learn which courses are available and at best get über-useful advice from someone who knows your school's system. Perhaps even more importantly, most colleges require a counselor recommendation. Granted, most high schools, particularly the very large ones, do not have counselors that know their students particularly well. That's why it is important to set yourself apart. Admissions officers will be wowed when they read the letter of recommendation from your counselor saying how special you are.

Breaking It Down

When meeting with your counselor, you need to find out exactly what requirements you must fulfill. After all, you will have a tough time getting into your dream college if you can't even graduate from high school because you failed to fulfill certain state or high school requirements. Sure, there are ways of getting around certain courses: Do them by correspondence, take summer school courses, or get a waiver by attending vocational courses. Doing so will allow you to take classes in subjects that you really care about instead of wasting time in classes you have absolutely no interest in, just because the government or your school feels that you should have to take them to graduate. Of course, often what your school requires for graduation is part of what any college will require.

Make a list of the high school classes you plan to take along with the number of units (parts of a school year, be it semester or trimester), so that you can see your course plan at a glance. The following is a list of the bread-and-butter classes that most selective colleges recommend (see www.collegematters.org for examples of real sample schedules):

Number of Years	Class
4	Math (preferably one unit of calculus)
4	English
4	Science (including Chemistry, Physics, and Biology)
4	Foreign Language (preferably four years of the same one)
2	History

Some colleges recommend that you take additional courses like economics or government. A lot of what you decide to take will depend on what your school can offer you. The paragraphs that follow give a breakdown of different types of schools and how to approach designing a schedule for each one.

Public School: Kind of Like School for the Proletariat— Um, Yeah...

Most public schools offer different tracks: "honors" classes and "regular" classes at the very least. Classes designated honors will probably have more work, which can be a bummer. What's the payoff? You'll learn more, your grade point average (GPA) will usually be higher, and colleges will definitely notice. The moral of the story: *Take as many honors classes as you can.* If there is one thing that successful college students have in common, it's that they worked hard during high school and pushed themselves to take as many of the most challenging courses that they could. In case you're wondering, I attended a very large public high school, with a graduating class of 1085 students. Despite the enormity of my school, I made it a priority to personalize my schedule (read on to find out more).

3

Students from public high schools are not necessarily at a disadvantage when it comes time to apply to selective universities. In fact, some public high schools have well-established connections to selective universities. Examples include Stuyvesant and Hunter high schools in New York; Lexington High School in Massachusetts; Thomas Jefferson High School in Virginia; and Saratoga, Gunn, and Palo Alto high schools in California. However, the vast majority of students at selective colleges do not come from these high schools. In fact, students who come from "underperforming" schools who have been successful nonetheless sometimes get extra attention in the admissions process because they have overcome obstacles. Apply the advice that follows in this chapter and you'll be in good shape, whatever the status of your public high school.

Private School or Preparatory Academy – $$$ cha-ching! $$$

The same philosophy of succeeding in public schools applies to private schools: Take the most rigorous schedule that you can handle without killing yourself. Going to a private school as opposed to a public school will neither hurt nor help your chances of getting into your college of choice. Students at elite prep schools are both advantaged and disadvantaged. Many of the counselors at these schools are former admissions officers at top colleges, so they often help *a lot* in the process. They may even call up their buddies—current admissions committee members—at their former schools to put in a good word for the most stellar candidates.

Nevertheless, students at top boarding schools and prep schools (for example, St. Paul's, Exeter, Andover, Milton, Groton, Deerfield, and Harvard-Westlake) are compared to their classmates. These ultracompetitive "feeder schools" (that is, schools that send most of their graduating class to selective colleges) often have rigorous entrance exams and thus are comprised almost entirely of top students. More of the students will have their eyes on the really top universities and will be working hard to build a great résumé and transcript. That means that being a student at these schools isn't a guaranteed ticket into your college of choice. Elite colleges will check to see that you have taken the hardest classes possible while still performing well. Since the majority of students at these schools are stellar, you have to find your own way to shine even when compared to your classmates. As any admissions officer will tell you, regardless of the type of high school you attend, the selection of high school courses and your performance in them will serve as fundamental criteria when decisions are made about who gets in and who doesn't.

Magnet School—Attractive Prospect? (Pun Intended)

Interested in arts? Sciences? Whatever your interests, there's likely a magnet school out there for you. These institutions draw talented students in subject-specific areas from far and wide. If you're already sure you know what you want to do later in life, the advantage of magnet schools is that you get to develop specialized skills without having to take as many classes in subject areas that you might detest. Magnet schools will allow you to specialize in a specific area such as science or performing arts, which could give you a head start if you want a career in one of these fields. However, some magnet schools may require you to sacrifice the broad depth of curriculum that you get in a regular high school. Others require you to live away from home (which means you will have to pay to do your laundry and eat nasty dorm food even earlier than normal).

Some of these magnet schools may even offer programs where students concurrently receive college credit while still in high school. Examples include the Texas Academy of Math and Sciences (TAMS) at the University of North Texas, and, Bard High School Early College and Simon's Rock College of Bard, in New York City. Check out a complete list of schools specializing in math and sciences at www.ncssmst.org. Students at these and similar university magnet programs bypass the standardized exams and receive college credit immediately on a college transcript from that university. Of course, following graduation of that magnet program, the student may eventually choose to attend a different, perhaps more elite, college. Other universities will not necessarily accept college credit from the magnet school, but there is a good chance that some of it will transfer. Admissions rates into selective colleges vary depending on the particular university magnet program, and these statistics are usually available directly from the program you might have in mind. These magnet programs may or may not charge tuition, so check with each individual school for details.

If you attend a specialized university magnet school, you'll have the opportunity to interact with really smart students in a university-like setting. However, one disadvantage may be the need to compete with your high-achieving classmates (the small fish in a big pond effect), which could hurt your chances of getting into an elite college. At the same time, colleges recognize the talent pool at magnet schools and often adjust accordingly. Furthermore, potential disadvantages of missing out on the typical high school experience could include things like not being able to go to the prom, participate in sports teams or events, or be part of a well-developed music program. The tuition may also be a potential barrier to attending magnet schools, although many are public and thus free.

I advise that you take the time to research your options thoroughly if you are thinking of attending a magnet school. Visit the campus, sit in on a few classes, and ask professors and students questions. Kick the tires a bit, and do all the things you would do during regular college visits. (See Chapter 9 for more information on college visits.) After all, attending a magnet school will define several years of your life, so you should be sure that you'll be happy.

If you've decided that you want to attend a magnet school, then developing your schedule will follow similar guidelines. Take as many advanced courses as possible. Chances are that there will be some sort of set requirements that the magnet school has in addition to state graduation requirements, so inquire about these. Again, ask your counselors for advice and direction.

For the Homebodies

Home schooling is yet another option for students. As with any other option, there are many pros and cons when it comes to home schooling. It is about the most personalized curriculum that you can get, with a variety of options and flexibility at your disposal. One common reason for opting for home schooling is that it frees the schedule for students who also happen to be especially serious in an extracurricular endeavor. I remember meeting people at piano competitions who were home schooled and thus were able to practice four to five hours a day! (And yes, they were *really* good.) Maybe you are home schooled for religious reasons. Or perhaps the schools in your area don't meet the standards that you'd like to set for yourself, and developing your own curriculum would be more challenging. Home schooling takes a lot of self-motivation, but it can absolutely be a great idea for some high schoolers.

One disadvantage to home schooling in the eyes of admissions officers is that getting your high school credentials from home doesn't give selective universities an idea of how you thrive in competition as compared to your peers. Home schooling means no chance for getting a high class rank, and translates into no really good frame of reference for how prepared you might be for college courses. In addition, your social, athletic, musical, student-government, and other extracurricular resources will often be limited. Make sure if you and your family elect to pursue home schooling that you venture outside the house to gain some broader experiences in areas such as community service, athletics, the arts, etc.

Supplementing School

Another way to make your application shine among the rest of the stack is to take supplemental courses. You can do this during the school year by taking a night class at a local community college or nearby university while high school is in session. Alternatively, many people opt for summer fun. If you check out my schedule later in this chapter, you will see that I took a bunch of courses during my summers to supplement my education. I thought it would be useful to learn how to touch type before I started high school (and it did help, a lot). I also accelerated my mathematics track by taking Algebra I in three weeks, which helped me to free up time for other courses during senior year. You likewise might wish to consider accelerating your coursework so that you can take college-level courses in a subject that really interests you by the time you're a high school junior or senior.

Many students are invited to participate in precollege programs after having taken part in an invitational SAT/ACT (Scholastic Achievement Test/American College Testing) program (for example, the Duke Talent Identification Program), where you take the SAT or ACT in middle school or junior high, way before the "real" time that counts for college admission. Even if you didn't participate in such programs, many opportunities are still available. Most programs are offered during high school summers. Examples include the Research Science Institute with the Massachusetts Institute of Technology (MIT) and the California Institute of Technology (Caltech) or College Experience (CE) at the University of North Texas. You may even want to consider a musical program like Tanglewood Music Festival in Massachusetts. Most universities will have these types of programs, so call them up and inquire about research opportunities or official summer programs for high school students.

If your standardized exam scores or course grades are high enough, then you can even apply for scholarships to these programs, if your family can't afford them. Furthermore, summer school programs offered through the local public school system are often paid for by tax dollars, and can thus serve as an alternative when finances are a consideration. The point is that you should take the initiative to figure out what excites you academically. This will show admissions officers that you don't mind supplementing the minimum requirements. It's impressive to colleges if you choose to attend extra classes, even when you aren't forced to do so by the state. Also, it shows colleges that you can thrive away from home.

An added bonus is that you may be able to get concurrent high school credit (see the "Grades, Grades, Grades" section later in this chapter). Of course, even if you don't get concurrent high school credit, you still win: You earn college credit hours (which may or may not be transferable), explore a subject at the college level, and gain exposure to college-style learning.

So, You're Asking for Punishment ...

Part I: Advanced Placement (AP). Regardless of whether you attend a public school, a private school, a magnet school, or even if you opt for home schooling, Advanced Placement (AP) tests are key. The Advanced Placement program is coordinated by the College Board (that is, the people who bring you the SAT) and gives you the opportunity each May to earn college credit while still in high school by taking exams in as many as thirty-four subjects (at the time of printing) across nineteen subject areas. Many schools in the United States offer Advanced Placement courses that will prepare you for the exams at the end of the year. Ask your counselor which APs are available at your school. Some schools don't have courses officially titled "AP," but students can elect to take the exams anyways. The tests cost almost $100 a pop, but this figure can be reduced, if need exists; see your counselor for details. Keep in mind that while this figure may seem expensive, a typical college class often costs thousands of dollars, so taking APs can save you and your family big bucks. For more information on AP programs, check out the official Web site for students (www.collegeboard.com/ap) and Chapter 4.

Part II: International Baccalaureate (IB). International Baccalaureate (IB) is a two-year advanced program of study that requires you to take advanced courses in six subject areas, write a 4000-word extended essay, and perform a certain number of hours of creativity (for example, music and literary publications), action, and service. The great thing about IB is that by the time you graduate, you'll already have under your belt certain things colleges really look for in a student: a rigorous, well-balanced schedule; independent research; and extracurricular involvement. If you're interested in graduating with an IB diploma, check out the Web site www.ibo.org.

So Why Take AP or IB Classes? A word of advice: If your school offers AP or IB classes, *take them!* You won't stand a prayer of getting into super-selective colleges like Columbia or Stanford if you don't take the most rigorous classes available. Here are some advantages of taking APs or IBs:

- They will demonstrate to admissions officers (as long as you do well) that you are not afraid to work your butt off to be successful.
- They will boost your GPA (most AP/IB classes are scored on a 5.0 scale instead of the traditional 4.0 scale).
- They will help you think analytically, develop good study habits, learn how to write well, and gain other skills that will be useful in college. By taking APs or IBs, you'll be one step ahead of your college class-mates who didn't take these courses.
- They might just get you out of that tantalizing 8:00 A.M. organic chem-istry class during your first semester of college or the oft-dreaded for-eign language requirement.
- They will help you win scholarship competitions by boosting your GPA and standardized test preparedness.

AP versus IB. The AP and IB programs are not mutually exclusive. I opted to do the IB program at my school while supplementing my schedule with AP courses like government and psychology. Also, if you opt to take IB courses, nothing stops you from taking a corresponding AP exam at the end of the year, and that's what most of my classmates did. Just be sure that you're mentally prepared to take exam after exam at the end of the year.

Grades, Grades, Grades

One superimportant consideration for college admissions is GPA. It might seem like a cold, woefully inadequate rubric to use to evaluate your many talents and limitless potential, but the truth is that your chances of gaining admission to selective schools, not to mention of winning any type of schol-arship, will be slim without a high GPA. Why? To some extent (certainly

Searching for Information

If you have your heart set on going to a particular school, then check out its Web site for information about recommended high school courses. Most college Web sites have a frequently asked questions (FAQs) page, where you can read up on the school and get answers to some of your burning questions. You could also call the admissions office, or even ask some students who attend the college what kinds of courses they took in high school. Finally, it is always a great idea to ask older students at your high school about the courses they took— which ones they enjoyed; which teachers were awful, enjoyable, amusing; and so on.

enough to make it one of the more important determinants of admissions), your GPA does show your capacity to study, to take notes, to score well on exams, to turn in your homework, and to "play the game of making the grade."

I like to view the GPA as a game, because adopting that attitude certainly beats viewing it as daily drudgery or a rat race. The object of the game is to make those numbers (on a 4-point scale, a 4.0 equating to an A; a 3.0 to a B, and so on) as high as possible. Different schools have different policies, so when you talk to your counselor, be sure that you understand how your school's grading scale works. Honors and AP/IB classes are usually scored on a 5.0 scale instead of a 4.0 one (like traditional classes), so strong performance in these classes will cause your GPA to go through the roof. University classes taken during the summer can sometimes count as part of your GPA as well. Inquire about your school's policy and be sure to get something in writing before you take the class.

Students often ask if it is better to take easy classes and get As or hard classes and get Bs. The classic answer that any admissions officer will give you is take hard classes *and* get As. What kind of grades you need depends on what tier of college you want to attend. For the most selective schools (and the most competitive scholarships), you'll need a very high GPA, although it doesn't necessarily have to be perfect. To attend schools that are still selective but not as selective (that is, those that accept between 20 and 50 percent of applicants), you'll still need a solid GPA (aim for above 3.0). According to the University of Virginia (UVA) Web site, the entering class of one of their schools had an average GPA of 3.4, but the range of GPAs of accepted students went from 2.8 to 4.0. A poor GPA may be offset somewhat by awesome standardized scores (SATs or ACTs), but try not to depend on that. Regardless of the selectivity rating of your dream college, remember to choose rigorous classes, study hard, and show admissions officers that you aren't afraid to meet a challenge. Your grades don't have to be perfect, but if you work hard and do well, it will pay off.

Senior Slackers Beware!

Try not to succumb to senioritis, which happens when students in their final year no longer care about their grades or coursework. This especially applies if you are taking APs—remember, you will have to take all those exams in May! Plus, colleges will not hesitate to rescind admissions decisions if your grades drop significantly.

Real Examples and Sample Schedules

Below I've inserted several course schedules, representing varying degrees of difficulty, to give you a few examples of how planning a schedule works. Remember, these are only sample schedules intended to give you an idea of the classes that students admitted to selective colleges take. They are by no means meant to be followed as a model.

Hard-Core

Table 1.1 shows a sample hard-core class schedule. (And I mean really hard-core; don't be worried if this seems a bit overwhelming.)

TABLE 1.1 HARD-CORE CLASS SCHEDULE

Plano East Senior High Official Transcript
Student: Joanna Chan

9th Grade	10th Grade	11th Grade	12th Grade
Honors English I	Honors English II	IB English III	IB English IV
Honors Humanities (gifted program)	Honors Humanities	AP Psychology	IB Biology II

TABLE 1.1 HARD-CORE CLASS SCHEDULE (continued)

9th Grade	10th Grade	11th Grade	12th Grade
Compacted World Geography with Humanities	Compacted U.S.History with Humanities	AP U.S. Government	IB Biology II laboratory
Honors Biology I	Honors World History	IB Economics	AP Statistics
Honors Algebra II	Honors Chemistry I	IB Physics I	IB Spanish V
Honors Spanish II	Honors Pre-Calculus	IB Calculus	IB Theory of Knowledge
Orchestra	Honors Spanish III	IB Spanish IV	Honors Orchestra IV
Physical Education	Medical Science Careers	Honors Orchestra III	Honors Mind Journeys II
	Physical Education	Honors Mind Journeys I (independent study)	

9th Grade Summer	10th Grade Summer	11th Grade Summer
Southern Methodist University (TAG program):	University of Salamanca, Spain.	University of Texas at Dallas.
Public Discourse (debate)	Coursework in: Culture	Coursework in: General Chemistry
Psychology for college credit	Conversation Grammar	General Chemistry Laboratory

Comments about Joanna's Hard-Core Schedule: Many (but not all) of my classmates at Harvard took a similar level of AP/IB classes. They didn't all do summer work, however, and many students accepted to selective colleges have as rigorous a schedule. If this schedule seems overwhelming to you but you still want to go to a highly selective school, I recommend that you aim somewhere in between this and the medium-core example.

Medium Core

Table 1.2 shows a sample medium-core class schedule.

TABLE 1.2 MEDIUM-CORE CLASS SCHEDULE

St. Paul's Official Transcript
Student: Aaron

9th Grade	10th Grade	11th Grade	12th Grade
Honors Biology	Chemistry I	Honors Chemistry II	Honors Physics
Honors English I	Honors English II	AP European History	U.S. Government
Civics	Geometry	Honors English III	AP English
Honors Algebra II	Honors American History	Honors Pre-Calculus	AP Calculus
French I	French II	French III	French IV
Physical Education	Choir	Choir	Choir
Choir	Studio Art	Independent Study: The U.S. Civil Rights Movement	Independent Study: France Under Napoleon

Comments about Aaron's Medium-Core Schedule: This schedule, while not as hardcore as the last, is still very solid. If Aaron's school had offered twelve AP classes and he'd only taken advantage of three, this wouldn't bode too well for admission into top schools. However, because his school only offered three AP classes, and he took all of them, he was still competitive for entrance into highly selective colleges. (His grades and other parts of his application were excellent.)

Soft Core

Table 1.3 shows a sample soft-core class schedule.

TABLE 1.3 SOFT-CORE CLASS SCHEDULE

South High Official Transcript
Student: Josh

9th Grade	10th Grade	11th Grade	12th Grade
English I	English II	English III	AP English
Algebra II	Honors Geometry	Honors Pre-Calculus	AP Government
Physical Science	Honors Biology	Honors Chemistry	Choir
Honors World History	Honors American History	Geography	French II
Choir	Choir	Choir	Home Ec
Physical Education	Psychology	French I	Anatomy and Physiology
Keyboarding	Business I	Business II	Logical Reasoning

Comments about Josh's Soft-Core Schedule: Unlike the previous examples, this schedule didn't take full advantage of all the AP offerings of the school. Compared with the schedules of other students attending this same high school, Josh's schedule might appear less rigorous, which is disadvantageous when it comes to applying to über-selective schools. This schedule also shows a classic case of senioritis. Despite these potential areas for improvement, Josh had very good grades, high standardized test scores, and solid extracurriculars, so this schedule might be enough to get into a midrange selective school.

Think It's Too Late?

So let's say that you're already in the middle of your junior year, or are already starting senior year. If you're reading this section, you might think that all this advice is pretty much useless at this point. While it's true that the best efforts are made early on, you can still learn a thing or two. First, you should not succumb to senioritis. Go ahead and challenge yourself by continuing that foreign language, and take honors or AP/IB class that you have the prerequisites for. Also, there are plenty of AP classes that don't require prerequisites, such as government, economics, or psychology. If you work hard, you're going to learn something and you might even end up with some college credit.

If your school has an independent study option, you can even design your own semester project, which could be related to community service or whatever academic subject you may be interested in pursuing. The final grade might be assigned based on the creation of a new organization, a service day, or an essay describing some independent research at the level of a minithesis. The bottom line is that you don't want to quit while you're ahead, and you don't want to lose steam during this final stretch. There are plenty of options for you to pursue, so start brainstorming and have fun designing your master plan.

Studying Smart

There is no maximally efficient way to study smart during high school. All of us are pulled in different directions every day, and it's so easy to become distracted by the Internet, television, extracurricular activities, and all that other fun (nonschool) stuff. Fortunately, we're not robots and we don't have to study in a perfectly efficient manner every day to be successful. However, having good study habits does help. The following are some guidelines for studying smart.

What to Do

- Take detailed notes in class.
- Start assignments early.
- Schedule your time.

- Study each subject every day.
- Drill the information with vocabulary lists or flash cards.
- Study with friends, if it's not too distracting.
- Utilize your weekends (how else are you going to finish all that reading?).
- *Unplug*. (Instant Messaging (IM), Hotmail, Kazaa, your cell phone, and so on).

What Not to Do:

- Overcommit.
- Pull (near) all-nighters.
- Cram at the last minute.
- Be disorganized with your books and assignments.
- Space out during class.
- Compare yourself to others.

And on That Note ...

I'd like to <u>underline</u>, **bold**, ***asterisk, and bloody emphasize as much as possible that how well you perform in your high school courses is important, but there is not a single "perfect" or "best" transcript or class schedule. Take courses that spark a genuine interest, and you'll be more likely to work harder and make better grades anyway! The most important thing is to challenge yourself. Admissions officers can spot determination in a transcript and appreciate the difficulty level of your classes. People reading your application will appreciate *you* and consider you as an entire individual. So have fun, study hard, and go for it!

HIGH SCHOOL ACTIVITIES

Jacquelyn Kung, Harvard

In high school? Involved in activities? Well, then, you know the drill: scrambling from the classroom to after-school practices to meeting after meeting after meeting. On weekends, there are volunteer projects and competitions (math, science, music, sports: take your pick). Oh, and sleep? What's that?

Whoever you might be, this chapter gives you the skinny on activities. It begins with an explanation of why the Activities section of the application exists and how much it is worth in college admissions. Next, it tackles my personal pet peeve: the "fluffy" advice that people give you when they find out you're applying to college. After that, the chapter breaks down each year of high school and talks about what you can do to set yourself up with fun, meaningful activities. Finally, it ends with advice on how to package your activities and awards, with a heavy emphasis on creating a great résumé. Got all that? Okay, let's get started.

Activities Overview

Why the Activities Section of the Application Exists

When the college admissions officers rip open your hefty application packet, they know nothing about you: neither how incredibly hilarious you are nor what a stud you may be. In a way, it's like your slate has been wiped clean, and you get to introduce them to the "you" that you want them to see. Of course, when you're actually mired in the application itself, it's easy to lose sight of this "big picture" view and get caught up in trudging through the process of completing all the sections.

All the sections on the application, frivolous as they might seem, contribute pieces to the puzzle of "you" for the admissions team. For example, the way you describe activities and the order you list them in shows the relative importance that you place on each one. Ultimately, the activities you participate in serve as a reflection of what kind of person you are.

Here's an important note up front about lying: Just don't. Not only is it wrong, but admissions officers have lots of experience and funny ways of sniffing out when something isn't quite right. You will be automatically rejected if it is discovered that you have lied, and from the way admissions people at colleges seem to know each other, you might be blacklisted from more than one school.

The Activities section is critical to the college application because it gives the admissions committee a sense of the energy that you dedicate to your interests and therefore what you can contribute to their college community. It's important to the selective colleges that you can juggle multiple activities in high school along with your coursework, because they reason that you will be able to handle the tougher load at college (and still be able to save the world on weekends).

Elite colleges also have a duty to make sure that they stay as prestigious as possible. They always want their campuses to be abuzz with life and activity. A dynamic college campus attracts media attention, especially when reporters can gush on and on about student-sponsored charity events on campus or world-class conferences promoting social awareness. With this positive attention, the status and prestige of the college goes up. This translates into an increase in the number of applications from crème-de-la-crème students. Alumni are happier with their alma mater, and giving rates increase. The same goes for scholarship competitions. The more impressive the winner bios that scholarship funds can publish in their newsletters and read aloud at their banquets, the more donations they'll get to fund more scholarships.

Although better recognition and media attention is probably not at the forefront of admissions officers' minds, you'd better believe that they're envisioning your niche within their lively campus. Your activities say something about your role in your school and community. (Just remember:

They want world leaders, they want mini–Mother Teresas, and they want the best.) If you're just getting by with classes—even if you're getting by with very good grades—that shows someone who lacks drive, is a total nerd, or both.

How Much Is the Activities Section Worth?

The Activities section, like almost everything on the college application, is important, but just how important it is will vary from college to college. Some schools put equal weight on activities and the other areas of the application, while other colleges might specify an approximate percentage for activities in the admissions rubric. The general rule of thumb is, the smaller the school, the more important the personal elements (essay and activities) of the application will be. In addition, the more selective a college is, the more important the Activities section becomes for distinguishing one applicant from another.

In general, students shooting for the über-selective colleges (such as Harvard, Stanford, Princeton, and other Ivy League or lofty sorts) should have stellar academics and a host of solid activities. Students aiming for schools in the 25 to 50 percent selectivity range (such as The University of California–Los Angeles (UCLA), University of Virginia, or Emory) should have good academics and good activities. So in either case (superselective or just plain selective), you should show that you are involved with activities. However, the more selective the school (or scholarship), the more exceptional your activities and talents should be.

Most of the students I've met at Harvard were involved with one or more mind-boggling activities in high school. Granted, some of them were superstars in one field only, flagged by some special national or international title (for example, top-ranked South African golfer). Others were just involved in a lot of cool things in high school. It makes for diversity and a fun weirdness among students.

My classmates were definitely diverse, fun, and weird. For instance, during my sophomore year, the guy who lived upstairs from me in my house (Harvard lingo for "dorm") was a world champion juggler. He could juggle something like twelve or more objects at the same time (and here I am, a klutz with just three). Top colleges also boast more than a handful of Intel Science Scholars, Teen Jeopardy Champions, Geography Bee Winners, NFL (National Forensic League) Champions, and America's Junior Miss winners.

On the other hand, one of my best friends in college was a well-rounded, non-title-holding high school student. He organized his high school blood drive, played some basketball and volleyball, and was involved in a splattering of activities. With this quick snapshot of students in my college class, you can start to see that the admissions officers are trying to combine all sorts of flavors together to form an interesting, dynamic class.

One important piece of advice to remember is to do something unique. Being student body president at a huge high school or captain of your state-winning football team often just isn't enough for admission to über-selective colleges. Admissions officers have told us that you really have to have something unique about your activities. Not superweird, just unusual. This will make you stand out in the pool of applicants, leaving a lasting impression with the admissions team or scholarship committee that makes decisions two weeks and three hundred applications later. On a personal note, I quickly discovered that my violin and piano talents weren't unique, as every Asian girl I knew who was applying to colleges was an accomplished violinist *and* pianist. I had to differentiate myself with unique activities. In particular, I used my musical talents in community service, which was a little out of the ordinary. In addition to being unique, strive for excellence with your talents. Try participating in a music festival or trying out for all-region. Even an ordinary activity can become something special when you achieve something extraordinary with it.

Defluffing the Fluff

It's amazing the number of people who will try to offer you advice once they find out you're applying to college: parents, relatives, neighbors, teachers, high school counselors, women in line at the post office, and so on. You'll hear things like: "Oh, you're applying to a selective school? Then you should have some activities under your belt. Just be involved with things you like, and you'll be okay." And, "Don't get involved with too much—just one or two high-profile things should be fine." Or, "You should go start something to show them that you've got initiative."

I wanted to scream when I heard all this chatter, especially when I probed behind the surface and nobody had any substantial answers. To me, this advice all sounded so vague and fluffy, like things that I had heard a gazillion times from the five corners of the world. But how could I act on it? I didn't really know. Let's pick apart these fluffy sayings and explore how they all relate to your actual life.

"Get Involved in Things That You Like, and You'll Be Fine"

Applying this piece of advice is tricky; it is the true-false paradox of activities. True, it's great to get involved in things that you enjoy. A Girl-Watching Club, for example. A lot of guys would love to be involved in a club like this. However, how will The Girl-Watching Club hold up when compared with The National Honor Society and the National Youth Movement for Volunteerism? Not very well. The reason is probably obvious to you. The merits of the Girl-Watching Club are minuscule compared to that of other, better-known clubs with slightly more altruistic objectives.

This brings up an important point: Some clubs are better than others. Most clubs out there are good, but some are simply not as good as others for the purposes of your application. Let's look at another scenario.

Take, for example, the Math-Science Club and the National Honor Society. Which of these two clubs would be considered "better"? To answer this, you must first ask yourself to what kind of schools you're applying. If the colleges you are interested in are geared toward the math-science areas—the Massachusetts Institute of Technology (MIT) or the California Institute of Technology (Caltech), for instance—then the math-science clubs are likely to have more clout with the admissions officers. As a side note, while you definitely want to be involved with the math-science club for schools like MIT, having something else unique (but not generic like the honor society) would also be good. If the college is geared toward the liberal arts, the admissions folks probably won't differentiate between the Math-Science Club and National Honor Society, unless of course you've indicated that you're interested in a math or science-related program on your application.

Another factor to consider is your personal involvement in these clubs. If the rest of your application is all about your math and science awards, or if you were president of the math club, then you should definitely feel confident listing the Math-Science Club as a major activity because it goes along with the "package" that you're presenting of yourself. If you are more specialized in one particular area, it could be considered an asset to your application. It all depends on the overall look (or focus) of your application. For instance, if you have been a big teen scientist, highlight that in your activities by demonstrating your contributions to science-related activities, publications, and organizations. The key is to be able to back up your areas of specialization with lots of accomplishments.

The notion of "specialization" brings us to the next common bit of "fluffy advice" that you've probably heard:

"Choose to Be Really Involved in One or Two Things Rather Than a Lot of Things ... and Then You'll Be Fine"

Again, this is true and false. (I know, these kinds of answers are annoying, but hear me out.) For this piece of fluffy advice, it all goes back to what "really" means. If "really" means that you are at the state or national level for something, then it's great that you are putting so much time into this one activity. Understandably, you probably need to devote all your time to one thing if you are excelling at the national level. If you are at the state level, that's great, but you need something else, perhaps one or two more activities. This is especially true if you are applying to the upper echelon of the selective colleges.

Let's say, for instance, that you are on the National Junior Tennis League team. Because you have to travel all over the place and you have to practice for endless hours every week, that doesn't leave you much time to do other things. No problem. Being on the national tennis team, and perhaps even winning an amateur competition or two, will suffice for the Activities section. The focus of such an applicant is clear: tennis. You would put down "National Tennis Team" as well as other tennis-related activities, like high school varsity tennis captain and teaching tennis to community children, on the application.

But what if you're not on the National Junior Tennis team? (Most people aren't, by the way—I can't even hit the stupid ball.) Instead, you're a piano player who has won numerous local competitions and even advanced to the district or state level (but not past that). Great, that's very cool, and something colleges will pick up on. They will be impressed by this activity. But you definitely need more if you are applying to the most selective colleges.

There are thousands of local competitions across the country in any given month. This isn't to discount your musical or other abilities, but only to serve as a reality check for you (like it was for me). Thousands of students will be filling out some version of this on their application: "I got the highest rating at the Fort Worth Guild Festival." You need to put this, plus more. A high local status is rarely enough for the top-tier colleges; sometimes even state-level status isn't enough.

An Aside about the "Tiers" and "Expectations" of Colleges

Some colleges are more demanding of their applicants than other colleges. Also, some colleges are known for preferring students who are well rounded as opposed to students who are stellar in one area. For example, the urban myth is that Harvard tends to accept "stars" (students that shine in one area in particular) over well-rounded students and Yale and Princeton accept well-rounded students over stars. Do I believe this? Well, not really. I don't think that admissions officers limit themselves by only accepting a certain "type" of student.

I do, though, certainly believe that there are "tiers" of colleges. The rule of thumb here is that that the higher the tier of the college to which you are applying (and thereby the lower the admission rates), the more activities and interests you should have on your application, and your achievement in these activities should be at higher levels (for example, state and national awards or having a substantial impact on the community, like organizing the construction of five playgrounds). This knowledge is likely intuitive to you already: The stronger an application—made strong by having interesting activities, good academics, and great essays—the more likely it is that a student will be accepted by a top-tier school. Keep in mind that students accepted to top-tier schools will also get accepted to second-tier colleges. This just goes to show that it never hurts to be a brighter star than you think you need to be.

The good news is that an activity that has a strong impact on the community can be *more impressive* than doing well nationally and perhaps more accessible for most students. One example from my life is C.A.R.D.S., described in the "Go Start Something to Show Initiative" section.

"Go Start Something to Show Initiative"

Yeah, that's great. But what does "something" mean, and how do you go about starting "something"? First of all, before you think about starting something, ask yourself why you want to do this. Is it simply to make your college application shine? If so, that's a silly reason to go start something. There are other ways to get involved in your school and community in order to make your application strong. Plus, you'll save yourself time and a major headache in the long run. However, if you feel like you can make a difference in your school or community because you've identified something that doesn't exist and should, then go for it! Start something to fill that missing niche if you're feeling particularly entrepreneurial *and* there is genuinely a need.

This "something" can be a school club, a community service project, a nonprofit incorporated under the laws of your state, or a small business. Most people start a school club or a community service project because of the messy legal and tax implications of an incorporated non-profit or business. Certainly, it is most popular (and easiest) to start a school club. At most schools, you just need to find a sponsor and some students who want to be in the club, maybe fill out a sheet for the principal or counselor's office and one for the yearbook, and then you're all set. Of course, you'll have to hold a first meeting, and since you're the organizer, you'll want to bring materials to pass around that describe why the club should exist. Next, you and your clubmates should brainstorm together ideas for events, projects, and so forth. You'll also need to choose leaders (usually a president, vice president, secretary, treasurer, and any other necessary positions). The benefit of being the founder of the club is that you're most likely going to be chosen as president. That's the upside; the downside is that you're charged with making sure that the club gets off the ground and that you set a precedent for future leadership teams.

I think starting a club is exciting. In fact, I started a poetry club in high school that met every month to read and discuss poetry. It was fun, and it was personally fulfilling. However, I did not organize it very well, and it died when I graduated from high school. On my application, it didn't look particularly impressive, since we did not do very much. If I had wanted it to contribute significantly to my application, I could have made it more "useful" by establishing a poetry day at school or having the club sponsor poetry readings at the local library. Also, I could have found successors: younger students who could take over leadership of the organization once I graduated.

Another initiative you could lead if you see a need for it is a community service project. This doesn't have to be tied to a particular high school; in fact, you could ask students from many area high schools to get involved.

There's no actual paperwork tied to starting a service project (unless you partner with a community organization, then you have to fill out applications and informational sheets), but you should be mindful of any legal ramifications, should something go awry.

In high school, I started a community service project called C.A.R.D.S. (Children's Art Remembering Distinguished Seniors) that brought children to elderly residents in nursing/retirement homes. I recruited a team of students from area high schools, then called day care centers and signed them up for deliveries to a nearby nursing/retirement home. I also had to create "materials" (brochures to fax or mail to the day care centers and nursing/retirement homes). Most people will want to know what it is they are getting involved with, and while a one-page flier is a pain to create, having one helps give you credibility.

By signing up over a dozen day care centers and nursing/retirement homes, I got over six hundred people in the area involved in the project. Hundreds of children delivered their homemade cards to hundreds of elderly residents in the nursing/retirement homes. It was a great success, covered by the local TV stations and newspapers. If you are organizing a project that is warm and fuzzy like C.A.R.D.S., the news media will love it. Create a press release with the "what, when, where, why, and how's" of your project and fax the page over to local TV stations and newspapers. It helps to recruit more people to get involved with your project, and it gives those people who are already involved exposure in media. Plus, it's fun to have cameras following you around.

The liability for C.A.R.D.S. was associated with the possibility that a child or a resident could get injured during a delivery. After all, this is the United States, and you never know who is going to sue you. Since most day care centers and nursing/retirement homes are insured in case of injury of their students and residents, we were covered if anything went wrong during a delivery. It's a very small possibility that something bad will happen, but be sure to consider the worst-case scenario and have a plan of action prepared just in case.

As mentioned earlier, you can also incorporate a nonprofit under the laws of your state or start a small business. Both involve a lot more than starting a club at school or organizing a community service project. I've done both, so if you are truly interested in doing either of these, please email me (get my current contact information through www.collegematters.org), and I'll help you get started.

Timing and Time

Long-Term Stuff

The Activities section, like the grades portion, requires long-term planning and effort in order to reflect well on your application. Whereas you could feasibly churn out the essay in a day and test scores in a morning or two, building a strong résumé of activities and talents usually takes three or four years of high school involvement (or even before high school, in the case of a musical instrument or an athletic activity). The Activities section technically starts with freshman year activities, but there's a catch: Many colleges don't ask about ninth-grade activities and choose to start with the tenth-grade stuff instead.

Part of this long-term stuff relates to the supposed personal growth and maturity that you've gained from participating in activities. Think along the lines of organization, discipline, leadership, and self-confidence. This section should show the growth and maturity you have achieved—or appear on paper to have achieved—through your activities. This concept of personal growth in your activities is very important. You can show that you've achieved personal growth through holding higher and higher offices in clubs over time. You can also explore your personal development through your personal essay(s). Keep this in mind (and refer to Chapter 6 on essays for more details).

What Grade Are You In?

Because the Activities section of the application requires long-term preparation, let's go year by year and talk about what to do or consider during each of the four years of high school.

For Freshfolks (and Younger). You are in a good position when it comes to activities. At the beginning of the year, you should start getting involved with a bunch of activities and "feel" your way around. However, do not be a "yes" man or woman. (Translation: Do not say "yeah, sure" to everything that the club wants you to do.) You are, after all, just a regular member and are not running the show—yet. Poke around and find the activities that you're interested in *and* that you can probably do well in, whether it's heading it up in a few years or winning some sort of award or medal through competitions. On the other hand, if doing well in something will require overcoming some sort of disability or obstacle, this could also be particularly impressive. It requires taking a risk, but is definitely worth the try. Most importantly, choose something that you know you will be happy doing for the next three or four years. And remember, if you hate it later, you can always quit. Once you have settled these decisions, then consider taking on more responsibilities in the organization, whether it is making posters, creating emails, coordinating an event, or recruiting more students to join.

For Sophomores. This is the year to build up your activities. Evaluate your activities, and decide which ones you want to stick with. If you are going to drop or add activities, now is the best time to do it so you can still get in a solid three-year commitment. If you decide that a particular club isn't really worth your energy, then get rid of it because it's just sucking up your time. Choose a few key activities to spend your time doing (be sure to have a mix of academic and nonacademic activities)—and start looking for opportunities to lead. Consider running for an office or organizing a project.

This is also the year to begin creating your résumé so that updating it over the next two years will just be a matter of entering in the new activities and accolades. There's a section at the end of this chapter on creating your résumé, from formatting to content.

For Juniors. By junior year, you should have your activities set. Check to make sure you have a mix of academic and nonacademic activities (unless your strategy is to show complete dedication to one thing, such as tennis). This is the year to be vice president of your favorite organizations. This way, you are positioned to run for president at the end of the year.

On that note, keep in mind that the most selective colleges have thousands of presidents of this and that applying every year. Also remember that you don't have to have an official leadership title to be an amazing leader; you just need to see a need and try to meet it. Sometimes, students who get admitted weren't president of anything, but they did something that was simply awesome, such as founding their own successful organization or organizing an amazing service project. Sure, being president won't hurt you, but you need to make sure that you have more than just a title.

This is also the year to be racking up on those awards, whether from competitions or within the school. Keep in mind that applications are due early senior year, especially early action/decision applications, so you won't have much time to win further accolades senior year. (Sure, you could write the admissions office and let them know what award or position you just got…and sure, you would look like a dork.) The key is to win offices and trophies junior year; you'll then have them for your applications come senior fall.

For Seniors. Congratulations. You've made it to senior year. No doubt, this is your busiest year of high school. You have umpteen activities to head up as president, editor, captain, and so on; umpteen applications to complete; things to see; and people to meet (or date, if you're so lucky).

Load up on activities during the first semester (or in the first few months, if your school doesn't go by semesters). The reason is because applications are due in these first few months, and you want to be recognized for the effort you put in, earlier rather than later. Believe me, it won't matter what you did in high school once you're in college. The recognition won't come then. Get them on your college applications, where they will do you good.

Having your résumé updated will be incredibly helpful this year. (See the last section of this chapter on crafting a résumé.) You'll have a record of what you've done over the last few years and you can see what the "major" activities have been. These, by the way, are the ones to list in the Activities boxes on the application. There is more on this later on, as well as in Chapter 5.

Already a Senior but Not That Involved? "Uh-oh," you might be thinking, "I haven't gotten too involved in extracurriculars." The good news for activity slackers like you is that the Activities section could be less emphasized than the other sections if you can compensate for it in other ways (such as having a killer essay, amazing recommendations, or being renowned and recognized as absolutely brilliant). If you've been an activity slacker in high school, and you're a senior now, don't pile on the salt and pepper now that you're in your last year. It'll be obvious to the admissions officers looking at your application that you're just trying to make up for lost time.

Instead, if you're in the not-so-involved category, consider getting involved in a couple of activities. It would be especially good if at least one of them was related to community service. Rather than use up all your time joining a zillion activities during your senior year, use that time to perfect the strengths of your application: the essay, recommendations, grades (senior year first semester), test scores, and other sections. Showing up strong in other areas of your application can shift attention from the few blank boxes in your Activities section.

A Senior and Too Involved? If, on the other hand, you're totally drowning in activities, there's good news for you. The Activities section can be the distinguishing part of your application. Keep in mind, though, that there are thousands of other National Honor Society presidents, student government treasurers, and other titled students who will be applying to the same college. I was amazed by how many valedictorians, salutatorians, student council presidents, band drum majors, and so forth I met during my first week of college. Sure, mention all your officer roles, but make sure to emphasize what sets you apart from the rest of the bunch.

A Warning to Students of All Grades

If you are superinvolved in activities and see your grades slipping, stop! You can't let that happen. Pull to a safe and legal stop, and get your grades in order before proceeding. Be sure to choose quality over quantity in your activities. Consider limiting the number of activities that you do, but aim for really high officer positions, choose activities with something to show at the end, like an event, or both.

Summer Opportunities

Some applications will ask about activities you have pursued during the summer, be it study abroad, a summer job, or taking summer classes. Granted, this section is not likely to be given as much weight as the general Activities section, but every little bit counts! So think about what activities you will do during the summer as well.

There's no denying it: A lot of students at the selective schools went to "dork" camps during the summers between grade levels. You know, the math camps or the summer camps where the "tents" are actually dorms in universities and the "activities" are classes that you sit in for hours every day.

Beyond that, summertime is a great time to do other things. You could be a counselor in a dork camp for younger folks. You could study abroad. You could study for standardized tests, read the novels for next year's AP

English class, or both. You could work and save up some spending money. Between these activities, don't forget to relax (my personal favorite).

Tricks of the Trade: What I've Learned

Now, a few "tricks of the trade," or pieces of advice, which will help you to make sure that you don't really kill yourself. The following are some strategies that helped me avoid disasters.

Appearing Like You've Done a Lot

1. Go for offices that don't take that much time. Why break your back ten hours a week as vice president of Club A when you can spend one hour a week as president of comparably interesting Club B?

2. Run for offices that are relatively easy to win. Is nobody running for a certain position (VP or president)? Then step up! It's a guaranteed win for you. Then do something great with your new role.

3. Put time into the activities that you really care about (colleges often want to know how much time each activity takes per week). Have one or two time-intensive activities, things that take five to ten or ten to twenty hours per week, but not too much more unless it's pivotal to the success of society (like AIDS research) or if you are on the national or international level (like training for the Olympics). Also, have a lot of fringe activities in which you hold offices. This will make it appear like you've killed yourself (that is, done a lot) in high school.

Keeping It All Together

1. Pack your backpack and bags the night before. Getting into this routine helps you get ready faster and makes you less prone to forget things than if you haphazardly pack your bags as you're running out the door. In the same spirit, keep things in one consistent place, such as keys in the bowl by the door. To save sore shoulders, it's nice to have two sets of textbooks: one for school and one for home. (Ask your teachers if they have extra copies you could borrow for the year, or consider purchasing the textbooks, then reselling them later.)

2. Keep a notepad by your bed. Post-it notes work well, too. If you're anything like me, your brain is still truckin' at 100 miles per hour with things to do and things to remember as you're dozing off at night. Keeping paper and a pen by your bed will help you to write it down (however illegibly), get to sleep, and remember it again in the morning.

3. Have a central reference point, be it a Personal Digital Assistant (PDA) or a planner. Random little pieces of paper do not work well. Write things down. Keep it centralized. And just keep one to avoid overlap (and possible mishaps).

Managing Your Time

1. Synchronize and centralize. Sync your PDA/organizer with your computer, forward all emails to one address, and keep books and studying supplies in one consistent place.

2. Estimate the time that it will take to do tasks and activities. Build in buffer time of an additional 50 percent on top of what you've estimated. (So, for example, if you've estimated it will take two hours to do something, assume it will take three.) Then put these estimated times into the blocks of time in your day and stick to it. Be sure to build in transportation time to and from places!

3. Prioritize. Schoolwork always comes first. Then activities. No, scratch that. Your sanity comes first. And so do your health and your family. Then comes schoolwork, followed by activities.

4. Make daily to-do lists and carry them around with you. These are those pieces of paper or lists on your PDA where you write down all the little things that you have to do that day (things like reading assignments, emails to write, people to call, and so on). Then as you do things, cross them off and feel good about being so productive.

5. If you are particularly hardcore, schedule things by the hour. Estimate schoolwork/tasks/activities using hours (and sometimes half-hours). I consider myself medium-core, so every now and then in an especially busy week, I use Outlook's calendar feature to schedule the week at a glance. This way, I can slot to-do's into the hours of each day and set reminders, which will sound off an alarm and a pop-up box on my computer so I won't forget that all-important deadline or call that I need to make.

Working with Money Constraints

You can't fork out three or four thousand dollars for a summer study abroad program? Well, join the club. Most of us can't afford those kinds of luxuries. The good news is that selective colleges like Harvard, once filled with only rich kids, now have students whose financial situations run the gamut from coming from families who were brought up on public assistance to those with summer homes in the Hamptons. Moreover, the admissions officers will take your personal situation into account. Sure, they won't know exactly how much money your family makes if admissions are need-blind (that is, you aren't admitted or rejected based on your ability to pay). But, they will see your parents' occupations and level of education, which will give them an idea of your family's financial situation.

No matter what your economic situation is, it is important that you take advantage of opportunities presented to you. Granted, it's much easier when you have loose purse strings and a sea of opportunities in front of you. But money constraints can provide you with an opportunity to shine. It will strengthen your application if you show that you overcame challenges and grew stronger, wiser, and more interesting in the process. Let's talk about three ways to work with money constraints.

Earn Money

This is perhaps the most obvious thing you can do. Aside from bringing in some extra dough, jobs help strengthen your application because they show that you are willing to work (literally) toward a goal. You could write a great essay about it: how you earned money, what you learned, and how you used the money you earned to achieve your dream of going to Guatemala, for instance.

Getting a job can be difficult before you are fifteen or sixteen years old. I remember having a lot of trouble because nobody would hire me. When I turned fifteen, though, my mother helped me get a hostess job at the local Chinese restaurant.

My best friend was smarter. She initiated a unique way to earn money, which was more lucrative and more impressive in college admissions. She started a string quartet to play for weddings. Each person in her quartet would earn about two hundred dollars *per wedding*. Another person I know started a lawn mowing business in high school and worked at it during the spring to fall months for nearly four years. If you're more brain than brawn, you could start a test prep business. Just put up some posters and charge $20 to $30 per hour for prepping other students.

Ask for Money

No, I don't mean going to the nearest street corner and putting out your hat. Asking for money simply means if you can't afford to pay for something (for example, a summer program), call the administrative office, express your interest in the program, and explain your financial situation. Then ask if they have any scholarships that you could apply for, if you could get a special discount, or both.

Asking for money could also mean asking for free services that you then use to make money. In college, I called up a photographer, offered to model for him so that he could add to his own portfolio, then asked to use those pictures for my own portfolio in exchange. He agreed, and I got a set of beautiful pictures that would have cost five hundred dollars—for free. I then signed up with an agency and made some money modeling (which then paid for the College Matters Web site).

Eschew the Need for Money

To be perfectly honest, you don't need money to do some of the most interesting activities. If you were to take up juggling, for example, you would just need a few pairs of rolled-up socks to toss around. After you become pretty good at something, you could use that talent to make some money through performances or teaching, which you could then use for more advanced equipment, and so forth. If you need a service for your project, you can ask a local business or organization to donate it (copies, refreshments, and so on).

The bottom line is that money constraints shouldn't constrain you from getting some great activities under your belt. In fact, you could use this to your advantage in the admissions game—being creative and working with what you have gets you places!

Presenting Yourself on Paper

Filling out the Activities Section of the Application

Let's assume you've done too many activities. In fact, you have too many activities to fit into the boxes on the application. So you are freaking out.

But the good news is that this is not a problem. Just fill in your "major" activities (translation: activities for which you were president or vice president, from nationally recognized down to locally recognized activities), and then attach your résumé to the application itself, so that the admissions folks can see how busy you have been.

Okay, that was just the bare basics. Filling out the application is a chapter unto itself, so for more information, please refer to Chapter 5.

Creating a Usable Résumé

A résumé, or list of achievements and accomplishments, is a must for college applications. For one, you can reference it when filling out the application forms. Moreover, you can attach this résumé to the Activities section on the application, and admissions officers can quickly skim through it for a comprehensive overview of your activities and achievements.

I should note two things here. The first is that this sort of high school résumé can be more than one page. Mine went on for six pages. The second note is that a few colleges do not allow résumés to be attached to the application itself. This can be really annoying for those students who have a lot of activities under their belts, since it means they must fit their three or four years of high school activities inside a few measly boxes on the application.

That said, let's talk about *when* and *how* to create a résumé. You should start creating a résumé sometime during your sophomore year. Keep it updated, and add new activities, offices (president, treasurer, and so on), awards, and distinctions as you get them or once every few months. If you are a junior or senior reading this chapter, you should definitely still create a résumé; just be sure to think about and remember all the activities that you are or have been involved with in past years.

The following steps are for those of you who do not have a résumé already created. Please keep in mind that there are many ways to make a résumé, and all are good as long as it includes the pertinent information: years, offices, etc.

Start with your name and include your social security number, address, phone number, and email address at the top. Many colleges ask for your social security number on your résumé, so you can either choose to put it on when requested or just always include it. Center or right-justify all this information.

Include a section at the very beginning entitled "Significant Achievements." By the time the reader gets to page six of your résumé, his or her

FIGURE 2.1 SAMPLE RÉSUMÉ.

(Optional: Social Security Number in the header for ID purposes)

Phoebe B. Peabody
100 Main Street
Austin, TX 10000
(123)-123-1234
phoebe@peabody.com

Significant Achievements

2003 Horace Mann Scholar, chosen as one out of 10,000 applicants

Governor's Medal for Public Service, chosen as one of six youths in the state

School Rank: 3 out of 635

High School Courses (optional—this is already on your transcript, so why repeat it?)

Activities

12th   Honor Society (President)
        Student Council (Secretary)
        Band (Lead Trumpet)
        Environmental club

11th   Honor Society (Vice President)
        Student Council (Class Rep)
        Band
        Environmental Club
        Math-Science Club

10th   Honor Society
        Student Council (Class Rep)
        Band
        Environmental Club
        Math-Science Club

9th Band
   Environmental Club
   Math-Science Club

Community Service

12th Habitat for Humanity
   Volunteering at hospital (helped train new candy stripers)

11th Habitat for Humanity
   Volunteering at hospital

10th Habitat for Humanity
   Volunteering at library

Work Experience

12th Pat's Coffee House (server)
11th Local Grocers (cashier)

---

attention has probably waned or died. Having this section at the beginning highlights what *you* consider to be the most significant of your achievements.

Next, you should organize your accomplishments under categories like "Courses," "Activities," "Awards," "Community Service," "Work," and "Other." Under each section, list things in reverse-chronological order, starting with your current year of high school. For instance, under "Activities," have subheadings for each grade, and include *all* the clubs in which you have been a member. (You decide whether this section features only school clubs or includes nonschool clubs as well.) Beside the name of the club, be sure to include in parentheses what office you held, if you held a position.

Some people may also want to include how much time they spent each week on the activity. Applications ask for this information, so it is helpful to document it for easy access later. However, doing so is optional. If you include times, add up the hours spent on each activity and make sure it sounds believable and reasonable (don't exaggerate, it'll be obvious). After all, there are only 168 hours in a week!

So basically, your résumé should look something like what's shown in Figure 2.1.

Quick points about looks

Font: 11 point font or greater Spacing: at least 1.5 spacing (no single-spaced résumés!)

Margins: white space looks good, the default margins of Microsoft Word are fine

Length: there is no minimum or maximum (as long as it's not all just fluff)

It All Boils Down to Readability

The test is to put the printed résumé a few feet away from you. Then look at it and ask whether it's something you might want to pick up and look at. If something looks too cluttered or choked full of small, cramped words, most people would rather not read it.

Another test is to give it to an adult you know who is brutally honest (you know, the ones that aren't saying "oh, you're so great" to you all the time—my piano teacher was this reality check for me). Ask for suggestions and comments. In this test, I wouldn't recommend giving it to one of your classmates or friends from school. Your résumé is something that you probably don't want to pass around, as it's your competitive advantage. It also makes you look like you're showing off, especially if you have an extremely long résumé, and that's a big social no-no.

Conclusion

So you've let me yack on and on about activities, and now we're at the end of the chapter. Let me conclude by simply reminding you that activities are important, but they should not be your be-all and end-all. Being involved with activities helps you develop personally, and when it comes to admissions, activities act as an indicator to colleges and scholarships that you are an interesting, multidimensional person. Getting a big head or having a mental breakdown as a result of being involved in lots of activities should be an indication that you've taken it too far. Everyone has limits, and you will know once you've hit yours. At that point, you should pull back and remember that there's more to life than activities and competition.

That said, activities can be really fun and result in amazing personal growth experiences. You can do a lot of great things through your talents and activities, and I'm sure you'll have some good stories to tell about them once you're in college. I hope you've found this chapter to be helpful—best of luck!

WHY BOTHER?

College Matters Editors

Let's not kid ourselves. Applying to selective colleges and for scholarships to pay for them takes a lot of time and effort. The question in your mind might be, "Is it really worth my while?" After all, does it really matter where you go to college?

Even if you think you want to attend a selective college, you might be intimidated by the admissions process, either to get into college or apply for scholarships, both of which may seem out of your reach. Moreover, you are a shoo-in to the local college(s), the ones that everyone around you seems to go to (if they go to college at all). So why even bother applying to or going to selective colleges?

All of us on the College Matters team wrestled with these questions when we were in high school. (What's more, many of us came from families where very few people or nobody had attended college.) Now, when we give College Matters seminars around the world, we get these same questions from our audience again and again.

Sometimes these questions take the form of bold statements, and frankly, we hear a lot of things that don't ring true with our experiences or that we know simply aren't true. These popular misconceptions can deter students from investigating schools that may be a good match for them, so we want to set the record straight here. With these myths laid to rest, the rest of this book will serve to help you successfully navigate through the admissions and scholarship application process.

Myth Number 1:

It Doesn't Matter Where You Go for Undergraduate School; It's Graduate School That Really Counts

To address this myth, we need to differentiate between "success in life" and "opportunities." Greater success does not come from being a graduate of a selective college. Success in life is determined by how you define success and how hard you work to get there.

Nevertheless, greater academic opportunities and more diverse experiences *are* often available at more selective colleges. Name recognition goes a long way, and students at elite universities often have more connections and clout to invite well-known speakers to conferences, initiate national movements, and find internships. This ability to get your foot in the door extends to the types of jobs that will be available to you upon graduation. This fact is also important for admission to graduate school, especially for disciplines like law and medicine, where coming from a selective college certainly helps.

Furthermore, selective colleges have the reputation necessary to draw stronger students and more renowned professors. This prestige often means a more rigorous learning environment. Not only will it attract a higher-caliber teaching staff but it will also have better resources, such as larger libraries, better labs, and nicer on-campus housing. Finally, these schools also have more (and often higher-paying) companies come to recruit their graduates.

We could go on and on about the ample opportunities available at selective colleges, but perhaps it would be better to give you examples of some of the opportunities readily available to College Matters students at top schools:

Academic Opportunities

- Taken an introductory economics course with a professor who has chaired the U.S. president's Economic Council
- Gotten paid to do research about their community service organizations
- Been taught by professors who worked alongside Albert Einstein
- Traveled to China, Mexico, Zimbabwe, India, and many other places to do research (fully paid for by their college's research funds)
- Taken a field trip to Nicaragua to monitor elections with a freshman seminar class

Extracurricular Opportunities

- Toured six continents with a college a capella group
- Worked as the chief editor of an international relations magazine sold on six continents
- Organized yearly conferences hosting former Nobel laureates, the Senate Chair of the Science Committee, and world-renowned scientists from multiple continents
- Met dozens of world leaders and former world leaders at their university's forum
- Led government simulation conferences in Europe and Latin America
- Interned at top-secret places like the Central Intelligence Agency (CIA) and supersecret places like the National Security Agency (NSA)

Postgraduate Opportunities

- Landed six-figure salaries upon graduation
- Wrote speeches for Bill Clinton, Al Gore, and George W. Bush
- Been awarded fellowships specifically available to students at their school for postgraduate study abroad in places like the United Kingdom
- Wrote for the *Simpsons* and other Hollywood sitcoms

So do we think you should only apply to selective colleges? Not at all. We hope we don't sound like that, because selective colleges aren't the best fit for everyone. We simply want you to consider and compare the options for college that are available. It is just too easy to default to the local favorite (where all your friends and classmates seem to go), without considering the many options—and opportunities—available to you.

Myth Number 2:
Only Rich Kids Go to Selective Schools

Yes, that was the case—in the 1940s. Many of the selective schools now admit U.S. students on a need-blind basis. (Translation: Admissions officers do not consider whether you can pay for their college when deciding on candidates.) Plus, most colleges have great financial aid programs for those who need help. If you come from a typical middle class family, attending a selective university could cost less than attending a state university. (Turn to Chapter 12 on scholarships for more details.)

Furthermore, it so happens that all three of the editors of this book attend(ed) Harvard. Speaking from our personal experiences, none of us on the editing team has found Harvard to be a snobby or elitist environment. And most of our friends at other top colleges wouldn't describe their schools as snobby, either.

In fact, one of the most interesting tacit taboos around campus is talking about how much money your family has. Those people who go around and flaunt their family's wealth are often pegged as the arrogant suckers to avoid. So it's hard to even know who is rich, who is poor, and who is in between.

Myth Number 3:

People at Selective Schools Study All the Time and Never Party

Are you kidding me? Have you ever seen the movie *Animal House*, inspired by Dartmouth's frat scene? What's more, in 2003, the City of Cambridge reduced city party hours because of a wild party that involved a room full of shaving cream and 1300 (mostly Harvard) students! Wherever you go, you will have a choice about how much you want to party. Even at the dorkiest of colleges, if you look around on a Friday or Saturday night, you're bound to find some parties. We should highlight, though, the most notable difference, which is that it is acceptable to use schoolwork or other work-related excuses for not partying at many selective schools, an excuse which is far less common at other colleges.

Myth Number 4:

No One from My School or Family Has Attended a Selective College Before; I Don't Stand a Chance at Getting in, and I Don't Even Know Where to Start!

Actually, you can make this work to your advantage. Admissions officers are looking for people just like you! Don't be afraid to state this fact in your application. Of course, it means you might not have as much information about the admissions process available to you, but that is where this book—and College Matters students—can help! If after reading this book, you still have questions, please email us at info@collegematters.org. We are more than happy to help address your situation.

Myth Number 5:

I Shouldn't Bother Applying to Selective Colleges or Scholarships Because I Won't Get in or Win

How do you know? If you don't try, you never will! If you are not yet in twelfth grade, you still have time to work on your grades and activities. If you're a senior, you can still improve your test scores and essays. We recommend that you go for it! This book helps to lay out how. The rewards can be life changing.

CHAPTER THREE

RESEARCHING COLLEGES

Mitch Ginsburgh, Northwestern

Close your eyes and imagine that it's dorm move-in day, the start of your freshman year of college. Your parents can't stop crying. You have a million boxes littering the floor. You've just met your roommates, Ned Nerd and Joe Jock. But then, there's the exciting stuff. You're away from home. You get to take the classes you want to take. You get to stay out as late as you want. You feel like you're on your way to becoming a doctor, lawyer, scientist, businessperson, or whatever. Of course, one huge thing is missing from this picture: You're still in high school and you have no idea what college you're going to go to. So, where do you think you might be? And how are you going to get there?

All right, let's press the Rewind button on your dream. You drove or flew to campus from home. Before that, you were relaxing in your last summer after high school. Before that, you were deciding which college you would attend. Before that, you were jumping up and down when you got the acceptance letters. Before that, you were filling out the applications and taking the SAT or ACT. Before that, you were narrowing down which schools you would apply to. Before that, (it's a long rewind—two years) you were receiving a load of mail from every college in the solar system. Before that, you were about to take the PSAT (Preliminary Scholastic Achievement Test).

Stop! This is where my schpiel starts.

No, I'm not telling you to do well on the PSAT; see Chapter 4 for more information about that. The important thing I *am* telling you to do on the PSAT is to check that tiny box that says that you want to receive information from colleges. This is where the ball starts rolling. Check the box! If you don't, you'll have to request information on your own, which will take up your time and money. You don't want to call long distance every time you need to receive information. (You wouldn't use your mom's cell phone and risk her cell phone carrier dropping your call with an admissions officer, would you?) A few months after you take the test, you'll start noticing the mail from colleges piling up. If you've already taken the PSAT and didn't check the little box, no worries—it just means that you're going to have to request information from your colleges of interest by phone or email.

Mount Mail

Ever wish you were getting lots of mail? Well, your wish is about to come true. The post office will definitely be able to tell that you're applying to college by all the mail you will be receiving. By your junior year, you'll probably start getting at least one brochure a day. You'll get form letters that ask you to think about your future and letters that say how wonderful you are. One letter I received even said that if the PSAT were the Olympic Games, they would be playing the Star Spangled Banner for me right then!

Save all the material from schools in which you are even remotely interested, even though 95 percent of it will eventually end up in the trash. If you are organized or have the time, you should alphabetize or otherwise categorize the material, for easier access later in the process. If organization is not your strong point, find two shopping bags where you can separate the mail into two piles: interesting and not-so-interesting. As you sort through your mountain of mail, decide which bag each brochure deserves, and toss it in there with the rest of its kind.

At this point, you're probably asking, "Why am I saving all this?" There are at least two good reasons to allow a good bit of junk mail to enter your life. First, it's just good record keeping. You will know what you have received from where. You can list the schools you like, along with the schools you definitely don't like. As you read through their fan mail, you'll be getting ideas about what does and doesn't appeal to you about college in general. Take note of these gut feelings. They can be deciding factors later on. Second, and more importantly, you never know when today's junk mail will be tomorrow's prize. What looks like a loser school with a nice brochure may look better after you read about it more than once or when you compare it to other schools. The basic rule of thumb is this: *Open your mail and keep almost everything.*

Once you know for sure which colleges you are applying to, then—and only then—can you get rid of your shopping bags or files that have information about schools that are no longer of interest. But you'll need to create a file for each school to which you are applying that contains all the information you have. And yes, it is important to be organized at this point. Having everything in one central location will be really useful when you need to read up on a school for an interview or look up a relevant statistic for your admissions essay. It may also be useful to create a book with your personal notes for each school in which you are interested. Then, you can take this book on college visits and add to its notes at that time. But wait, we're getting ahead of ourselves: How do you even know what schools you're interested in?

How Do You Know What's Interesting?

This is where your unique qualities and preferences are very important. I'll call it your *college criteria*, your list of interests and activities that are important to you in your search for the perfect college. Your college criteria are supremely important, and to keep them all straight, I would highly recommend using the appendixes in the back of this chapter to organize them. Maybe you're looking at schools based on their size or population. Do you want a small school with a homey, nurturing atmosphere? Or how about a large university with every department under the sun, thousands of people to meet, and a Division I football team?

Are you looking for opportunities in music, athletics, or politics? Would you rather live in a big city or a small town? Is it important to have access to bungee jumping and karaoke? What type of dating scene do you want? Remember to consider your academic interests as well. Got the urge to study Arabic? Are you absolutely sure about going premed? If so, you might want to consider whether a school has an associated medical school, nearby hospitals, or good premed advisors. How about a traditionally African American college? What are your expectations in student diversity? Would you like to be in an honors program? Do you want fries with your diploma?

With your college criteria handy and organized, you can quickly skim through your mail to see whether a school meets some of your requirements. If you see one or two clues that make it look like a good possibility, then search for more information. This is how I found out about Oberlin College. I got the brochure and took a quick look to find, to my surprise, that it had lots of things for me: a great music school, a Jewish community, wide academic options, a diverse campus, and a unique winter term that allows students to take one subject of interest during January (and have a relaxed time otherwise). All I did was skim the brochure for three minutes, and I saw that it looked interesting. So remember—skimming helps you find potential in schools you never would have considered without having received a mountain of mail.

What Are Some Examples of What Might Be in a Criteria Listing?

My English major friend Eric was looking for the following criteria:

- A school that offered a diversity of experiences and options
- Access to media (radio, television, and film)
- Good financial aid
- Flexibility (easy to change your major)

My personal college criteria looked something like this:

- Music opportunities—I eventually chose my university based on this factor
- Jewish community
- Proximity to a big city
- A variety of dorm options

I also wanted a school with great academics, professors, and facilities; but so many schools that were interesting and many others that weren't had all these things. It really came down to distinguishing between the finer points such as the following:

- Career advising
- Climate

- Alumni network for when I graduated
- Study abroad programs
- Size and quality of dorms
- Sports teams
- Percentage of students living on campus
- Political atmosphere
- Crime rates
- Pollution
- Entertainment options nearby (opera, major league sports, symphony, nightclubs, ballet, art museums, movie theatres, and so on)
- Number of restaurants nearby (to escape school food)
- Special programs—this criterion can be really important for minorities and women especially

Since You Know How to Read, Try These Books

There are two types of college guides: big, fat ones that give you lots of boring statistics for every college from Podunk U. to the Ivies, and skinnier ones that specialize in colleges in a particular region or of a particular caliber. The latter kind tend to have more interesting qualitative information, in addition to statistics. Guides like these may be written by current or former students of a school. Detailed guides can be useful to find out some things about colleges that interest you, such as SAT score ranges, tuition costs, and what student life is like. Make sure the guide you use is up to date, especially if what you are looking for is tuition costs, which increase substantially every year. Get these books in your local library, at your favorite bookstore or online bookseller, or from your guidance counselor.

Personally, I was scared the first time that I saw the admissions statistics for the colleges I liked. They all had more undergraduate freshman applicants than students in the entire university! You should know the numerical chances of getting into your dream school, but also remember that your application will be judged on an individualized basis. For example, an applicant with pretty good grades, not-so-bad test scores, and highly specific interests and skills may have a much higher chance of getting through a selective school's admissions maze than what the raw data might suggest. If you like what you see in a school, your chances could be better than you expect!

Ideas Invading Your Life from All Directions

Parents, friends, teachers, and counselors will probably make some suggestions on colleges they think will be good for you, often because either they or someone they knew attended those schools. It never hurts to do a bit of research based on their suggestions, because it may lead you to something good that you had not considered. Take it all with a grain of salt, but take it graciously.

When you hear about interesting leads, get more information! Email for brochures, course catalogs, concert calendars, admissions bulletins—if only they would send you the sweatshirt, too. (They won't do that.) It doesn't take long to fill out a reply card or save trees and dash off a quick email to the admissions department of a school to request more information. In fact, that's half the reason admissions offices exist!

Selective Colleges: Just Pick the Most Expensive Item on the Menu

Even if you are admitted to your dream college, the price tag for the education might be enough to steer you toward a cheaper school. My tuition, room and board, books, fees, travel expenses, and spending money totaled about $35,000 per year—and that was in the late 1990s. When you think about all the movies you could see, all the sodas you could drink, and all the pizzas you could order.... Instead of paying $140,000 for an education, my parents could have owned two Porsches! What were they thinking when they signed me up for those SATs?

Well, if you attend a high-prestige institution, you'll face stiff academic competition, and you'll meet students from all over the world who have similar motivations and represent diverse interests. Is it all worth it? You must decide that for yourself. Overall, if you have high grades and a diversity and depth of interests and experiences, it is definitely worth it to investigate your options at highly prestigious colleges and universities. Not only are you likely to get a great education, but you'll probably meet people

Colleges on the Computer

You don't have to wait for schools to come to your mailbox. You can go to them on the Internet. Most schools have .edu Web addresses following the name of their school. If that doesn't work, just do a quick Google search on the name of the school and choose the "I'm feeling lucky" button—it's a good time to use it. College Web sites typically give lots of information, and it takes a while to find everything worth seeing and reading. It's always good to click on the admissions info and get the story from that page. This gets you information that the school wants you to know, and you learn about their "persona" and what kind of students they are hoping to recruit. Pay special attention to any mission statements that might be listed. They tell you the main goals that the university has in mind.

Going online can also answer your basic questions like "What majors do you offer?" and "Why are your buildings so old?" After you get the official word from the admissions Web page, get your own word from the rest of the site. Click on information for students to find out what's happening on campus. What are the dorms like? Which classes are offered this semester? What fun activities are accessible on campus? What is the range of activities to get involved with once you get there? Click on department links that just look cool—examples might be Art History, Asian studies, or Learning and Organizational Change. Does research take place at the school? What about off-campus resources and hangouts? Click and find out!

you'll want to be close to as friends and colleagues long after the archaeology class you took is over. Furthermore, the more well-known schools often have superior resources for advising and placement for the next step beyond the undergraduate degree, whether it's a job or more education. Remember, most selective colleges have great financial aid. If you have to take out a small loan, it will be pebbles compared to what professional grad schools (law, medicine, business) will cost you.

But all this raises two questions:

1. "What are the selective colleges?"

2. "How do I know which ones to apply to?"

Answer to Question 1

Selective colleges are generally described as those that accept fewer than 50 percent of their applicants. At this point, I want to clear up a big myth. Selectivity is often associated with quality, especially in college rankings, but just because a school is selective does not necessarily mean it's the best school for you. Keep in mind your selection criteria, and never decide to apply or not apply to a school based solely on selectivity rankings. Your college guides will give you what they think are the best schools. Also, *U.S. News and World Report* comes out with an annual ranking of "top-tier" universities. While the top-tier list is a good source of ideas and reports where a sizable number of the highest high school achievers are going, it doesn't (and can't) quantify one very important thing—a school's personality.

Answer to Question 2

"How do I know to which schools to apply?" Don't limit yourself to just top-ranking schools! There are probably a dozen schools that would be good for you, and plenty of them may not be on a top-tier list. Don't get hung up on the rankings. They change every year. Even if you're admitted to a higher-ranked school, you may still be better off at a different school because of a special program or different social scene. And not all top-tier schools are alike. Rice University is in a big city, but it's a small university. Cornell is in a small college town, but it's much larger than other comparable schools. Columbia is in New York City; it has lots of research institutes and graduate schools along with its undergraduate programs. Haverford College is in suburban Philadelphia. As a small liberal arts college, it has zero in terms of its own graduate programs, and thus it gives undergraduates lots of personal attention. You can find so many contrasts between all colleges and universities that it's best to take your "college criteria" and apply them to what you read about these schools. Using your college criteria, only you can judge which ivy-covered towers are the ones you want to climb for the next four years.

Liberal Arts Schools versus Research Universities: Why Do I Care?

In *U.S. News and World Report,* you'll see schools ranked according to two categories: liberal arts colleges and research universities. So what is the difference? *Liberal arts colleges* will still offer the normal majors, the normal activities (though probably not the high-profile athletics), and many aspects of the normal college experience. They are, however, likely to be much smaller than most universities, maybe even smaller than your high school! They will have a strong emphasis on teaching, and this means small classes. They may even be founded on explicit core values that seem to permeate the whole atmosphere of the campus. Providing undergraduate education may be the one and only goal of a liberal arts college. Viewbooks probably emphasize a "nurturing" educational atmosphere or a strong sense of campus community and closeness.

So, what about *research universities?* Their goals probably include research and graduate programs that compete for attention along with the undergraduate studies. Of course, undergraduates can often access these research opportunities, which may give you a jump start if you're considering certain career tracks or graduate school after college. You may even be able do research at the affiliated medical school or school of government. But the university administration may have a less explicit role in forming a community of students. It's not the rule, but research universities tend to be larger institutions compared to liberal arts schools. These universities usually have graduate students running around everywhere. This is something to think about if you're worried about getting "lost in a crowd" at a university or feeling "too cooped up" at a liberal arts school.

Let's Not Forget …

The Citadel. West Point. The Air Force Academy. Navy. At these military colleges, you can get a great education—*for free!* After graduation, you'll be an officer in the U.S. Armed Forces. The catch is that you'll have to get up around 5:00 A.M. and run, march, or perform whatever physical activity is mandated. These schools tend to be very "hardcore"—you'll still have a social life but perhaps not as much as you would have at a nonmilitary college. At the same time, you may have a desire to serve your country and home community, making these options the ultimate education for you. If you like discipline and free tuition and wish to serve in the military, then these government-run military colleges are a good bet. Note that upon graduation you will be commissioned and required to serve in the U.S. Armed Forces, with the length of time differing according to military branch and specific program.

You can also consider the ROTC, which stands for Reserve Officer Training Corps and is the training program for students who go to nonmilitary schools. If you are involved in ROTC, the government may pay for you to attend a nonmilitary school. ROTC scholarships are based on academics, extracurricular involvement, and an interview, so you'll need to apply and be solid in these areas. If you are awarded an ROTC scholarship, after graduation you'll be required to perform four years of active duty and two years of reserve duty in the Armed Forces. Like students at military colleges, you'll have plenty of drills to execute and orders to follow. You'll also have to take special classes in military science, which may take away from your elective choices. At the same time, you'll definitely have something lined up after graduation. And military service looks *very* impressive on a résumé. For more information on ROTC, check out the Web sites: Army (www.armyrotc.com), Air Force (www.afrotc.com), and Navy and Marines (www.rotc.navy.mil).

Or What About ...

Interested in cattle ranching and working on an alfalfa farm? There's Deep Springs College, a great school where the two years you're there are free. Unfortunately, as far as I've heard, it's only for guys. (Sorry girls, we all know that you can herd cattle too.)

Interested in reading works by Homer, Aristotle, and other great authors? Colleges like St. John have what is known as the "great books" program, where students enjoy these works as the central part of their education.

Girls, interested in going to an all-female school? There are fantastic all-female colleges like Smith and Wellesley. If you like the idea of going to an all-girls school but want to be around a significant number of boys as well, consider Barnard, which is the sister school to Columbia, or Bryn Mawr, the sister school to Haverford. Reasons why you would go to an all-girls school are very individual. Some girls may find that they do better in an all-female environment. Others may not care to compete against boys while in college. As an aside, even if you do go to an all-girls college, you will have opportunities to meet boys in local co-ed colleges. For instance, Wellesley students can cross-register with MIT and Harvard for classes, and on weekends there is a bus that takes Wellesley students to parties at these schools.

Interested in the performing arts? How about Juilliard or Northwestern for music, the California Institute of the Arts (CalArts), or New York University for theatre? These schools will give you a chance to study music with the best in your field. These schools may also have better resources for setting you up with a professional job after graduation.

Perhaps you'd like to take only one class at a time? If so, check out Colorado College. Here, you'll spend a month taking one intense class and have lots of time to enjoy all the outdoor adventure opportunities that the Rocky Mountains offer. Taking one class at a time is particularly useful for people studying things like ecology, because it offers ample opportunities for field research.

Interested in studying somewhere other than the United States? There are the famous colleges of England: Cambridge University, Imperial College, and Oxford University. Canada, too, has top universities—McGill University, in Montreal, and the University of Toronto, among them. In addition, other countries have good colleges, which are especially rewarding to explore if you are interested in working in that country later on. You may want to consider participating in the International Baccalaureate (IB) program if you're going to apply to these schools. Check out Chapter 1 for more information.

For those of you considering medical school, you may want to investigate combined medical school programs that guarantee acceptance into med school to high school students through an accelerated program. Some of the most well-known examples include Rice-Baylor Medical School (eight years), Brown-PLME (Program in Liberal Medical Education) (eight years), Northwestern-HPME (Honors Program in Medical Education) (seven years), Boston University (seven years), Penn State–Jefferson Medical College (six years), and the University of Miami-HPME (six years). Other schools, like Tufts, offer their undergraduates the opportunity to apply for a guaranteed spot in their medical program during their second or third year of college. The advantages are obvious. No need to fear the grading curve, ace the MCAT (Medical College Admission Test), or stress about getting into med school later. However, you may feel tied to a career you don't want, and most of these programs aren't at the absolute top med schools in the nation (which may or may not be an issue). If you're interested in applying to one of these competitive programs, taking laboratory sciences during high school, taking an SAT II in the sciences, gaining science research experience, demonstrating a commitment to medicine while still in high school by volunteering at a community clinic or hospital, and securing a recommendation letter from someone in the medical community are all important steps.

Anyhow, I think you get the point. I just want to flag your attention to colleges other than the ones that you keep hearing about. There is life beyond the Ivy League. There is life beyond the state schools. There are opportunities for you in so many places!

Dealing with Your Gut Feeling

You may see a campus or read a view-book that just "speaks to you." While it would be very interesting to find out the role of subliminal messages in college admissions, you should save that project for your Ph.D. dissertation in psychology. In the meantime, snap yourself out of the trance. If you're just really taken with a place for what seems to be an irrational reason, ask yourself what's really behind it all. For example, my family and I breezed through Harvard on a whim during my college trip to Boston. It was the most gorgeous day. It was the most beautiful, intriguing campus. You could hear a choir rehearsing. You could see light playing off the buildings. The atmosphere at that moment blew me away. After I left, I thought I might apply there on a whim. I'm glad that I didn't. The place just didn't have what I was really looking for—it didn't match my criteria. Keep that in mind when the sirens at University of the Earthworm start singing to you.

A First Date with a College

When a school really interests you, it's time to consider visiting the campus to see the complete picture. But have you spent enough time collecting information to start narrowing down the field and deciding which schools you want to visit? If it's only your sophomore year, give it some time. If it's your junior year, you're ripe to start visiting campuses from January till August before your senior year. If you have the time and money to spend on visits, it's definitely worth it. Refer to Chapter 9 for more information.

If you don't have enough money or time to visit all your schools of interest, try to talk to current students. Perhaps you or your family has friends who go to your schools of interest. If not, your guidance counselor might be able to put you in touch with someone. Barring that, the admissions office may even have a list of students who are willing to talk to interested prospects. Getting a current student's perspective is critical; it's the real inside scoop!

If you've done your homework (which, being a good student, you always do), you can probably find at least a dozen universities that match the "interesting" category. But once you have your list of interesting schools, your job gets harder. You have to take all your prospects and narrow them down to five, seven, but not more than ten schools that will actually have the honor of reading about you on an application.

Showtime

Well, you've read, visited, mailed, emailed, thought, and dreamt college. You have a list of places that interest you, and you want to choose the final group of schools to which you will apply. Here's what makes your short list: colleges with the best-looking student body. Or, maybe the ones with the best food. Okay, now here's the serious answer: You're looking for the schools that very closely match your college criteria. These schools could be well known, very different from the mainstream college, or both. You could easily end up with a wide variety among your list of schools. Use your college criteria to set up a pros-and-cons worksheet to help you choose which schools will make your short list.

Another thing you have to decide is the number of schools that will end up on your short list. Because I care about your sanity, I'm going to suggest that you apply to about six colleges, including one or two safety schools. Applying to more than six colleges can become overwhelming, with all the paperwork and essays required. Applying to fewer than six schools starts to limit your options, especially if a school turns you away. Your decision on a backup school should be based on the reality that admissions offices simply cannot admit every applicant to a particular school. Basically, if there's a school that you would be willing to go to, and where you will definitely be admitted (usually public schools in your home state), you should put it on your list just to be sure you'll have something to occupy your time after high school. Having a backup doesn't mean you're expecting failure. It's a decision based on the reality of what will happen in the inevitable competition for college. I had a backup. Just about everybody I know at college had a backup or are at their backup, and 99.99 percent of them are very happy. (If they weren't happy, they transferred.) If you've researched a college and see a good fit between you, the student body, and the school's environment, a rejection letter represents the school's loss, not yours.

Think about what your college criteria are. Write them down. Look at them and change them periodically, as your interests change. Then go after the colleges that are best for you. Good luck!

Appendix: College Criteria Chart

Criteria (list here)	Rank for Each School (from 0=terrible to 5=ideal)					Importance (from slightly=1 to very=3)	Total for Each School				
	A	B	C	D	E		A	B	C	D	E
i.e., Size	4	5	1	4	5	2	8	10	2	8	10
i.e., Athletic facilities	3	3	5	2	1	3	9	9	15	6	3
1											
2											
3											
4											
5											
6											
7											
8											
9											
10											
11											
12											
13											
14											
15											
16											
17											
18											
19											
20											
21											
22											
23											
24											
25											
						TOTAL					

Use the chart to the left to evaluate your schools of interest quantitatively, based on your college criteria list. Follow the steps below to get a rough estimate of how well each school performs according to your criteria. Remember, this is just a rough estimate. There are lots of qualitative things which are not easily ranked which should go into deciding which schools to apply to.

1. Assign your respective schools a letter (A, B, C, D, E) that corresponds with one of the letters at the top of the chart.

2. List your criteria in the vertical column on the left.

3. Rank how well each school that you are interested in performs for criterion 1, on a scale of 1 to 5.

4. Assign a weight to criterion 1, with 1 being slightly important to you to 3 being very important.

5. Multiply the rank that you gave to each school for criterion 1 by the weight for criterion 1. Record the result in the appropriate column.

6. Repeat this process for each of your criterion.

7. Add up the respective weighted scores of each of the schools and compare the results. Ask whether this makes sense with your "gut" feel for each school.

CHAPTER FOUR

STANDARDIZED TESTS

Melissa Dell, Harvard

I remember first hearing about the SAT from watching TV sitcoms in junior high. The picture they painted was of a mind-boggling, superimportant test. If you bombed it, you'd end up at Clown College instead of Stanford. Maybe, like some of the College Matters team members, you have to hear about the SAT or ACT virtually every night at dinner from your bordering-on-obsessed mother, who notifies you that you'd better start studying now, since Linda's daughter got a 1500 on the SAT and Cynthia's son made a 1470. Or maybe you heard about the SAT from your ever-so-informed guidance counselor, who told you that it was out of 3600 points. (It's not out of 3600—it's out of 1600 until March 2005, 2400 thereafter—and yes, this is a true story.)

Chances are that however well intentioned your mother and guidance counselor may be, they probably haven't taken the SAT since they were wearing orange-checkered bell-bottoms and listening to *Yellow Submarine* in the 1970s. So, they aren't likely to remember what it's actually like to face the pressure of taking the thing. If what you want is the *real* lowdown on standardized tests from students who have recently taken them and done well, then read on. This chapter will tell you what you really have to know to ace those dreaded tests—straight and simple, no B.S. about it. In this chapter, we'll expose the half-truths surrounding standardized testing for what they are, giving you the lowdown on the exams that you'll most likely encounter.

The SAT I

The Lowdown

- The SAT I is the test that most people take to get into college.

- You can take it more than once.

- Colleges will see all your scores, but most will count only the highest ones.

- Most colleges will look at your highest math score and your highest verbal score, if you take the test multiple times (that is, you can mix and match scores).

- Scores on each section range from 200 to 800 (1600 total pre-March 2005 and 2400 total post-March 2005). The mean score for each section is around 500.

Chances are that if you want to go to college, you're gonna have to take this test (or the ACT—flip forward in this chapter for details in the section entitled "The ACT"). What follows is a brief description of the SAT test, pre- and post-March 2005, when it will be changed.

A Brief Description

What's the format of the SAT I *before* March 2005? The SAT I (prior to March 2005) is a three-hour test with seven sections:

- Three *verbal* sections: Two 30-minute sections and one 15-minute section.

- Three *math* sections: Two 30-minute sections and one 15-minute section.

- One *equating* (or *experimental*) section: One 30-minute section of either verbal or math. The equating section doesn't count toward your score.

In order to make sure that want-to-be-good test takers don't cheat, the sections appear in different orders in different books. So don't freak out if you are working on verbal, and the person next to you is working on math. Also, there is no way to tell which section is the equating section, so treat them all seriously. By the same token, don't freak out if you think you didn't do so hot on one section, because it may be the equating one. This exam is more about preparing your state of mind than you think, so practice some Zen deep breathing.

What's on the SAT I *before* March 2005? Three types of *verbal* questions are used on the SAT I:

- Analogies (nineteen questions)
- Sentence completions (nineteen questions)
- Critical reading (forty questions)

Three types of *math* questions are used on the SAT I:

- Five-choice multiple-choice (thirty-five questions)
- Four-choice quantitative comparison (fifteen questions that emphasize the concepts of equalities, inequalities, and estimation)
- Student-produced response (ten questions that have no answer choices provided)

What's the Format of the SAT I *beginning* March 2005? The new SAT will last for three hours and thirty-five minutes. (Ugh—the agony will be slightly prolonged. But, hey, its good practice for all you ambitious, soon-to-be pre-meds who will be taking the eight-hour MCAT in a few years—*groan*.)

- One *writing* section of fifty minutes
- Three *critical reading (verbal)* sections, two of twenty-five minutes and one of twenty minutes
- Three *math* sections, two of twenty-five minutes and one of twenty minutes

What's on the SAT I *beginning* March 2005? Three types of multiple-choice *writing* questions and an essay:

- Identifying sentence errors
- Improving sentences
- Improving paragraphs
- An essay

For those of you who have taken the SAT II Writing test (see the next section, entitled "SAT II Subject Tests," for more information), this section may seem very similar (and it should). The questions *and* the essay are basically testing your grammar ability (you know, all those annoying rules you started learning in second grade, but no, you won't have to diagram sentences). In addition, the essay tests your ability to write in a clear and organized fashion.

Three types of critical reading (verbal) questions:

- Reading comprehension
- Sentence completions
- Short paragraph reading comprehension

This is just like the old SAT verbal section, except that the analogies have been replaced by short paragraph reading comprehension questions, which consist of brief paragraphs, (which are basically like the longer passages, but broken up into shorter chunks) followed by a question. Trust me, replacing the analogies is the best thing that the College Board folks have done since they "dumbed down" the SAT in the 1990s. You have to have a gargantuan vocabulary to get all the analogies questions right. Short paragraph comprehension questions, on the other hand, will be much easier to prepare for. See the section entitled "Studying for Standardized Tests" for more info on how to prepare for the SAT.

Four types of *math* questions:

- Numbers and operations
- Algebra and functions
- Geometry and measurement
- Data analysis, statistics, and probability

Whoa! Functions? Data analysis? While the new SAT math section might sound as if it is going to be way more difficult, the changes aren't actually as big as they seem. The test will include a couple of things from Algebra II (for example, functions), for which you can easily prepare, and even fewer things from statistics (once again, easily prepped). Quantitative comparisons have been eliminated—trust me, a good thing.

If you go to www.collegeboard.com, you can get lots of specific information on what each type of question is supposed to "measure," in theory. While the people at College Board have lofty-sounding descriptions about what the test measures, in reality SAT verbal questions test your vocabulary and SAT math questions test how good you are at basic arithmetic, algebra, and geometry (and how good you are at avoiding the silly, incessantly annoying traps that College Board folks set). The Web site also contains information about fee waivers and accommodations for students with disabilities and allows you to register online. If you need accommodations for a disability, be sure to send in the required paperwork several months in advance, as processing accommodation requests takes time.

Demythologizing the SAT I

True/False: Guessing on the SAT won't hurt my score.

True (probably): You've probably heard that there is a guessing penalty on the SAT. The good news is that as long as you can eliminate at least one answer, it is *to your advantage* to guess from the remaining choices. Any test prep company will tell you so (and they don't make millions of dollars for giving bad advice). Even College Board, the company that wrote the test, will tell you that while it doesn't make sense to spend time randomly filling in bubbles, you should guess whenever you can eliminate at least one choice.

True/False: The new SAT is going to be so much harder. Algebra II and an essay—the College Board wants to destroy my life!

False: Okay, so maybe the College Board does want to destroy your life. But redesigning the SAT is a lousy attempt to do so, at best. The number of people receiving each particular score on the SAT will remain the same (that is, it's a curved test). But for people who study (like you), the essay will be even easier to prepare for than the analogies section, which the College Board is throwing out the window. You can learn a few simple techniques to send your essay scores through the roof, whereas analogies are killers and very hit-or-miss. Flip to the section of this chapter entitled "Studying for Standardized Tests" to learn more about how to get ready for the writing section of the test. As for the Algebra II, it will replace the quantitative comparisons. For all of you who have taken the SAT before, you know that quantitative comparisons are horrific. They are full of booby traps and have a bigger guessing penalty. Give me straightforward Algebra II any day.

If you are class of 2006, you have the unique opportunity to take both versions of the SAT and see which one you do best on. So register to take the SAT now, and then register again to take it in March once it has changed. (Of course, don't do so if you do fabulously the first time around. However, you may have no choice if, for some reason, the college you are interested in makes you take the new one, which will be made crystal clear in their application materials.)

True/False: The SAT is a very important test. If I don't do well on it, I will not get into the college I want and will not be successful in life.

Both: Hah-hah, trick question. Yes, the SAT is important, and yes, as lousy as it may be, it's necessary to face up to the fact that how well you do on it will affect which schools you will be able to get into and which scholarships you will be able to win. But, there are *lots* of things that go into making admissions and scholarship decisions and *tons* of things that determine how "successful" you will be in life, including your personal definition of success. In sum, the SAT is important and you need to take it seriously, but it's not everything.

How Many Times Should I Take the SAT?

How many times you take the SAT depends on what sort of school you want to go to. State U. will often just look at your highest score when they award scholarships based solely on SAT scores, so it probably wouldn't hurt you to take it multiple times. However, if you're applying to a selective or liberal arts school, I wouldn't take it more than three times. Admissions officers will see all your scores, and the fact that you took the test a zillion times will not impress them. You should show that you have more productive things to do with your time. I knew a couple of people in high school who took the ACT eight or nine times, and very few of them improved their scores. If you want to practice, take real SATs under real testing conditions (for more information, turn to the prep section). Don't pay some exorbitant fee to take the actual test.

SAT II Subject Tests
The Lowdown

- Most selective colleges (that is, colleges that admit less than 50 percent of applicants) require that you take *three* of these one-hour subject tests.

- Some colleges give college credit for certain scores on the SAT IIs. Nearly all will use them for language placement purposes. Check out the Web sites of colleges in which you're interested.

- There are eighteen different subject tests (at the time of printing), ranging all the way from Hebrew to standard mathematics.

- They fall roughly into five areas: English, History, Mathematics, Science, and Languages.

I'm a Senior, My Dream College Requires the SAT IIs, and I Haven't Taken Any — What Do I Do?

Okay, no big deal, you'll be fine. It would have been easier on you now if you'd taken a couple earlier, but there is absolutely no reason why you can't still ace them. Yeah, it's gonna be extra work to prep for these exams, but I have lots of friends who prepped at the last minute (that is, at the start of senior year, not the night before the exam, smarty), did well, and are now at fabulous colleges. If you are a senior and currently taking fourth year or above in a foreign language, strongly consider taking the corresponding SAT II, as the material will be fresh in your mind. If you're good at math, take the Math IC or IIC exam (the differences are explained in the true/false questions in this section). If you're good at English, take the Writing and Literature exams. If you are still short on exams, consider reviewing material from junior year Chemistry, American History, or last year's whatever class—it'll all come back more quickly than you think.

- Each test is scored on a scale that ranges from 200 to 800. Median scores vary by subject.

You should find out which SAT IIs the schools in which you are at all interested require, as early on as possible. Most schools require Writing, and science/tech schools usually require Math as well as Chemistry *or* Physics. It makes the most sense to take an exam right after you finish taking the corresponding class (this means signing up for the May or June administration), beginning sophomore or junior year. For example, I took World History after I finished the class sophomore year. Tests in languages, Math, and English should be saved for later on in your high school career, after you've taken more related classes.

The Format of the SAT IIs

SAT IIs are one-hour examinations that test your knowledge in a single subject area. They are all multiple-choice, with the exception of the Writing test, which contains a (fortunately very brief) twenty-minute essay. Like the essay that will soon appear on the SAT I, the essay on the SAT II Writing exam is graded by overworked English teachers and is easy to prep for, if you have the guidance of a good SAT II prep book or class.

Demythologizing the SAT IIs

True/False: I should take more than three SAT IIs because I will have a better chance of getting higher scores.

Depends: It will probably be to your advantage to take more than three if you meet both of the following criteria:

1. You have three scores already, but aren't happy with them.
2. You're pretty sure that you can do significantly better on other subject tests.

But just taking lots of SAT IIs will not make your application look good; in fact, overdoing it may hurt your chances of getting in. My interviewer for Harvard told me a story about a kid from a Tibetan monastery who thought that he had to take every single SAT II test, including the really random language ones like Modern Hebrew and Korean with Listening. So, when the

Harvard admission folks got his application, there were scores from every single test. This might have worked for him (hey, he's a Buddhist monk), but it won't work if you're some kid living in suburbia. You used to be able to choose which scores colleges would see, but those days are long gone. Colleges will see *all* your scores, so you need to seriously evaluate which subjects you're good at and then strategically choose which tests to take. This means thinking about which ones you'll do best on.

True/False: The best way to study for SAT II exams is by reviewing relevant textbooks.

False: It seems that studying your biology textbook would be the best way to prepare for the bio exam, right? Wrong! So many students fall into this trap. There is *lots* of stuff in your bio textbook, 95 percent of which will never show up on the exam. Why study stuff you don't need to know? Not only is it extra work, but it will detract your attention from what is actually relevant. Go to the bookstore or library, pick up a book that has been written specifically to prepare students for the SAT II, and study it well.

True/False: It is harder to get a good score on the Math IIC exam than on the Math IC.

False (if you're halfway decent at math): Quick crash course: There are two math exams, IC and IIC—the IIC is more advanced. But guess what— the curve is also *way* more generous to correct for this, so unless you really hate math, strongly consider taking the IIC. If you're borderline, buy a copy of each test from www.collegeboard.com, and see which one you do better on. If the scores are similar, take the IIC, because doing so will be more impressive.

True/False: It's best to take exams in a single area, so that I can show I am superstellar at something.

False (usually): It definitely looks best to take exams in diverse areas, so that you can show that you're a superstar in everything, but not at the expense of lower scores. Even techie schools usually require the Writing exam (in addition to one in math and another in science), because this is an important skill. However, if the extent of your Spanish is Taco Bell commercials, *puh-lease* do not take the Spanish exam. (It can be useful though, if you really do speak Spanish, to practice by listening to Spanish language commercials!) It's okay to take two exams in the same area (I took Writing and Literature) but try to make sure the third exam is in a diverse area (I also took World History and Math IIC). Many schools will waive your freshman year language requirement if you get above a certain score on an SAT II language exam, and SAT IIs are much easier than APs, so this is something to keep in mind when choosing which tests to take. However, if you want to use the SAT II to get out of a language requirement but don't want schools to see your score, consider taking the exam in May of your senior year (like I did with Spanish), so that it won't be used to make admissions decisions.

The ACT

ACT Lowdown

- The ACT can be taken *instead of* the SAT I.
- Like the SAT I, you can take the ACT more than once.
- Each section of the ACT is worth a total of 36 points.
- You *cannot* mix and match ACT scores like you can with SAT scores.
- The ACT is taken mostly by students in the South and Midwest, whereas the SAT is taken mostly by students on the East and West coasts.

Format of the ACT

The ACT tests your skills in four areas, and lasts two hours and fifty-five minutes:

- *English:* Seventy-five questions (forty-five minutes)
- *Mathematics:* Sixty questions (sixty minutes)
- *Reading Comprehension:* Forty questions (thirty-five minutes)
- Science: Forty questions (thirty-five minutes)
- *Optional* (surprising, isn't it?): A *writing test* (thirty minutes), beginning in February 2005

As you can see, some ACT sections are (much) longer than others. However, all will count equally toward your score (with the exception of the Writing test, which will be scored separately). Scores are calculated by adding your four subsection scores together, and then dividing by 4. Here's a more detailed breakdown, with some section specific study tips.

English. This section tests things like grammar and punctuation. Note that it *does not* test vocabulary like the SAT. So if your vocabulary is infinitesimally miniscule, but you're decent at grammar, you might want to opt for the ACT.

Math. This section consists of arithmetic, pre-algebra, basic algebra, geometry, and four trigonometry questions. ACT math is pretty straightforward (not tricky like the SAT). Review arithmetic, basic algebra (mostly stuff from Algebra I) and Geometry. And what about trig? "I haven't taken trig, my school doesn't offer it," you might be crying out in alarm. Basically, you can count all the things you need to know about trig on one hand. You should know the basic trigonometric identities (sin, cos, and tan) and the identity $\sin^2 + \cos^2 = 1$. If you are hazy on these concepts, ask your math teacher, consult the trigonometry chapter of an algebra book, or check out a test prep book. Trust me, if you know these basic facts, the trig questions are the easiest on the ACT.

Reading. ACT reading questions, unlike SAT critical reading questions, do not follow the order of the passage (which makes them a giant pain). The main key to doing stellar on the reading section is moving quickly and accurately, and the best way to do this is to practice, practice, practice. I can't emphasize this enough—you will improve your score through practice.

Science. The good news is that the science section requires no outside knowledge (that is, all the info you need to answer questions is provided on the test). While general knowledge about science learned in your classes will help, approach the ACT Science passages the same way you approach the critical reading passages. Look for the *assumption* underlying each experiment and the point of carrying out the experiment (the *objective*). Simply identifying these two things will help you to answer many of the questions. And remember, the *control* of an experiment is the variable that is not changed.

For more info about the test, registering online, fee waivers, and accommodations for students with disabilities, check out www.act.org.

Demythologizing the ACT

True/False: Now that the SAT is going to have an essay, I should take the ACT.

False: Don't let the essay deter you from taking the SAT. Doing the essay might sound like hard work, but you can easily prep for it. Many colleges may require you to take the essay part of the ACT (for more information, consult their Web sites), and even if you don't have to do the essay part of the ACT, you'll still have to do the science.

True/False: Colleges just look at my highest score, so it's usually good to keep taking the ACT until I get the score I want.

False: Colleges will see *all of* your ACT scores; if you have to take it a million times to improve your score, it's not going to look good. Come on, you've got to have something more productive to do with your time than taking the ACT eight times. That being said, taking it two or three times is not a problem, if you have studied hard and think you can improve your score. The following are some statistics about students who took the ACT a second time:

- 55 percent increased their composite score.
- 22 percent had no change in their composite score.
- 23 percent decreased their composite score.

So, it's up to you. But remember, a negative change just isn't impressive, so make sure that you prepare a lot if you're going to try again.

ACT versus SAT

If you are from the South or Midwest like I am, you are probably wondering if you need to even waste your time learning about the SAT. You might be uncertain if you should take the SAT, the ACT, or both. Once again, the answer to this question depends on several factors. I went to high school in the Midwest, in Oklahoma, and was virtually the only one at my high school to take the SAT. Why did I bother to take it? Well, I did so for three reasons:

1. I had already put a lot of time into studying for the PSAT for the National Merit Scholarship program (see the section entitled

"PSAT/NMSQT" later in this chapter for more details on the PSAT), so it required just a little extra effort to take the SAT.

2. National Merit semifinalists must take the SAT to advance to the final-ist stage.

3. Some people do better on the SAT, others on the ACT, so I decided to take both.

So, what should you do? If you have already put significant time into study-ing for the PSAT or are planning on doing so, I would focus your energies on studying for the SAT. Take a practice ACT to see if for some reason you do much better on it. (Perhaps your school district specifically prepares stu-dents to take the ACT.) If that's the case and you bomb your practice SAT, then take the ACT. At the end of this chapter you will find a chart that will allow you to compare your SAT score to your ACT score.

If the PSAT has already come and gone, and you don't quite remember what it was (that is, you didn't study at all), you should probably take the ACT. You should do so because, if you come from an area where students mostly chose this option, you are more likely to be familiar with it. Of course, you can take both tests. Before you do, though, listen to someone who did. It takes a lot (I mean *a lot*) of time to study as hard as you need to for both the ACT and the SAT (especially if you have to take SAT IIs and APs as well). Do you really want to take more tests than you have to? Don't spread yourself too thin. Focus on doing one thing well.

If you do decide to take both tests, use the conversion chart at the end of this chapter to see which score is best. Only send the score of the test on which you did best to colleges. 99 percent of the time, colleges have no preference between the SAT and the ACT. Check the Web sites of colleges of interest to make sure that this is the case.

PSAT/NMSQT

The Lowdown

- It's like the SAT but shorter (yeah!) and no essay.

- You take it during October of your junior year (and many schools let sophomores take it as well, just for practice).

- It you do well, you can get lots of money for college by being a National Merit Scholar (amounts ranging from small scholarships to a full ride).

- Colleges will never see your scores (unless you tell them).
- It will help you prep for the SAT I and the SAT II Writing test.

Format of the PSAT

Starting in October 2004, the format of the PSAT will change to reflect the new format of the SAT. The entire test will last two hours and five minutes. It will contain the following:

- Two 25-minute *critical reading (verbal)* sections
- Two 25-minute *math* sections
- One 25-minute *writing* section

Like the new SAT, the critical reading section will contain short paragraph reading comprehension questions and no analogies. The new math section will incorporate most of the new changes to the SAT math section (for example, no quantitative comparisons), but it will *not* contain Algebra II (a.k.a. "higher-level") math questions. The writing exam will contain multiple-choice questions similar to those that will be on the SAT, but no essay.

PSAT Recognition Programs in a Nutshell

National Merit Scholarship Corporation (NMSC). The National Merit Scholarship Program is a privately financed academic competition based on the PSAT scores you receive during junior year. To participate, you must be a U.S. citizen or a permanent resident who is in the process of becoming a citizen. Of over 1.2 million test takers, 50,000 will be selected to advance in the competition. In April following the test, these students will be invited to select two schools to which National Merit will refer them. In late September of senior year, more than two thirds, or about 34,000, of the approximately 50,000 high scorers on the PSAT will receive letters of commendation, but they will not continue in the competition for Merit Scholarship awards. What does this mean? Commended students are those who have very good scores but not quite good enough to qualify for as many big scholarship bucks as finalists (darn!). Notably, commended students will not qualify for scholarships offered by the National Merit Foundation, but they may qualify for certain scholarships sponsored by their parents' employers.

About 16,000 students, or approximately a third of the 50,000 high scorers, will be notified that they have qualified as semifinalists. If you are a semifinalist, you will have to write a couple of essays, have your guidance counselor send your transcript, and have the College Board send in your SAT I scores. Most semifinalists become finalists. Basically, National Merit wants to ensure that students who have lousy grades and don't try in school but who are brilliant test takers (you know, those superannoying geniuses who never bother to attend class) are not rewarded as much as those of you who have actually put some effort into your education.

Translation: What this all means for you is potential big bucks. If you do well enough on the PSAT, universities will *pay you* to go to college. (In addition to offering a scholarship to cover tuition, room, and board, some schools also award National Merit Finalists with a stipend to cover things like books.) Even if you choose to go to a college that doesn't pay people to attend (for example, an Ivy League School), private companies or the National Merit Foundation will give you money.

Here's one possible scenario: You win a National Merit scholarship worth $20,000 per year that is renewable for four years. That means college will be *$80,000 cheaper*. If you study for twenty hours, that is $4000 per hour. If you are more ambitious and study for forty hours, that's still $2000 per hour. If you only study for five hours, you probably won't be a National Merit Scholar. So, unless you have a job that will pay you thousands of dollars per hour, I would suggest studying—hard (see the section entitled "How to Study" for more info). Sometimes colleges will give you other stuff too— mere pennies compared to the scholarships, but still a fun reward for studying so hard. For example, a big state university that heavily recruits National Merit Scholars gave me three free football tickets for coming to visiting day (and their team was ranked number 1 in the country at that point).

Okay, so here is the important question: If you are selected as a finalist, how much money can you expect? Well, there are three different types of scholarships—you will be offered one and only one. They break down as follows:

- *College-sponsored merit scholarship awards.* A lot of public universities and some liberal arts colleges sponsor these. I have friends who were basically paid to attend their universities because they were National Merit Scholars. You qualify for this award by naming a participant school as your first choice.

- *Corporate-sponsored national merit awards.* If your parents work for one of 1700 sponsors, you might qualify for a corporate-sponsored merit award. For example, my mom worked for a sponsoring company so I got a $4000 scholarship. It was not as big as the scholarships sponsored by universities, but since I chose a college that doesn't sponsor the National Merit Program (Harvard), I qualified and saved myself $4000 worth of debt.

- *National Merit $2500 awards.* If you choose to attend a university that does not sponsor the National Merit Program, and your parents don't work for a company that sponsors National Merit, you will probably get a National Merit $2500 award.

So which award do you want? Well, that depends. If you want to attend an institution that sponsors the National Merit Program (oftentimes a public university), you have it made. But don't feel as if you have to attend a college that sponsors one of these programs. People ask me all the time why I would pay so much money to go to Harvard when I could go to a public school for free. The short answer is that Harvard has great financial aid. Colleges calculate how much you pay as a percentage of your parents' income and assets. If you come from a typical middle class family (one with an income of $40,000 to $60,000 per year), a selective school could very well cost less than a state university. Some of my friends have to pay the $40,000 per year Harvard price tag because their families have too much money to qualify for financial aid (usually over $150,000 income per year). Yeah, their families make sacrifices, but I don't know any of them who regret it. And, a great job after graduation can make up for extra money spent on tuition in a short amount of time. See Chapter 12 on financial aid and scholarships for more information.

For more information about the National Merit Scholarship Competition, visit www.nationalmerit.org.

The National Achievement Scholarship Program. The National Achievement Scholarship Program is another academic competition that is a lot like the National Merit Scholarship Program except that it specifically provides recognition for outstanding African American students. African American students can enter both the Achievement Program and the Merit Program, can qualify for recognition and be honored as scholars in both, but can receive only one monetary award. About half of the eligible students (50,000 out of 110,000) are recognized by the program. Fifteen thousand of these students will be selected as semifinalists and 12,500 will be named finalists. Finalists are then eligible for the same types of scholarships as National Merit Scholars.

For more information on this program, visit www.nationalmerit.org/nasp.html.

National Hispanic Recognition Program. The National Hispanic Recognition Program (NHRP) recognizes 4000 academically outstanding students of Hispanic origin. You won't get any money for being a NHRP scholar (darn!), but names of all qualifying students are provided to admission offices at top colleges across the country to encourage them to recruit exceptionally talented Hispanic students and provide scholarships. Doing well on the PSAT and getting on this A-list of high-achieving Hispanic students means getting recruited. In short, being an NHRP Scholar is a great opportunity.

For more information on the NHRP, visit www.collegeboard.com/student/testing/psat/about/scholarships.html.

Demythologizing the PSAT

True/False: I shouldn't check the little box on the PSAT that asks permission to send my name to colleges. If I do badly, it will hurt my chances for admissions and the College Board will sell my name to sleazy telemarketers.

False: Colleges get lists of students who score within a certain range, so if your score was lower than your dream college's range, all that means is that they won't see it. PSAT scores are never used to make admissions decisions. And the College Board will only sell your name to sleazy door-to-door salespeople. (Just kidding! I promise, they won't sell your information to anyone.) You will, though, get mountains of mail from colleges after you check that box—be ready to kill a tree.

True/False: I know that I won't qualify for a National Merit Scholarship, so I shouldn't bother to take the PSAT.

False: In the first place, your high school will almost certainly require you to take it. In the second place, taking the PSAT is great practice for taking the SAT, no matter what score range you fall into. In the third place, you might just surprise yourself with a brilliant performance!

True/False: If I live in Alabama, I don't need to score as high on the PSAT to win a National Merit Scholarship as I would if I lived in California.

True (usually): National Merit Scholarships are awarded at the state level. If your state has 1 percent of the nation's college students (that is, if 1 percent of all college students in the United States are legal residents of your state), it will have 1 percent of the National Merit Scholars. If your state has 20 percent of the nation's college students, it will have 20 percent of the National Merit Scholars. So, it seems like qualifying scores should be pretty equal throughout the country. But the catch is that most students in the Midwest prepare for the ACT, so they are less likely to have seen the material that will be on the SAT (and hence on the PSAT) than students who live in regions where the SAT is predominantly the test of choice. Thus, qualifying scores in regions where students usually take the SAT tend to be higher. So if you come from the Midwest or South, use this to your advantage by familiarizing yourself with the PSAT before you take it. And if you're from California, I feel your pain, but there's nothing that you can do about it, besides studying harder.

True/False: I must know my first-choice school when I am first selected to compete in the National Merit Program. Once I choose a school, I can't change it.

False: The folks at National Merit will ask you to name a first-choice school, but you will be able to change it as late as May of your senior year. Thus, if you are applying to any schools that sponsor the National Merit Program, you might wish to name one of them so that you will receive cool stuff (free football tickets, food, trips to campus, fee waivers, and so on). Just make sure to notify National Merit of the college you finally decide to attend.

Studying for Standardized Tests

There are four options for studying for standardized tests:

1. Don't study at all.
2. Study on your own (using books, practice tests, and so on).
3. Take a test prep class.
4. Get a tutor.

Some students opt for option 1, and a few of them occasionally still do really well on standardized tests. However, consider the type of student that does this successfully—someone who is absolutely brilliant, who never needs to study for anything, who never reads prep material (that is, who most likely won't be reading this book), and who is a big risk taker. Before you decide not to study, you'd better be darn well sure that you fit into this "brilliant" category. Very few students get perfect or near-perfect scores without studying, and not studying involves taking a *huge* risk. Also, be aware that your friend might say she didn't study for the SAT and still did well in order to look smarter, but you can bet that she was taking practice tests every Saturday for a month.

Furthermore, some people say nobody needs to study for standardized tests like the SAT because they test intelligence, not how much you study. This is the biggest lie/scam/myth ever. Reliable studies have consistently shown that studying for the SAT will dramatically raise your score. In fact, one of our College Matters team members improved her score *680 points* after studying over a period of two years!

If English is not your first language, it is even more important to study than it is for native speakers (and it's still pretty important for native speakers). I have lots of friends at Harvard who didn't speak English that well when they first began high school, but they buckled down, studied, and aced standardized tests.

Many students fall into category 2. Tips about studying on your own are in the next section, "How to Study."

Some students fall into category 3—in fact, deciding whether or not to take a test prep class is a fairly common dilemma. I have taught for a national test prep company so I know that these classes can be useful. However, they are very expensive, so for many students, including myself, enrolling in test prep classes just isn't a realistic option. They also tend to help students who either (*a*) have a score below 650 on each of the SAT sections or below 29 on the ACT or (*b*) cannot motivate themselves to sit down and study on their own. If you fall into either of these categories and have the money, you may want to consider taking a class. If you cannot afford a class, consider buying the bookstore-version of the prep material of a specific test company. The tips and tricks taught in class are described in detail in the book; it's just that a lot of people are willing to pay someone who will discipline them to sit down and study.

One of our College Matters team members, a high-scoring, motivated test taker, had a 1500 on the SAT and decided to take a prep class that guaranteed a 100-point improvement or your money back, because he never thought he'd get a perfect score (1600). He found the class totally useless because he was already motivated to study on his own, and he *did* increase his score by 100 points (because he studied on his own), so he had to pay the $1000 fee (ouch). Keep in mind as well that the guarantees may not be as good as they sound. When you read the fine print you may discover that the "guarantee" is for you to retake the class if you don't improve your score—it's not a guarantee of money back.

Increasingly, school districts are offering classes to prep students for standardized tests. If your school district offers a class, definitely take it. But keep in mind that these classes usually will not be as good as classes offered by the big, expensive prep companies, unless you go to a very good school. (Hey, you get what you pay for.)

Finally, you could select option 4: private tutoring. Unfortunately, private tutors, at least the good ones, usually make the price of test prep classes seem equivalent to a blue-light special. Private tutors are extremely expensive, so unless your family is very well off, private tutoring is simply not an option.

How to Study

How you study for standardized tests will depend on how much time you have. It's clearly better not to cram, so if you have a while before you have to take standardized exams, definitely follow the long-term strategies. The good news is that there is a lot you can do to improve your score, even if you have just a month or so to prepare for the exam.

Short-Term Strategies

- Go to your bookstore and buy a book that is specifically geared toward helping students study for the particular standardized test that they— and you—are taking. (The exception is the PSAT, for which you can use SAT books to study for since it is a shortened version of the SAT.) Sit down with the book and study it well. Actually do the questions instead of just reading them and thinking, "Yeah, I know, I got it." Ask older friends what books they like or go to your local library and flip through several books to see which one you like best. Stick with reputable companies.

- Buy *10 Real SATs*, *Real SAT IIs,* or practice ACTs online. All these publications contain actual tests that will allow you to practice, practice, practice. And remember, practice, as your grandmother says, makes perfect (or near perfect). Practicing will allow you to become familiar with the test and to try out all the great tips suggested by your test prep book or class. While you might not need to take a dozen practice tests, take *at least* two or three; taking more will probably be useful, especially if you are a weak or even only a moderately strong test taker. Virtually everyone can improve, and those extra 2 points might be necessary for that $70,000 National Merit Scholarship. When you take a practice exam, try to simulate a real test-taking environment. This means *turning off* the IM and not stopping to answer the phone.

- If you have smaller blocks of time that you wish to use to take real exams, take individual sections under testlike conditions. For example, spend twenty-five minutes taking a verbal section. Circle the questions that you missed, and see if you can get them right the next time. If you make a personal copy, then you can reuse the questions. Take it from us veterans, practice will pay off.

- Using old SATs to prepare for the new format SAT is fine—just be sure you are familiar with the new format, and skip the quantitative comparisons and analogies (yea!). Study for the writing section using an SAT II Writing prep book.

- Don't panic. It's just a test or two. Remember the Zen deep breathing.

Long-Term Strategies

- *Read, read, read.* Whether you like it or not, the SAT/PSAT verbal is a vocabulary test, and the best way to improve your score is to read. By simply studying vocabulary words during the month before the test, you can improve your score substantially. However, very high scoring students (above 750) are almost always prolific readers. Reading will also significantly improve your ACT English, Reading, and Science scores. So find something you enjoy and read as much as possible. Make a list or create flashcards of new vocabulary words that you come across and study them.

- *Start studying early.* I would recommend that you start studying the summer between your freshman and sophomore years. Just take a practice test or two and buy a book about the SAT to browse through. That way, you can *take the PSAT your sophomore year* when your school offers it. This early PSAT taking is important, because it allows you to practice for the all-important junior year administration for the National Merit Scholarship. Even if you don't have a chance to take any practice tests, at least start learning vocabulary words and familiarizing yourself with the format. Definitely start to study more intensely the summer between your sophomore and junior years. Doing so is not a sign of being overcompulsive. It just makes good sense, as you will most likely be taking the PSAT and the SAT or ACT during fall of your junior year.

APs (Advanced Placement Tests)

The Lowdown

- You can get college credit for scoring well on AP exams.
- Getting 4s or 5s (out of 5) on APs will help you in the college admissions process.
- There are thirty-four exams in nineteen subject areas (at the time of printing); check out www.collegeboard.com/ap for specifics.
- Exams last three hours and contain multiple-choice and essay questions.

Finally, a standardized test that is good for something beyond just getting in! AP gives you the chance to do college-level work in high school. If you get good enough scores on AP exams, thousands of colleges worldwide will grant you course credit or even sophomore standing.

Benefits of Taking APs

- You'll study a subject in greater depth and may gain insight into what subject(s) you are interested in studying in college.
- APs will help prepare you for the college workload. If you take AP classes now, later on, when you are in college, you will be ahead of your classmates who do not take APs.
- You'll improve your chances for getting into a selective college. Colleges like to see that you have enrolled in the most demanding classes available (like, say, AP classes).

- You might save loads of money. A course credit at some private universities costs over $3000. By comparison, getting credit from AP tests is dirt cheap.
- You'll have more time at college to take classes you enjoy, as opposed to boring (yes, boring) prerequisites.
- You will learn a lot of interesting information while studying with other talented students.

Demythologizing the APs

True/False: If my school doesn't offer AP classes, I can't take AP exams.

False: Just because your school doesn't have AP classes doesn't mean you can't take AP tests. In fact, taking AP tests despite the fact that your school does not offer AP classes will be particularly impressive to admissions officers and scholarship committees. Of course, you will have to put in extra time on your own studying for the exams (as you should even if you are enrolled in AP classes). You can do this by buying or checking out books specifically designed to prepare students for AP tests.

My school didn't offer AP classes, but I took lots of AP tests anyway. This significantly improved my high school experience (I learned so much more), and it is an important reason why I was able to successfully compete for admissions and scholarships. Yes, prepping for AP tests on your own is a lot of work, but if you're going to be taking a class in an AP subject area anyway, why not put in that bit of extra work now and save yourself lots of work and money later? Once again, trust me, AP tests are (much) easier than college finals.

True/False: I'm already learning about the exams in my AP classes, so it's not necessary to spend extra time studying on my own.

False: Maybe you have a brilliant AP teacher or maybe your teacher is boring, entirely ignorant about the subject, and just makes you watch conspiracy theory documentaries about how we didn't land on the moon (true story). Regardless, I would suggest buying or checking out a book that is specifically written to prep students for the particular AP exam you will be taking. APs test a limited body of knowledge, and there are great books out there like the *Five Steps to a Five* series published by McGraw-Hill that will help prepare you for the tests.

The TOEFL

The Lowdown

- The Test of English as a Foreign Language, or TOEFL, is an English test for those who did not attend high school in an English-speaking country.

- If you were not educated in an English-speaking country, you will usually be required to take the TOEFL if you wish to attend a college or university within the United States. Yes, if you are in an American or international school in a non–English speaking country, you will likely have to take the TOEFL too.

- The TOEFL is scored on a range of 0 to 300.

- In most countries, you will take the TOEFL on a computer. However, if you live in a region without access to computers or in China, it will be necessary to take a pen-and-pencil version of the test.

- The computerized TOEFL is adaptive. This means that the more questions you answer right (or wrong), the harder (or easier) later questions will be and the higher (or lower) your scores.

To register for the TOEFL and to access information for students with disabilities, go to www.toefl.org. At the time of printing, the cost of registration was US$110, worldwide.

A Brief Description

What's on the TOEFL?

The test consists of two types of *listening comprehension* questions:

- Short conversations between two people followed by one question.
- Long conversations followed by several questions.

Also included are two types of *structure* questions:

- Incomplete sentences (where you must fill in the blank with the appropriate choice).
- Error corrections (where you must pick the incorrect word or phrase from four options).

There is a wide variety of *reading comprehension* questions:

- These questions ask about the theme of the passage, to what nouns certain pronouns refer, where a sentence should be placed in the passage, and so on.

A *writing* section contains the following:

- One 30-minute essay. You must write about the topic provided. For examples of essay topics, see www.toefl.org.

In September 2005, the College Board (yup, the same people who bring you the SAT) will be adding a speaking section to the TOEFL. (You know how they love to change those tests.) The spoken section of the TOEFL will replace the Test of Spoken English, or TSE. It is therefore even more important for you to practice speaking English, not just reading and writing it.

What's the Format of the TOEFL?

- *Listening* (forty to sixty minutes): Thirty to forty-nine questions, computer adaptive
- *Structure* (fifteen to twenty minutes): Twenty to twenty-five questions, computer adaptive
- *Reading Comprehension* (seventy to ninety minutes): Forty-four to fifty-five questions
- *Writing* (thirty minutes): One essay

The listening and structure sections are "adaptive": When you answer a question correctly, the next will be harder, and when you answer a question incorrectly, the next will be easier.

Studying for the TOEFL

English is a fairly difficult language to learn, because of the wide variety of vowel sounds and the bizarre way in which words are spelled, among other difficulties. The best way to learn English is, of course, by practice. Team up and study for the TOEFL with classmates. I have lived abroad (in South America) and helped students study for the TOEFL and TSE. Based on my experience, I recommend improving your ability to read, write, and correct errors by reading English language books, newspapers, and Internet sites. Furthermore, the best way to improve your listening comprehension, vocabulary, and speaking skills is by watching English language cable TV or movies that are subtitled (not dubbed). You should also buy a book specifically written to prepare students for the TOEFL and take practice, computerized TOEFLs online at www.toefl.org. Students who have been educated abroad in schools where the primary language of instruction is English are likely to find the TOEFL to be very easy. If you are fluent in English, spend your time studying for the SAT Verbal instead.

Test Logistics

The Lowdown

- Be sure to *register* for your test by the deadline, available from your guidance counselor or on the test's Web site.

- If possible, chose a *test center* with which you are familiar, so that you will be more comfortable on test day. Be sure to have directions to the test center as well as the contact number in case you get lost.

- Organize your *supplies* the night before to avoid panic on the morning of the test when you can't find your calculator or admissions ticket.

- Get plenty of *sleep*. Cramming is not an effective way to study for standardized tests.

- On the day of the test, be sure to eat a good *breakfast*. But don't drink too much, or you'll have to go to the bathroom within an hour!

- Bring *acceptable identification* (a driver's license or a variety of other combinations—check out the back of your test ticket for more information).

- Don't forget your *Number 2 pencils* and a *calculator,* if permitted for the test you are taking. Make sure your calculator has fresh batteries!

- You may also want to bring sinus or pain *medication*, in case you get a nasty headache in the middle of the exam.

These tips should be pretty self-explanatory. Just be sure to follow them for a (nearly) painless test day.

Whew! Got that? Take a deep breath. Don't panic. Worry about each test one at a time, study hard, and everything will fall into place. Good luck!

SAT/ACT Conversion Chart[1]

English ACT	Verbal SAT	English ACT	Verbal SAT	Math (ACT)	Math (SAT)	Math (ACT)	Math (SAT)
36	800	23	530–540	36	800	23	540–550
35	790	22	520	35	790	22	520–530
34	760–780	21	500–510	34	770–780	21	500–510
33	740–750	20	480–490	33	740–760	20	480–490
32	720–730	19	460–470	32	720–730	19	460–470
31	700–710	18	450	31	690–710	18	430–450
30	680–690	17	430–440	30	670–680	17	400–420
29	650–670	16	410–420	29	650–660	16	380–390
28	630–640	15	390–400	28	630–640	15	350–370
27	610–620	14	370–380	27	610–620	14	310–340
26	590–600	13	340–360	26	590–600	13	270–300
25	570–580	12	320–330	25	570–580	12	250–260
24	550–560	11	300–310	24	560		

Composite (ACT)	V & M (SAT)	Composite (ACT)	V & M (SAT)
36	1600	23	1060–1080
35	1560–1590	22	1020–1050
34	1510–1550	21	980–1010
33	1460–1500	20	940–970
32	1410–1450	19	900–930
31	1360–1400	18	860–890
30	1320–1350	17	810–850
29	1280–1310	16	760–800
28	1240–1270	15	710–750
27	1210–1230	14	660–700
26	1170–1200	13	590–650
25	1130–1160	12	520–580
24	1090–1120	11	500–510

[1]Source: College Board, 1999. Conversion tables for the new format SAT are not yet available. Simply multiply the combined score in the above table by 3/2 to get a rough idea of how your new SAT score compares to your ACT score.

Testing Timeline

Sophomore Year

Fall: Take the *PSAT* with the juniors (in October).

Spring: Take appropriate *SAT IIs* (for classes you did well in and have just finished).

Take *AP* tests in appropriate subjects.

Summer: Start studying for the *ACT* or *SAT*.

Junior Year

Fall: Take the *PSAT* (in October).
Consider taking the fall administration of the *SAT* or *ACT*.

Winter: If you haven't taken the *SAT* or *ACT* yet, take whichever you prefer now!

If you took the *SAT* or *ACT* in the fall and aren't happy with your scores, start studying to take it again in the spring.

Take appropriate *SAT IIs* in general subjects (like the Math IIC or Writing) with which you by now have extensive experience.

Spring: Retake the *SAT* or *ACT*, if necessary.

Take appropriate *SAT IIs*.

Take appropriate *APs*.

Summer: Study for *any standardized tests* that you plan to retake in the fall.

Senior Year

Fall: Retake the *SAT* or *ACT*, if needed.
Take necessary *SAT IIs* if you do not yet have three scores that you are happy with.

Winter: The December administration is your *last chance* to improve your scores!

Spring: Don't let that senioritis set in too deeply. You may still have *APs*!

Summer: Congratulations! You're done! Now is the time to chill!

CHAPTER FIVE

THE APPLICATION

Jane Feng, Stanford

So you've pulled off good grades, aced your SATs, and shone through your extracurricular activities. Are you done? Hardly! Now it is time to package all those achievements for your college application. Yes, it is both the most important and the most aggravating thing you'll have to do during the college admissions process. The application, with the possible exception of the interview, is the only representation that colleges will have of you. Therefore, *how you present yourself on paper* is absolutely critical. The amount of time and effort that you put into the application will show admissions officers how much you want to attend their school. So don't get so caught up in perfecting your résumé and acing standardized tests that you don't have enough time to polish those applications!

Before we proceed with the details of the application, heed this word from the wise: Do *not* procrastinate. A good friend of mine had near-perfect test scores, got fantastic grades, and was involved in tons of activities. He was über-competitive for the schools he applied to, but he did his applications at the very last minute without putting much effort into them. He forgot to make extra photocopies of the applications to practice on first, so his applications were covered with Whiteout. Only later did he realize how many typos and little errors he had made and how sloppy his applications looked. He ended up not being admitted to any of the private colleges he applied to—all those little errors added up to a big mistake that cost him the schools of his choice. Don't let this happen to you!

Nuts and Bolts

There are two basic types of applications. The first is the common application (usually with supplementary materials), which many schools accept, and the second is the specific application from each school. The common application is fantastic for students applying to multiple universities, because you can send the same application to many schools. However, most colleges that accept the common application also require supplementary information, including essays (bummer). If a college accepts both, it is completely your choice which one you want to fill out. Filling out the school's specific application will not give you a competitive advantage. I would recommend filling out the common application if you are applying to more than a couple of schools. To download the common application and see a list of those schools that accept it, visit www.commonapp.org.

Both the common application and school-specific applications have similar parts: (1) biographical information, (2) test scores, (3) academic awards, (4) extracurricular activities, (5) work experience, (6) short and long essays, and (7) optional attachments. School-specific applications may also ask very detailed questions about your life (colleges are very nosy). For example, schools might want to know what books and magazines you've read, what movies you've seen, why you want to go to their school, and even what other schools you've applied to. Thus, filling out the application could be a totally revitalizing experience that forces you to delve into your inner self and to discover deep new insights, or it could just be that annoying thing you have to get out of the way so that you can start enjoying your senior year! In either case, the advice that follows will make the process less time-consuming and painful, and help ensure that you blow away the admissions officers at your school(s) of choice.

Nearly all colleges now allow you to submit your applications online. This is a fantastic innovation! It means no running to Staples to make copies of the application, no rushing to the post office in a mad dash to make the postmark deadline, and no hefty overnight express postage bills. If you do submit your application online, it is essential to remember that perfecting the finer details of the app is just as important as if you submitted it in paper form. Don't get sloppy! Print out a copy of the application after you've filled it out and comb through it with an eye for perfection. Did you remember your periods, commas, and spaces? Are there typos? Did you use consistent abbreviations (abbreviate only if you are crunched for space and/or character limits)? All abbreviations should be easy to decipher. Did you upload the right documents? Remember, using slang is not acceptable. These are things the application checker function does not catch. Apply online only if you have a decent connection speed (that is, not modem dial-up). It's incredibly frustrating to sit in front of the computer as your online application loads or saves.

For those of you who choose to apply by paper, you will need to request the application by going to the school's Web site or calling the admissions office. Once you have a copy of the application in hand, pay attention to the following advice: Make a copy of the application as soon as you get it and practice filling it out on the photocopy. You should not fill out any of the fields on the actual app until you know exactly what you are going to say. This way, you can avoid whiting out on the actual application you will submit. Think of your neat-freak English teacher—your admissions officer could be even stricter about neatness, so make sure your application isn't sloppy!

You should always type anything on your application that is longer than a few lines. Admissions officers don't have time to decipher your scribble. If they can't read your application, it will go straight to the reject pile. Once all your information has been transferred onto the real application, proofread it to make sure there are no errors, put it away for a day, and then proofread it one more time. Make sure that you've signed and dated the application in all the required places.

Once you have completed and proofread your application, there are still lots of important details to attend to. Be sure to make or print a copy of the completed application for your records. That way, if it gets lost in the mail or fails to transmit electronically, you won't have to do it all over again. Moreover, you will be expected to discuss any and all parts of your application at any interviews that you might have. Having a copy on hand will allow you to easily review what you wrote.

Try to send all the parts of the application together, in one package. This includes the actual application as well as recommendation letters, transcripts, and supplementary material. Make sure that your application is postmarked by the deadline. If a college must receive it by a certain date, it may be necessary to send it via certified mail if you procrastinated and are nearing the deadline. After a couple of weeks have passed, and regardless of what method you used to send it, call to confirm that your application has been received.

All these details may seem overwhelming. Refer to the College Application Checklist at the end of this chapter for an easy-to-use checklist, so that you can make sure that everything is requested and turned in on time. The deadlines that colleges set are not flexible. Thousands of applicants get their applications in on time; to be considered for admissions, you must be one of them. Use this chart to make sure that a missed deadline doesn't prevent you from attending the school of your dreams.

Early versus Regular Application

Most schools have two different rounds during which you can send in your application: an early round (applications due around October 15) and a regular round (applications due around December 31). The principal difference is that if you decide to apply early (by the October 15 deadline), you are obligated to attend the school if admitted and must withdraw all other outstanding applications. In the early round, your application will either be admitted, deferred to the regular decision round (where you'll get a second chance), or rejected. In the regular round, you will either be admitted, rejected, or wait-listed (that is, if fewer students matriculate than expected, you may have a chance to attend after all).

So what are the pros of applying early decision as compared to regular decision? First, admissions rates tend to be substantially higher for early decision. However, many admissions officers argue that because the early round is binding, it draws the most serious students who are best matched to the college. This, not easier standards, could lead to the higher admissions rates. Second, you'll save yourself a lot of work. Filling out one application will be so much easier than filling out six. Third, if you're deferred during the early round, you'll have another chance to be admitted during regular decision. Finally, if you're admitted, you'll know by Christmas break! Your plans for the next year will be settled earlier, leading to a more stress-free senior year.

The principal drawback to the decision to apply early is that it is binding. You must know absolutely, positively, beyond a doubt that a particular school is right for you. Furthermore, applying early *could* negatively impact your financial aid. Colleges will use exactly the same formula to calculate your financial aid award. (Financial aid officers are generally nice people who are not out to stab early applicants in the back.) However, you will have less negotiating leverage if you apply early because you're required to attend (so, for example, you can't pit one school's financial aid offer against another's). Nevertheless, if it is absolutely your dream to attend a particular college and you know *for sure* that it is the one for you, apply early to take advantage of the admissions boost.

Note that a few schools (such as Harvard, Brown, Yale, and Stanford) have what is called early action. This is different from early decision. You still apply by the October deadline; you are still notified of the status of your application by December; and your application is still admitted, deferred, or rejected. However, early action is not binding. You can apply to fifteen other schools if you want (but don't, because you'll kill yourself), and you have until May 1, the normal deadline, to decide where you want to attend. Note that there is not an admissions boost from early action; admissions rates are exactly the same as for regular decision. If a school you are interested in has early action, I would recommend taking advantage of it. You will know at an earlier time what your application status is, and if admitted to your dream college early, it could save you the work of filling out other applications.

So what happens if you get deferred? The bad news is that admissions rates of deferred applicants at most colleges during regular decision are very low. However, you will at the least get another chance for admissions. You will also have the opportunity to send a supplemental update. If you are deferred, you really need to do something amazing that will make your application stand out even more than it did the first time around (for example, being a finalist in a national science contest or bringing a humongous community service project to fruition).

And what if you get waitlisted? Well, the best thing to do is simply to wait. You will be asked if you wish to remain on the waitlist. If you got admitted to a school you would rather attend, graciously decline so that other more interested students can move up the waitlist. Otherwise, say yes. There is, after all, no commitment on your part.

Since colleges have a waitlist just in case fewer admitted students accept a college's offer of admission than expected, most waitlisted students who get in usually receive the news within a few weeks after admitted students send in their accept/decline cards. Nevertheless, waitlisted students will continue to be accepted in small numbers throughout the summer as spaces open up (as others change their minds, get off the waitlist elsewhere, and so on).

If you are waitlisted, you can do some things to help your chances of getting in. Do not, however, let your parents ceaselessly call the admissions office. This will only hurt your chances of getting off the waitlist (after all, no one likes to be pestered). However, if there is a new development in your life that didn't make it onto your original application to the college (for example, you received a major award or led a large, successful project some time during senior year), you can send this new information into the admissions office. Also, we know students who wrote letters to colleges that waitlisted them, explaining how badly they wanted to go to that particular college—and they got in. If you especially want to go to a school that waitlisted you, consider writing a heartfelt letter pleading to be let in (and cite good reasons why).

If you get off the waitlist, then great! But sometimes being waitlisted may leave you with a negative feeling about the college. One student we know wanted to go to the Massachusetts Institute of Technology (MIT; first choice) and Yale (second choice). But he was waitlisted at MIT. In the meantime, he got into Yale and decided to attend. Despite getting admitted off the MIT waitlist at the end of May, he declined MIT's offer. If a school is still your first choice when you are offered a spot off the waitlist, don't be embarrassed about attending. No one will ever know that you were waitlisted unless you spill your beans, and chances are that you were just as qualified as the students who were admitted the first time around!

As a note, some students get accepted to a college under the condition that they take time off, usually a year, to go do something and grow personally. It doesn't happen that often, but there is a tiny chance that you might end up in this situation. Take this as a blessing in disguise, as you can use this year to do something that really interests you.

And what if you get rejected, without even the hope of being put on the waitlist or admitted on condition of deferral? Yes, it stinks—nobody likes rejection. But you should remember that there is a certain amount of randomness to the application process, and some of the most brilliant students are rejected. (Stories abound of people who were admitted to Harvard or Princeton and rejected from somewhat less selective schools—these things do happen, and they don't always make a lot of sense.) Hopefully, you will have been admitted to another school you like. Please refer to Chapter 10 for more information on what to do if not admitted to any schools (and how to avoid this problem by having a safety!).

Now that you have a general overview of how the application process works, let's dive into the specifics of each section of the application.

Fifteen Schools Just Ain't Enough for Me

Some students who are indecisive, horrified of mass rejection, or spurred on by pushy parents apply to a ridiculous number of schools to increase their chances of admissions. I strongly urge against doing so. Filling out a large number of applications will consume so much time that the quality of your applications (and perhaps your grades) will go down, thus making you more likely to be rejected across the board. The recommendation in Chapter 3 is to apply to six colleges, and I second this recommendation. Apply to two reaches (colleges that will be pretty challenging to enter, given your profile—that is, GPA, test scores, and activities), two matches (colleges that match up well with your profile), and one or two safeties (colleges that you know you will get into). If you are particularly ambitious and willing to dedicate a large amount of time to the applications process, it is probably okay to apply to a couple more (like eight). If you go beyond this number, you are entering the danger zone.

The Bio: Not the Stats Again!

To begin with, colleges want to know all about you and your family: your ethnicity, your preferred major, where your parents went to school, when they graduated, what jobs they have. Make it easy on yourself and write all of this stuff down before you begin to work on your applications, so that you don't have to keep bugging your parents for information each time you start a new one. The following is a list of the things most schools ask for regarding parents or relatives:

- College and graduate schools for each parent
- Their years of graduation (and sometimes majors)
- Their current job title
- Their current employer (use the official name: for example, Hoffmann–La Roche instead of Roche)
- Any relatives who have attended the college (name of relative, relationship to you, and his or her year of graduation from the college)

As a note, it does help to have a family member, especially a parent, who attended the school. This is because schools expect alumni giving to increase if a relative (especially a son or daughter) is accepted to the college. While your chances for admission are higher if you have alumni connections, the vast majority of students who are accepted to top schools don't, so there is no need to fret about it.

Following is a breakdown of frequently asked questions in the biography section:

What Is Your Racial/Ethnic Group?

Colleges classify minority groups as those that are underrepresented, usually meaning African Americans, Native Americans, and Latinos. Women are also considered to be "minorities" at colleges where they are significantly underrepresented, usually engineering or military schools. Asian Americans, however, are not considered by most colleges to be a minority group, since they are not underrepresented. You might be thinking, "Man, it stinks to be Asian/Caucasian." But don't worry about something that you can't change. Identifying with a minority group could indeed help you in the admissions process to top colleges, because the most selective schools are looking for a diverse student population. However, it all depends on the needs of the college itself. Generally, to be considered part of a particular ethnic or racial group, you must be at least one eighth that race or ethnicity. The bottom line: Check all the boxes that apply. And don't lie about your ethnicity (or anything else on your application)! It would be pretty sad to get your admissions offer from the University of California–Berkeley rescinded if the admissions office found out that you were Norwegian, not Hispanic like you said on your application. However, if you choose not to answer this question, then you are assumed to be in the majority, and this does not hurt you in any way! Please refer to Chapter 14 for more information.

What Is Your Anticipated Major?

Some universities, particularly large public ones, recruit people for certain departments, making those departments much less competitive than the more popular ones. It could, on rare occasions, give you a slight advantage if you apply to a department that is less popular (like nursing instead of business). A friend of mine got in contact with the music department at the university to which she was applying. After the faculty found out about her singing talent, they put in a good word for her at the admissions office, telling them that she would be a great asset to the university. While success stories like this do exist (most often for students who are superstellar in a certain field), getting in because of a stated major is more the exception than the rule. Most colleges are just trying to estimate how many people will be in each department, so don't agonize over this question. And don't leave it blank or put that you are undecided because some schools have scholarships for students in specific departments.

Are You Applying for Financial Aid?

It is fine to check the box asking if you are applying for financial aid. Most colleges work on a need-blind basis, meaning that they do not consider your financial situation in evaluating your application for admissions. The top colleges usually have great resources for financial aid, so finances should never be a factor in your decision to apply to a top school. The problem is getting in. If you get in, the school will work with you to plan a financial aid package. If you are applying to a school that is not need-blind and you do need financial aid, there is no choice but to apply. Just because you require financial aid does not mean you won't be admitted. See Chapter 12 for more details on financial aid applications.

What about Your Test Scores?

When you write your SAT scores down, choose your highest math and verbal scores. It is fine to mix and match on the SAT, but not on the ACT, since colleges usually just ask for your composite ACT score. If you've gotten a lower score before or after your highest score, you don't have to write it down! Admissions officers will probably see it on your score report, but make them notice your highest score on your application. Many competitive colleges ask for SAT II subject tests. While some ask for Writing, Math/Science, or another subject, others just ask for any three, which means you should pick the ones on which you have scored the highest.

Academic Honors: Don't You Wish You Could Fill Up Those Lines?

This is the section I hated the most when I was filling out my applications. Since my high school didn't give out awards, and I wasn't involved in academic competitions, I never had any academic awards. But before you freak out on this section, just remember that it's only a tiny piece of the entire application. But if you are a genius with a long list of awards that can't fit in the space (of course I'm not bitter), be very concise but clear on exactly what you have accomplished. If the title of your award is not evident, *add a brief description.* Do not clutter this section with insignificant awards, such as perfect attendance (what a nerd!). If you have more awards than you can fit on the little lines, choose the ones that show your specialty and your diversity (for example, Intel Science Scholar, State Chemistry Contest Finalist, and National Council of English Teachers Essay Contest Finalist). Furthermore, use strategies to conserve space. For example, you don't need to write Academic Quiz League on three separate lines for three separate awards. Instead, put it on one line and follow with Second Place (tenth), First Place (eleventh), First Place (twelfth). Then you'll have room to put all those other awards that you have won!

Activities: What's Up with the Little Boxes?

Ugh! And you just thought the Academic Awards section was a pain. In the Activities section of the application, you get to fill in little boxes with a select number of your activities (your most important ones), the number of hours dedicated to each activity, and your current position or responsibilities (and sometimes whether you were elected or appointed to your roles). The following are some tips to make this section as painless and stellar as possible. See Chapter 2 for more information.

- Make a résumé before you start filling out your applications (instructions are found in Chapter 2). Résumé in hand, this section should be fairly quick and painless. If you haven't written a résumé, you'll spend hours on each application trying to figure out what you've been doing during high school.

- Fitting all of your activities into these tiny little spaces can be a challenging task, so abbreviate when you have to! Don't cut off an important description of your activity because you run out of space!

- Make sure it is clear what your abbreviations mean. And don't write in tiny script in an attempt to crunch your activities into boxes that weary-eyed admissions officers won't be able to read. Remember, highly illegible applications go straight to the reject pile. Also, typing your application helps, but be sure to locate a typewriter before you need it. They are becoming increasingly obsolete!

- Always put your activities in order of importance to you, in order of the amount of time that you have dedicated to them, or both.

- Make sure you describe what you have accomplished in the "positions, honors, letters earned" box even if you did not have a leadership position. For example, you could write "tutored elementary school students" or "organized book drive."

- Don't sell yourself short. Even small leadership positions count as leadership, like "chair of school welcoming committee."

- Use action verbs and strong words. Doing so can make the difference between being perceived as just getting yourself involved in a lot of activities and being seen as actively participating in them. Examples of such active verbs include created, initiated, spearheaded, led, and organized.

The Work Experience Box

This shows admissions officers how much outside, real-world experience you've had and is an indicator of your maturity. It is good to have a job or two to write down, because this will demonstrate that you haven't had everything handed to you and that you have had to work to support yourself in high school. It doesn't have to be a glamorous job—baby-sitting, checking groceries at a store, or helping out on the family farm are all fine. An admissions officer once told a College Matters team member that his favorite application had come from a boy who had to work twenty hours per week in a shoe store to support his mother, who had cancer. Sure, your story may not be as dramatic as this, but regardless, you need to show admissions officers that you haven't had everything handed to you on a silver platter.

Essays: Uh-oh, I Have to Write?!

Aw, my favorite part of the application: the essays. The essay is a whole monster in itself that just can't be tackled in one short section; see Chapter 6 for the essay lowdown.

Transcripts, Test Scores, Recommendation Letters, and Financial Aid Forms: Don't Forget These!

The application will also require you to send in your transcript, test scores, recommendation letters, and financial aid forms (if you need financial aid). Be sure to request your transcript early, to leave plenty of time for processing. You should send an official copy to all schools to which you apply. You must have your scores sent directly from the College Board or from ACT. You can request score reports (for a fee) with a single click at www.collegeboard.com or www.act.org or by filling out a form available in your guidance counselor's office. Be sure to leave six weeks for processing. Also, remember to get your recommendations! See Chapter 7 for more details. And finally, absolutely do not forget financial aid forms. Forgetting these could cost your family as much as $35,000 per year, and deadlines are strict. See Chapter 12 for lots of details on filling these out.

Extra Attachments: Should I Send Them in?

The last part of the application is the optional supplementary attachments. If you have special talents or skills, showing them can only help you. You might include pictures of artwork from your portfolio, musical recordings that you were involved with, a copy of a literary journal that you edited, and prose or poetry that you've written. Do realize that oftentimes the people who judge what you submit are specialized professors in that field. Make sure your work is excellent (perhaps you've won district, state, or national recognition). If you've spent a lot of your time and energy on it, then show the college what you've accomplished. But do not waste people's time by sending in silly talents (like a picture of you holding your breath until you turn blue). And keep extra attachments *brief*. Admissions officers are already overworked looking at thousands of other applications. If you send in too much stuff, they won't look at any of it or will remember you as "the kid that …[*fill in with unflattering description*]."

For instance, Harvard admissions officers will recount the tale of a student who sent in thirty-something recommendations, including one from his dentist. (I don't know about you, but my dentist can write about my brilliant teeth and great gums and not much else.) There are also those students who have *way* too much time on their hands, sending in boxes of pencils with their names printed on them or baked goods with subliminal messages written across them in icing. And please don't send newspaper clippings about yourself, except when you wrote the articles or except when asked. Any extra attachments should display your talents so admissions officers can judge them for themselves; leave shining commentary about your greatness for your recommendations.

Fees

Unfortunately, applying to college requires more than mere pocket change. For each school, you can expect to fork out a $40 to $100 college application processing fee and a test reporting payment (if you have the testing agency send score reports to more than four schools). The good news is that for families with financial need, these fees can be waived. Simply obtain a letter from your guidance counselor or principal explaining why paying the fee would create financial hardship for your family. Fee waivers from the Educational Testing Service (the folks who bring you the SAT) can be obtained from a guidance counselor and require that your family be below the nationally defined poverty line. Request a fee waiver only if you genuinely can't pay. If the admissions office discovers that you have abused the fee waiver, it could jeopardize your chances for getting in.

Basically, those are the main parts of the application! It's not that bad, is it? Don't forget, this is the opportunity to let a person (an admissions officer, that is) get to know you. After you've completed your application, have someone who knows you well look over it and ask these questions:

1. Have I accurately depicted myself?

2. Have I presented many different facets of who I am?

Then have someone who doesn't know you that well (perhaps your English teacher) review your application. Afterwards, ask him or her to tell you what kind of person is being represented on those pieces of paper. Remember, college admissions officers don't know you personally. You have to make them want to know you by showing them what a unique, talented, and multifaceted person you are. In other words, you must make the application come to life and scream, "Take me, take me! I'm smart, mature, and interesting!"

College Application Checklist

College	Application Requested|Sent|Received	Transcript Requested|Sent	Test Scores Requested	Rec Letters Requested|Sent	Financial Aid Forms Sent	Fee Paid

THE STORY OF AN APPLICATION

College Matters Editors

What happens to your application once it hits the mailbox or inbox of the admissions office? We asked two different people: the Assistant Director of Admission at Brown and a college admissions expert at Harvard's Graduate School of Education. Their answers are similar but reveal different details. Together, they tell the story of an application:

Brown University

Every application is read at least twice and sometimes more. The applications are randomly distributed among the eighteen admission officers on the board, so we can get a better sense of what the whole pool is looking like that year. For this first read, we try to offer our opinions and initial reactions to an application.

The first thing we always look at, no matter who is reading the file, is the transcript. We want to compare the applicant's courses to the school profile, meaning: Is the student taking the most challenging courses offered at the school, and how well is he or she doing in those courses? We also take into consideration the student's performance in class through what his or her teachers say in the recommendations. Furthermore, the essays not only provide personal information but also offer us another chance to see how the student thinks and writes as well as how he or she has contributed to the community and school.

Halfway through the season, we switch gears, and we are given the applications from the areas from which we are in charge. For instance, my first year, I was responsible for Long Island, Michigan, Indiana, Kentucky, and Texas. There's not much logic in how we distribute the world among all of us on the board. As the second reader, I have to determine which applicants are the best ones for Brown by taking into consideration what my colleagues recommended on their first-reads, but also by evaluating my files within the context of the school and area.

Usually, we have a week to "prep" for committee, meaning that we need to have completed reading every single file from a given area and be prepared to talk about each one. So, if I have one hundred files for a committee, I could go in recommending all of them (which never happens) or I could go in recommending none (which also never happens).

With our admit rate being 15 percent, it's very difficult trying to decide who will be admitted. Thankfully, the decision does not rest solely on the shoulders of the second reader. Each student recommended for admittance has to have the approval of the entire committee. There is no quota per school or per geographic location. We will simply accept the best kids who are the best matches for Brown. And since there is no such thing as a "typical" Brown student, the "best match" means a lot of different things from academics, athletics, music, and theater to community service, scientific research, personal stories, hobbies, and passions.

C. Darryl Uy
Assistant Director of Admission
Brown Admission Office

Harvard University

In many parts of this volume, authors have told you about the wonderful experience of being a college student, the new ideas you will encounter, the friends you will meet, and the skills you will acquire. What they have invited me to discuss is getting there: the process of admissions from a behind-the-scenes perspective. As you can understand, moving several million students each year from secondary schools to colleges and universities is complicated, especially since we have in this country no centralized bureaucracy for organizing the process. Frankly, I think it works best that way. It does, however, require that you take charge of the process and make it work for you. The rest of this book outlines how you can do this.

Let me turn to the process from the admissions office's perspective: When all of your application materials arrive in the admissions office, they are gathered together both electronically and in hard copy. Your scores, your secondary school record, recommendations, your essay, the interviewer report, and any extra items you might like to add (such as a picture you've painted or a tape of your violin solo) will be collected in your personal file.

At Harvard, where I happen to work, your completed folder is given to a member of the staff. This staff member is responsible for the first reading of files from any applicants at your school or area if you were home schooled. She or he writes a paragraph or two summarizing your case and giving a rating on a series of scales such as academic strengths, personal qualities, and extracurricular activities. Then another staff member reads your folder for a second time, also writing a paragraph summarizing your strengths and weaknesses and giving you ratings on these scales. The third reader, who is one of the senior people on the staff, does the final reading. In complicated cases or special cases, there could be more readings. For example, students with special musical abilities are often sent to the music department for assistance in reviewing the file, or files from budding writer applicants are sent to the English department.

The decisions are made in committee meetings. Since the applicant pool is large, subcommittees are set up to discuss and review all candidates. Each member of the committee has a docket before him or her containing all of the relevant data. The person responsible for the school presents the cases for that school, frequently reading from the recommendations and the candidate's own statement, which brings the data on the docket to life. Eventually a recommendation is made and voted on.

What are the bases of the decisions? Clearly there are many, and these differ from staff member to staff member. At the top of the list are a few very intellectually gifted candidates; students who are potential intellectual leaders. These students are considered so strong that they may well influence a total scholarly domain during their lifetime. We often argue about how many really fall into this category; typically it is 5 or 10 percent at the very most. The largest group of admitted candidates are students who did outstanding work in secondary school and have lots of other things as well that commend them. School leaders, for example, are a subset of this group. School leaders are those that have made a difference in their schools or at state and national levels.

After the first round of decisions are made, the committee as a whole reviews results from the subcommittee decisions. Discussions about individual candidates can be lengthy—up to an hour or more. Ultimately, the final decisions are made by a majority vote of the thirty-five-member committee.

After all of the admissions decisions are made, the financial aid office calculates an applicant's need and financial awards are made. This year, Harvard will ask for no parental contribution from any family with a total annual income of $40,000 or less, and only a minimal amount from families with a total annual income of $40,000 to $60,000. We hope that other institutions will follow these new guidelines and make it possible for more students who come from families of limited means to attend selective high-tuition schools.

If by chance you are not admitted to your first choice school, please do not get depressed by their decision. The college application process is one of the few times when you are judged by scores and records that may well have little to do with your adult contribution to society. Many of the great leaders in every field attended schools that were not highly selective. There are so many colleges and universities in this country where you can have a good experience growing, developing, and getting a good education that you need not be concerned by receiving the "thin letter," as it is known as in the trade. It is much more important to find a faculty member who gets you so fascinated with a topic that you want to learn everything there is to know about it. That's getting an education. College is a life-changing experience; it offers you the chance to help make yourself the kind of person you want to be.

The admissions process, while complicated in a number of ways for applicants, is a wonderful process. It virtually insists that those students applying think about what they have done in life and what they would like to do in their future. Most people seldom take time for this type of reflection, but the college application process encourages it in a number of ways. You must write about yourself and ask counselors and teachers to write references for you. Furthermore, you must take the responsibility of finding a college or university that will fit your personal and educational goals. Beginning this great journey is the first step in a liberating experience.

Dean Whitla, PhD
Director of the Harvard Summer Institute on College Admissions
Director of the National Campus Diversity Project
Harvard Graduate School of Education

COLLEGE APPLICATION ESSAYS

Manik Suri and Kiran Gupta, Harvard University

After hours of filling out personal information, squeezing accomplishments into narrow margins, begging teachers for recommendations, and attaching transcripts, you still have an incomplete application. The most intimidating part of the application process remains: the college application essay. The "how-to-get-into-college" shelf at your local bookstore is filled with books on how to write the admissions essay, yet writing it remains one of the most daunting tasks in the college admissions process.

Think of the college essay as a Rorschach test (you know, the kind where you're shown ink blobs and asked what you see). You're given a set of pretty general, broad questions and asked to use them to reflect on your experiences, goals, and values. That part may seem easy enough. The hard part is finding a way to convey some of the more meaningful reflections in lucid, lively, and concise writing. Trying to transfer your reflections to paper for others to read is often the more dreaded task. This chapter aims to help you accomplish both of these tasks. First, it takes a look at brainstorming, self-reflection, and topic selection; second, it presents strategies to help you to convey yourself on paper as effectively and positively as possible.

Does "The Essay" Matter?

You might be asking yourself why people make such a big deal about the college essay, and you're not alone. When everyone is talking about SAT scores, grades, and extracurricular involvement, it's hard to imagine that something as vague and subjective as "500 to 700 words on a topic of your choice" could possibly have a significant impact on your chances of admission to college. While there's no question that hard numbers and extracurricular involvement are large factors in most admissions decisions, there are some qualities that test scores and long lists of achievements simply can't convey. That's why the college admissions essay was created.

On the most basic level, the college application essay is a tool by which applicants can convey something meaningful about themselves to the admissions staff. It's a chance to add another dimension to your application. Ultimately, it's a chance for you to define yourself, rather than letting the grades, test scores, and achievements define you. Think of it as a bonus, because if you approach the college essay properly, it can be one of the strongest aspects of your application. Remember, it's harder for most of us, including admissions officers, to dismiss someone that we feel like we know. An application that coveys your personality will be less likely to get tossed into the reject pile with "Minnesota, football jock, 2.8 GPA, 880 SAT I" and "Jane Doe, the clarinet player." That's where a strong college essay becomes essential.

What Are Admissions Officers Looking for?

Your college application is essentially supposed to tell a story—a story about you—and the essay is a crucial part of that story. The application is like a jigsaw puzzle: It's a portrait of you, and the essay is the piece that completes your face. Like a jigsaw piece, your essay should "fit" within the context of the other parts of your application, supporting the strong case for admission that you have (hopefully) already made with your extracurricular involvement, talents, grades, and goals. At the same time, it should offer fresh insight into your character and present an aspect of you that hard numbers and lists can't convey.

For example, let's say that you are a student from an economically disadvantaged neighborhood in inner-city Boston who has had to work during the evenings to pay your way through high school. In that scenario, an essay describing your first visit to a wealthy, suburban country club and your realization that aspects of human nature transcend socioeconomic boundaries could enhance the "story" that your application is telling. On the other hand, writing an essay describing how you were clever enough to shirk your duties at your evening job while still getting an annual raise would not round out the admissions officer's image of you as a hard-working individual who overcame financial difficulties through dedication and a disciplined work ethic.

While your essay should complement the image that the rest of your application has presented to the admissions staff, it should do more than merely restate your obvious strengths and gloss over any weaknesses in your armor. Admissions officers reading your essay are hoping to learn something new about you, something interesting, touching, funny, provocative, anything that can help them better understand who you really are. The college essay represents your chance to walk up to the admissions officer at Stanford and tell her something that she'll remember about you when she gets out of bed tomorrow. You won't likely get that chance again, so use it well.

Don't feel that you have to awe the admissions staff into submissive acceptance of your candidacy; braggadocio rarely gets rewarded. Pity doesn't work much better. The admissions officer doesn't need to be sitting in a pool of tears after reading about the tragic murder of your pet goldfish (by your sister's cat, Cuddles, no less) to appreciate that you've faced serious hardship in your youth. Admissions officers aren't looking for essays about your extreme political views, your first kiss, or your favorite rock group. However, the fact that each of those topics has made for a successful college essay should bring home a central point: The admissions staff is looking for an honest and insightful perspective on who you are, what makes you tick, what you're passionate about, and why you're applying to their college. If an essay about your first pucker in eighth grade outside gym class conveys one or more of these ideas, then (and only then) it has the makings of a great essay.

How Much Weight Does the Essay Get?

It depends. That's probably not the answer you were looking for, but it's the honest-to-goodness truth. Some colleges place greater weight on the essay while others tend to focus more on class standing, grades, or standardized test scores. For example, many small liberal arts colleges like Williams, Smith, Amherst, and Claremont-McKenna consider the essay to be one of the most important single parts of the application. A few small schools even make the SAT optional, placing greater emphasis on the essay. But at some larger schools like the University of Southern California and the University of Texas at Austin, the college essay may play less of a role in admissions than, say, your grade point average and test scores.

Nonetheless, almost all of the elite colleges and universities place significant emphasis on the college essay—and so should you. If your grades and scores are less than stellar (particularly when compared with the average numbers for the school to which you're applying), a thoughtful and well-written essay can strengthen your chances of admissions. It might even be the deciding factor that pushes you over the edge and lands your application in the admit pile. On the other hand, a very strong academic candidate who is also student body treasurer and a member of the varsity women's basketball team may be denied admission to an elite college such as Princeton if she answers the four (in our opinion thought-provoking) essay questions flippantly. In conclusion, regardless of who you are or what you believe your chances of admission to a selective school to be, you should take the college essay seriously. Approach it thoughtfully, and you will likely be rewarded for your effort.

Essays: Who Said There Was More Than One?

Generally speaking, the "college essay," or personal statement, as it is often called, is the primary essay you will write and submit with all of your college applications. Some colleges also require that you respond to several other questions, ranging from short answers to complete essays, depending on the programs or majors to which you are applying. In addition, some applications ask the trite question, "Why is our school perfect for you?" or the ubiquitous "Favorite activity and why" question. Each type of question should be approached differently so that, as a whole, your responses work together to establish you as an individual with distinct interests, quirks, skills, and dreams. We will lead you through the different types of essay questions, offering suggestions for how to approach each type, and present general tips on writing all of the college essays.

Essaying 101: Beginning the Process
Pick Your Brain First, Not Your Topic

Arguably the most important step in the essay writing process is coming up with an idea that inspires you to write. Though your subject matter is often limited by the question you are answering, it still makes sense to choose a topic about which you feel passionately. Choose to write about something that deeply affected you personally because only then will your essay reveal something meaningful or insightful about you. Furthermore, most applications (particularly the Common Application) have an open-ended question that reads something like "topic of your choice." Because you'll likely have to answer multiple essay questions (some open-ended, others more delineated), picking a topic should not be your first goal. Rather, start by picking your brain.

Though you shouldn't pick a topic until you've had a chance to reflect, taking a look at the essay questions can often help to focus your brainstorming efforts. If the new applications aren't available when you begin brainstorming, take a look at the previous year's applications (they are almost always available online at each college's Web site). This will give you an idea of the nature of the questions that you'll be facing. When looking over applications to highly selective colleges, you'll find that you may be able to choose between as many as five different topics to write one essay. If any one of the topics jumps out at you screaming, "Write me, write me!" make a note of it, but don't skip the crucial brainstorming step and start writing immediately. The process of self-reflection will help you to distill your thoughts and come up with a number of potential approaches to the topic that initially caught your attention. And if none of the topics seem interesting at first, looking at them a second time through a self-reflective lens can often make a question as dry as *"Write about a summer experience"* sparkle with life.

Regardless of which topic you are considering, take some time before you begin writing (preferably on a number of different, nonconsecutive days), and imitate the Buddha. Think about life. Talk to yourself. Do whatever it takes. Here are some good questions to lead you on the path toward enlightenment (or at least toward picking a topic):

- What's important to me?
- What do I enjoy most about life?
- What do I see myself doing five years from now?
- Who inspires me and why?
- What are some of my most vivid memories?
- How have I changed since I was a kid and what made me change?

The Threefold Path to Enlightenment

The Path to Enlightenment is really an eightfold path, but to help you out we've distilled the essence of self-reflection into three general categories of questions. As you're rediscovering (or discovering for the first time) things about yourself—your interests, values, ambitions, accomplishments, talents, and traits—try to organize your thoughts around three categories:

1. Thoughts on yourself today: intellectual interests, extracurricular involvement, favorite books/bands/ movies/actors/relatives, close friendships, ethnic identity, religious beliefs, personal challenges or handicaps, and so on.

2. Thoughts on your past: childhood memories, memorable teachers, inspirational mentors, embarrassing experiences, obstacles overcome, emotional setbacks, and so on.

3. Thoughts on your future: college plans, career ambitions, heartfelt desires, relationship goals, and so on.

Reflecting around these three themes will help lend your brainstorming session some organization and flow. While the above-mentioned categories are by no means an exhaustive list, they are good "rough" guides to follow in the initial stage of the brainstorming process.

Honestly answering simple questions like these requires the kind of thinking that just might lead to the beginnings of a great college essay. For example, you might start thinking about what you enjoy most about life and before you know it you're thinking about an awesome jazz tune that you heard on a CD your friend lent you last week. Clearly, jazz is somewhere up there on your list of interests. You might even realize that you—the lead alto saxophone for the school jazz band—could write an essay about the intellectual process of jazz improvisation and how your passion lies in its unique blending of art and science (an essay that a current Harvard undergraduate successfully submitted). Indeed, good brainstorming will take your mind across the spectrum of your life, making you relive old experiences, dig up hidden memories, and crystallize your thoughts about your future ambitions. Don't worry too much about the college essay itself—that'll come later. For now, focus on getting your intellectual juices flowing and ideas going.

Often, people in your life can be a good source to tap into for essay ideas. Conversations with parents, friends and, yes, even teachers can sometimes bring ideas to the forefront of your mind. They know you well and might think of something you didn't as potential subject matter for an essay. Talk to them about your ideas and concerns, and don't hesitate to ask them for advice. However, remember that just because your mom suggests writing about your traumatic experience as a four-year-old running around naked in the shopping mall, it doesn't mean you should (it was probably more traumatic for her than for you). Ultimately, this essay is about you and *your* thoughts. Talking to people is meant to help inspire you, and if you find that their ideas aren't sparking your interest, you should stop listening! Also, remember that every essay is different, and that not all of them require as much internal reflection as others. Some of them will have much more personal themes, while others will require you to reflect outward on events, issues, the world, and even the college itself. How you come up with ideas will depend on which question you are responding to. Finally, you might find that some essays take you a long time to write while others, such as the short paragraph miniessays, may come to you a lot faster.

The Write-it-Down Rule

You know that frustrating feeling when you can't remember something exactly, but it's on the tip of your tongue? Well, you're going to feel that a lot unless you follow an important rule while brainstorming: Write everything down! The train of thought that comes your way during one brainstorming session can never be exactly duplicated. Write down your thoughts as you reflect on meaningful questions, and organize those thoughts around general categories or themes. By doing this, you'll find that brainstorming will be a far more productive exercise.

Get a Muse

The Romans and Greeks had muses and so should you. Your muse needn't be a beautiful woman; what's important is that your muse be someone who knows you well and ideally who also writes well herself (or himself). Some-one like your English teacher might make for a good muse. Other teach-ers, older siblings, and parents are other potential muses. Bring a piece of paper with your ideas sketched out and talk them through (in person or over the phone, not via email) with your muse. Use your muse as a sounding board for essay topics. Brainstorm ideas and explain what you're aiming to convey in the essay. Determine whether the particular experience or memory you're considering writing about is the most effective for getting your idea across.

Many of us feel uncomfortable talking to others about our works in progress, and if you're like most people, you probably do as well. It may be because you feel like you're being judged prematurely or because you're not happy with your work yet. But don't worry, you're not supposed to be! That's why it's called a work *in progress* and the exact reason why you should seek advice from someone! Choose someone you know who is smart and a good listener, and then tell him or her that you've been working on your college essay(s) and was wondering if you could ask for a little help. Chances are, the person you ask will be honored. That person may critique your work, but he or she will judge *you* positively: It takes a lot of maturity to recognize that others can help you improve your own work.

Topic Selection: So Many Choices, So Little Time

Unfortunately, there's no easy, painless way to pick a great topic, one that will write itself or that will lead to an essay that shines with stylistic bril-liance. If there's one lesson we've learned from the Great Writers, it's that good writing is the product of many revisions, edits, and crumpled pieces of paper. While choosing the right topic for you may not be sim-ple, it is an essential step toward writing a strong college essay. Simply put, a great topic—one that is right for you, not necessarily one that re-veals a previously unknown truth about life—makes for an outstanding essay. So, spend some time looking over your brainstorming notes and the essay questions. Consider all the possible topics you could write on before committing yourself to any of them. The strategies below will help you ferret out "bad" topics and hone in on "good" ones that would make for strong essays. Once you've narrowed your list down to a few topics, the only person who can make the final choice is the person who knows you best: you.

Topic X: Finding the Unknown Variable

A common misconception is that you need to write about something extraordinary or extremely dramatic in order to stand out in the application pile. This conception, however, is not true; it is usually the most sincere essays that leave a memorable impression on readers (in this case, the bleary-eyed admissions officers). At eighteen, not everyone has faced dire hardships or traumatic experiences in life, and you shouldn't feel compelled to make them up for a college essay. At the same time, don't be embarrassed to write about difficulties you've faced in your life, if those experiences have shaped a part of who you are. While there's no single, hard-and-fast rule when it comes to choosing a topic for the college essay, the following five tips should guide you as you begin thinking about potential topics.

Tip Number 1: Be Passionate About It. Good writing is inspired—by a woman's love, a beautiful sunrise, a memorable debate season, an amazing dramatic performance. If you want your essay to shine, make sure that the subject matter *matters* to you. If you want to impress on the admissions staff that you have a love for learning, don't do it by writing about the History Day project you did on Early American Film to earn extra credit in your history class just because you think it'll impress the reader. Instead, write about the time you spent seven hours at the Metropolitan Museum without even realizing it, pouring over the Impressionist Art displays because you love art history. No matter how unimpressive it may seem to you, your passion and the actions it leads you to take will impress the admissions staff far more than a lackluster essay on a seemingly "impressive" topic.

Tip Number 2: Be Smart About It. You might think that admissions officers will be more likely to remember your essay if you write about something provocative or shocking. You're probably right. But do you honestly want the admissions staff to be talking three years from now about the sixteen-year-old kid who peed in his pants? Though the shock strategy may work well in some arenas, it's probably not the best way to approach the college essay. Nevertheless, risqué or highly personal topics have the potential to become memorable essays. In one touching essay, an applicant wrote about her ongoing struggle to overcome anorexia nervosa, and how it had affected her academic performance and personal relationships in high school (she was admitted to Harvard). The thing to remember is that the shock value should complement, and not detract from, the message you're trying to convey about yourself through the essay.

Tip Number 3: Be Knowledgeable about It. Your essay is a reflection of yourself, and the quality of your writing should speak favorably about you. A quick way to tarnish your golden image is to write on a topic you know little about—and then get caught. If you don't know much about Confucian philosophy, don't try to expound on the striking parallels between traditional Confucian social hierarchy and your local high school bureaucracy in your essay. If you write an essay about the science fair project you poured your heart and soul into—when in fact your biology teacher did most of the work for you—it will likely become obvious that you don't know the difference between salmonella and salicylic acid. Stick with what you know best. If you don't feel completely comfortable with a topic about which you're thinking of writing, either take the time to learn more about it or ditch it. Basically, you don't want to give the admissions officer any reason to question your ability, intellect, or integrity. Which brings us to tip number 4.

Tip Number 4: Be Truthful about It. In the courtroom they say, "The truth shall set ye free!" In the college admissions game, we'd change that to, "The truth shall get ye in!" Nowhere in the college application is that principle truer than with the essay. Because college essay questions are so open-ended, it becomes very tempting for applicants to want to do whatever it takes to write a stellar essay. While no one can really double-check whether or not you did have a cat named Molly in ninth grade, who does it hurt to write an essay about how her death made you realize the fleeting nature of our fragile lives? The answer is, you. Tempting though it may seem to embellish or to invent stories and experiences, there are two reasons why it isn't a good idea to do so.

First, if for any reason the admissions staff suspects that you have lied on your application—which includes the essay—and decides to scrutinize it further, you may ruin your chances for admission. Admissions officers have read thousands of essays in their careers, and like highly trained jewelers, they can spot fakes as easily as they notice "diamonds in the rough." Second, if you attempt to write on a topic by inventing an experience you never had or by pretending to enjoy something you really don't, your writing will show it. Your essay will lack the genuine passion and conviction that comes with honesty. As a result, your essay will probably appear lackluster and only weaken your application. So, if you're debating whether or not to write about the time you saved a little boy's life at the local Y (when you actually pulled him out of the pool in the middle of his swimming lesson), don't do it. Your ability to write fiction is certainly a valuable skill that should be developed, but not through the college essay. In addition, do not have someone else write your essay, paid or unpaid. That is cheating and is just plain wrong.

The Only Word That Really Matters

There's one word that every college essay question has in common, one word that (whether it seems like it or not) is at the heart of every question's intended purpose: *you*. These three simple letters can unravel the mystery of the college essay, because they hold the key to its enigmatic purpose. Regardless of how creative or dull a college essay question may be, you can be sure that beneath the many variations lies a common theme: to get a better understanding of you, the applicant. While this may seem to be a rather obvious point, experience has shown that many applicants focus too much on the subject they're writing about (for example, the time your dad lost his job), and not enough on what those experiences reveal about the applicant (for example, the realization that material success isn't the only thing of value in life).

The admissions committee wants to learn about you, your interests, and role models. The admissions officers reading your essay probably don't care as deeply about the fate of western fence lizards in California as you do (if they do, count your lucky stars). Rather, they want your essay about the science program you participated in last summer to help them see your passion for scientific research, your dedication to the subject matter, and your love of learning for its own sake. So when you're considering potential approaches to the essay topic, remember to write on subjects that are interesting specifically because they reveal something about *you*.

Tip Number 5: Be Different about It. Clichés, clichés, clichés—avoid them at all costs! We've all heard of those topics, the ones that make you want to cringe. "Why I want to make the world a better place" or "The time my dog died, making me realize how short life really is" are topics that rarely allow you to make a powerful statement about yourself as an individual. For example, writing about your desire to be a doctor one day because you like helping people is a fairly mundane subject that is unlikely to be interesting enough to make your essay stand out from the pile in front of the admissions officer. A more interesting essay would discuss how your goal—to become a physician—has been shaped by specific life experiences that you've had and memorable people who have influenced you. Ultimately, the essay should lead the admissions officer to see how passionately you want to be a doctor and help people, but the quality of your message depends on how you convey it. Remember, there are many ways to approach any given topic, and not all of them are clichéd. Try to choose an approach to your topic that seems fresh, engaging, and informative, rather than couching your great idea in someone else's (already used) words.

Essaying 201: Writing Strategies for the College Essay

The Writing Begins

Even though your typical college application essay takes up only one page of writing, that single 8½- by 11-inch sheet of paper can at first seem huge and very, very empty. Let's face it, producing a polished, final draft of your college essay in a day, or even a week, isn't gonna be easy. But the process has to start somewhere, and as long as you've given yourself adequate time, you'll have plenty of opportunities to revise what you've written. So find that favorite pen, settle into that comfortable chair, and get started. Everyone is different, and you know your comfort zone best, so make sure that your environment is as conducive to the writing process as possible, whether that means playing classical music in the background or being in total pin-drop silence. Once you get settled, don't be intimidated. Now that you've decided on a topic and brainstormed some ideas, you're halfway there.

Remember, at this stage in the process, there are no mistakes (after all, the only person reading your words is you). The first words are the hardest, but it's likely that they won't end up in the final draft anyway, so don't try to create your magnum opus on the first attempt. For now, all you have to do is get your great idea into essay form, and that means using words and sentences. The best way to begin is to stop thinking and start writing; so take the first thoughts about your topic that come into your head and run with them. Before running too fast, though, it may be helpful to create an outline. Just jot a few words down for each point, summarizing what each paragraph may be about. This way, once you start writing, your thoughts will stay focused. If you change your mind midway through, it's okay to revise (or completely rewrite) your outline.

Show, Don't Tell

Once you've begun writing, you can initially get away with breaking grammar and punctuation rules. The one rule that you must remember, though, is what we call the "show, don't tell" rule. The key concept behind this rule is that actions speak louder than words. (That was a cliché and an example of what you shouldn't do!) Don't use sentences that simply tell the reader something by stating it. Show them exactly what you mean through concrete examples and vivid descriptions. For example, instead of telling the reader that you want to be a doctor someday, begin your essay with something catchy (but not a cliché!) that draws the reader in while revealing your interest in medicine. This could be a description of a memorable experience you had while volunteering at your local hospital, or an inspirational conversation you had once with a physician that you remember to this day.

Rather than merely stating the point, demonstrate it with an anecdote. Let's say that your years of volunteer experience in a local hospital and the relationships you have developed with several patients have convinced you that you want to be a doctor. You could begin by simply describing a typical day in your volunteer work: What does the hospital smell like? How does your scratchy uniform feel against your skin? What are the nurses and doctors around you doing? Set the scene, make the reader feel like he or she is there with you. Engaging the reader's senses through vivid description is a great way to demonstrate a concept rather than simply to tell it. Use words that describe smells, sights, sounds, textures, and tastes to bring the writing to life.

After you have done all of your "showing" in the body of the essay, you can use the conclusion to do a bit of "telling," explicitly reinforcing the message that your experiences and examples have demonstrated.

Proofreading and Editing

One of our good friends had a college essay that became infamous at her high school because it was a beast that had to be pared down from its original length of twelve pages to just less than one page of text over the course of about two months! The editing process does not have to be quite this severe or drawn out; in her case it was only because she adapted her college essay from a paper that she had entered in a creative writing contest in her junior year (hence, the length problem). But while you might not think so yet, many of you will face a similar problem—the need to "cut" your essay down to size. One page of 500 words, no matter how blank it seems right now, is a fairly small space in which to convey a significant aspect of yourself.

As you begin writing, don't worry too much about length, correct grammar, paragraph breaks, phrasing, word choice, or erasing. Just let the pen flow or your fingers type. The main objective in your first draft is to get your thoughts out coherently. Once you think you have a draft, put it away for a day or so, and don't even think about it. When you come back to your essay, bring with you a clear head and a red pen. Now you need to sit down, read over what you've written, and start the process of editing. Think about what you are trying to say, and what you have actually said as you read through your writing. This first edit should help to develop the basic structure of your essay, as you figure out things like whether you want to revise the number of paragraphs in your draft or modify the main points of particular sections. At this time, you should begin editing for word choice, phrasing, grammar, and punctuation.

Keep in mind that a college essay is not an English paper; you have a lot more flexibility in writing your college essay than you do in writing your English papers. While this flexibility can become an outlet for your latent creativity, be sure to still follow the conventions of good writing. The following are some important points to keep in mind when revising your essay:

1. Have a thesis (that is, the point your essay is trying to get across), and make sure that everything in your essay contributes to that thesis in one way or another.

2. Your introduction and conclusion should be the strongest parts of your essay. If you've ever been out on a date, you know the importance of first (and last) impressions.

3. Avoid contractions generally; they are too informal to use in something as important as the college essay!

4. Use transitional phrases like "consequently," "more importantly," and so on. They improve the flow of your ideas and move your essay along smoothly.

5. Don't start every sentence with *I*. This will make you sound conceited, which is never a good way to appear before strangers.

6. Vary your sentence type. Use a combination of simple sentences, complex sentences, and compound sentences to keep your writing interesting and fresh.

7. Avoid using superlong sentences. Admissions officers may skim your essay, so be sure that it is reader-friendly.

8. Never end a sentence with a preposition (we don't know why, but it's the rule).

9. Don't start sentences with "there is" or "there are," and generally, employ the active voice as much as possible; we've heard that the passive voice puts admissions officers to sleep.

When you've edited and reedited to the point where you think the revision process is complete, show the piece to someone whose command of English you trust and whose opinion you value. This is often one of the most useful parts of the editing process. Sometimes, working on an essay prevents you from seeing it objectively. That trusted friend, teacher, or family member will spot undeveloped ideas, unclear sentences, and of course, simple grammatical mistakes. Even more importantly, this person can tell you whether the essay paints an accurate and compelling portrait of the real you. Often in the process of revising your essay, your voice—the sparkle in certain turns of phrase or the twinkle in the writer's eye—can get blurred or lost. When you give your essay to a muse, mentor, parent, or sibling, ask him or her to read it with an eye toward how powerfully it represents you.

Be Word Wise: Diction and Syntax

Like clichéd topics, clichéd sentences are also a no-no. Examples include "better late than never" and "when one door closes, another opens." Because they are so commonly used, clichés sound awkward and detract from the individuality of your writing. Remember, the admissions officer reading your essay is trying to get inside your head. He or she wants to know more about you as a person. Using clichés makes the voice of your writing very generic. Ever notice how people say that they enjoy a particular author because he or she has a particular style of writing? Well, that's precisely what you should aim to develop in your essay, along with your great idea. Flow and style can help an essay just as much as clarity and thought. Clichés interrupt the flow and are often very jarring to the reader. You definitely don't want to make an admissions officer cringe and risk a trip to the reject pile.

While studying for the SAT, you might have learned a few grandiose words. Feel free to use them—in moderation. A few well-placed big words will sound impressive, but too many will, like clichés, make admissions officers cringe. This is a very common mistake that many overachieving applicants make, because in using too many big words their writing often sounds forced or pompous. Also, never use a word unless you are absolutely sure of its meaning. Misusing words may make your essay amusing, but it will also make you the butt of late-night jokes around the admissions committee table.

Deadlines, Deadlines, Deadlines

After all of your hard work is done and the essay is proofread and formatted, don't forget to get it in on time! Deadlines are terrible things that creep up on you when you least expect them. Unfortunately, with college admissions essays, there is no telling the admissions committee that the dog ate your essay and that you'll send it in tomorrow. There are thousands of applicants who will get their essays in on time, and you definitely want to be one of them. We recommend that you use the calendar at the end of Chapter 5 to keep track of when your various essays are due. Furthermore, set artificial deadlines for yourself and make it a goal to finish your first draft *at least* two weeks before the deadline, allowing for plenty of revision time. Also, remember Murphy's law: Anything that can go wrong will go wrong. So it's a good idea to mail things a couple of days early because you never know if the mail will get there exactly on time. You've worked hard on that essay, with all the drafts, editing, and proofreading, so make sure that it gets there on time, no matter what!

Recycling Essays

After working so diligently on your first or second college application essay, the thought of composing ten more for all of those other applications you still have to get to is probably more than a little daunting. The idea might even cross your mind to simply change the name of the college and use your personal statement for the University of California–Berkeley, for example, in your Stanford application. Such overt recycling of essays is tempting, but we advise against it. While many applications have questions that overlap with other colleges' applications, even similar questions are often different in subtle, yet noticeable ways. Furthermore, according to an inside College Matters admissions source, admissions officers are often familiar with other colleges' applications (they have to scope out the competition, too), and so their well-trained eyes will quickly spot a "recycled" essay in your application.

So does this mean you have to go through the entire process of essay writing ten times? Definitely not! Each essay you write builds on the last and the process gets easier every time, because you have already invested brain cells into thinking about your past interests, future goals, and accomplishments, as well as many of the other aspects of brainstorming and topic selection we discussed earlier. Don't create more work for yourself than you've already got. Instead, go over your notes and scribbled ideas from when you were choosing topics for earlier applications.

Generally, you should avoid recycling essays and treat each question individually (after all, don't you expect the admissions committee to do the same for you)? However, there are some cases, as with the Common Application, when you can actually use the same admissions essay for multiple applications. If you're applying to schools that accept the Common Application, we encourage you to take advantage of the opportunity and save yourself the time involved in writing another essay. These schools will often have supplemental applications with school-specific questions; for those, be sure to address each essay individually. Remember, in the context of the college admissions essay, even if you consider yourself to be an environmentally friendly person (which we hope you do), it is better to refrain from recycling.

The Scholarship Essay

Most of you are probably entering scholarship contests that require essays as well. The same tips that go for writing a stellar college essay go for writing a scholarship essay. One essential thing to keep in mind, though, is the mission of the scholarship fund. In order to write a successful scholarship essay, the message and content of your essay (your goals, anecdotes, and so on) should fit within the mission and nature of the scholarship fund to which you're applying.

Essay Editing Services

The Internet seems to be full of sites offering Ivy League–educated editors who will revise your essays. While this may seem like an attractive proposition at first, our advice is to seek a muse in person, not over the Internet. Why? Well, first of all, these services are very expensive. Secondly, and perhaps more importantly, communicating via email with a stranger is not nearly as effective as communicating with someone face to face. Your muse should be someone who will talk to you and ask questions that will stimulate your thoughts, not an overworked editor rushing to edit (that is, rewrite) your essay to make money and move on to the next one. Revisions like this will cramp your writing style; the essay will no longer be uniquely yours, and the writing will show it.

Since these editing services recruit editors from top universities, many College Matters team members know people who have edited, and a couple of us have even edited ourselves. The vast majority of people who use essay-editing services are wealthy individuals from abroad who are applying to business school (at the graduate level) and have *extremely* limited English composition skills. Few of the individuals against whom you will be competing for undergraduate admissions use these services, most likely because the services are overpriced and not particularly useful. Keep in mind that even if you get a great editor, very few high school students have the same compositional skills as an Ivy League–educated professional editor. It will be obvious to admissions officers that your essay was constructed by a professional, not by you.

One of the reasons why an essay is being added to the SAT is to make it even easier for admissions officers to tell if applicants had other people write their personal essays for them. Your writing style and skill level on your personal essay and SAT essay will probably be compared; if they are drastically different, it could jeopardize your chances for admissions.

Letting Go Is Hard, but Necessary

At the end of this long process, only so much time can be devoted to improving and revising your college application essays. As difficult as it can be sometimes, you have to avoid overthinking and overanalyzing your writing. Your voice is what the admissions officer wants to hear, and too much editing can compromise the originality of the essay. As we've said before, it's definitely important to get help from a friend, teacher, or family member, but remember that this is *your* essay and *you* should make all final editing decisions. Their comments are often helpful suggestions, but at the end of the day, this essay is *yours*. Let the words of Shakespeare, perhaps the greatest manipulator of the English language, guide you: "To thine own self be true."

What Now?

Congratulations! If you've made it this far through the chapter, we feel it's safe to assume that you've survived the process. (If you're just peeking ahead, get back to work on your essay!) Hopefully, the journey was both educational and entertaining, but most importantly, we hope that it revealed something about yourself that you hadn't thought about or known before. Now that you've completed the essay and feel satisfied with the result, put your pen and paper aside and move on to the next part of the application. No one said it would be easy, but you should be proud to know that you've gotten through one of the most challenging and rewarding parts of applying to college.

Sample Essays

The following are some sample college essays, submitted successfully by students to top schools.

Sample Essay 1

The author of this essay sought to demonstrate how his nickname, coined by his brother at a young age, reflects his underlying friendly and outgoing nature. He then used this event to explore how his name and the personality it represents led him to become involved with efforts to promote diversity and cultural awareness in his school and local community.

Question: Sometimes, seemingly insignificant moments in one's life can in fact leave a greater impact than one would expect. Describe such an instance in your life that has helped to shape your personality, way of thinking, or future in some way.

Perhaps I was not sprung from my father's head or conceived in any way that was even remotely immaculate, but in some ways I feel that my birth was of significance because it was that day that not only brought me into the world, but in some ways shaped my personality. On that late September morning in 1983, my parents decided to name me Neil. To my parents I was their second son, but to my two-year old brother I was his first best friend. My brother wrinkled his little forehead when my parents told him my name was Neil and then proclaimed with logic only a two-year-old could possess, "He's not Neil, he's my Buddy!" From that time on I was Buddy, and for better or for worse, the name has stuck. Although there seems to be little significance in the fact that some chunky infant renamed me, the name Buddy seems to have somehow molded my personality from a very young age. Although I am only half way through my first AP Psychology course, I think I can say that, in my case, some of Freud's psychoanalytic theories may be relevant. The name Buddy has fostered my development as a generally sociable, friendly, and caring individual. At the risk of sounding a bit arrogant, my name reflects strongly my personality, and I feel as though I am indeed everyone's buddy.

My ability to get along with all different types of people has allowed me to gain the respect and trust not only of students and teachers at my own school but of those from other area schools as well. These attributes could have been good for nothing more than making friends, but I am fortunate enough to have wonderfully caring parents who taught me to use my gifts as an instrument for positive social change. I am also of the mind that everyone is capable of making an impact on the current state of society, and that if I do not try, I am not only failing myself, but failing others as well.

With this frame of mind I set out to do as much as possible to help my community. As a member of student government, I was lucky enough to represent my school with other government members in delivering Thanksgiving dinners to less fortunate families. The summer after my sophomore year, I was accepted to College Misericordia's Diversity Institute's five-day seminar camp where I realized that despite the many admirable virtues our nation expresses, there is still the subtle, yet undeniably destructive curse of prejudice. The stories of discrimination I heard and the open discussions in which I participated moved me so greatly that I was convinced I had discovered where I wanted to concentrate my efforts. I wanted to help bring my community together, to help blur the racial, economic, and sexist lines that divide my small, predominantly white city. I wrote two articles for local newspapers expressing the need to instill in children the values of respect and tolerance for others. These articles caught the attention of local organizations, and without ever having planned it, I began to play a much larger role in a growing movement to promote diversity and cultural awareness in the community. As I grew more outspoken, I aligned myself with organizations like the Diversity Institute and the Peace Center's Dismantling Racism Committee, and was given the opportunity to speak alongside the District Attorney on a number of occasions, to both student and community leaders. I also had the honor of helping to organize and speak at a "Stop the Hate" candlelight vigil in Wilkes-Barre's Public Square with the Peace Center and the NAACP. These experiences that I have been a part of have shown me that I must continue to advocate unity among people. I know that bringing unity to such a diverse country is an overwhelming task, but I just want to be one person in what I pray will be an ongoing movement toward open-mindedness. Shakespeare once asked, "What's in a name?" For me, a lasting direction.

Sample Essay 2

This author approaches the question "topic of your choice" by exposing different aspects of himself—his passion for science, the influence of his family on his career goals, and his personal experiences in a foreign country—through a "frame story" set in a research laboratory.

The dopamine receptor model is nearly complete, its image revolving in front of me. The computer whirrs as it analyzes my results, offering me a short respite before the next set begins.

Today I am among researchers, a mind inquiring, in a niche I feel born to fill. Here at the Bioinformatics Lab at the University of California, Davis, I challenge concepts still evolving in biology. Professor Rosenquist calls for my advice on the most recent receptor alignments—not as her student, but as her collaborator and peer. I am honored to discuss my findings with such an accomplished group. I peer into the screen at a structure; its curves, loops, and turns each have a specific purpose, giving it a unique role in nature. Understanding that role is the focus of the paper I am now preparing for publication.

No one told me, though, that the work would be so painstaking. This I learned last year, humbled by the tiny flatworm. Eye to eye, we sat in contention, as Subject Four inched toward the fork in the T-maze. In moments like these, engaging in the process of scientific discovery, I found my research entirely fulfilling. The appeal of this monotonous exercise, worm after worm, lay in the fact that I was creating knowledge, contributing to the larger body of scientific understanding. But I wondered where it would take me. I want my work to matter—in a decade, in a lifetime. Though I enjoy the challenge of piecing together the details, it is the larger picture I hope to one day understand. By nature, then, I am a philosopher, savoring the journey, questioning, searching, pondering, even as I'm hoping to make a difference.

Waiting for the alignments to refine, I glance over at a book whose ruffled pages reflect my current pursuit—Atul Gawande's Complications. I am gripped by his experiences as a surgical resident and can relate to his writing, having myself grown up in a family of Indian doctors.

A cell phone interrupts dinner and a pager goes off. A nurse from the emergency room is on the phone——a patient has coded. My mom is swamped with a thirty-six-hour call. Dinner waits as my dad completes his dictation on an epileptic child. With a father and grandfather who are neurologists and a mother who is a nephrologist, I was brought up with medicine as a constant presence in our lives. If my father was delayed, I finished homework on my piano teacher's couch. Often, I read a book in the car, while my mom made rounds in the hospital. But no matter how busy, my parents helped me with science fairs and piano concerts, driving lessons and girlfriends. Over time, seeing them apply their knowledge to allay their patients' suffering, I came to realize that knowledge brings with it a responsibility, that its application is as important as its pursuit.

The receptor models are now rendering. Predictably, the computer freezes; I sit back, allowing the computer to reboot. Taped to the side of the screen, a photo of my family smiling at me from our home in India reminds me of the past.

Every year I return to that home, with feelings of nostalgia, melancholy, and at times guilt. Every year, the walk down to the market is more distressing. An elderly beggar with leprosy, missing his right arm, lies hopelessly on the median. A waif crippled by polio drags himself toward us as a truck nearly tramples his legs. I could have been that boy, he thinks. That could have been my life, I realize. Two minds, a world apart, come together. My grandma opens her purse for two rupees, her usual offering, and I silently wonder, "Can't we do more?" Every time I return to India, the realities become harsher, the disparities increase. The stark contrast awakens my conscience, beckoning me to help those less fortunate than myself.

As a researcher, I've found the intellectual freedom to innovate and the passion to pursue knowledge—an ideal blend for my mind. Still I am driven by the hope of improving the quality of life for those suffering elsewhere. I see myself applying my understanding as a researcher, searching for universal treatments for virulent diseases, or as a member of Doctors Without Borders, directly aiding those in dire circumstances and improving healthcare where it is nonexistent, or at best limited. Yet before I attempt to solve problems on a larger scale, I must focus on those in front of me. I hope that like the shape of the dopamine molecule I now try to understand, the curves, loops, and turns of my life will also have a unique purpose.

The computer beeps and the whirring stops—the results are ready. My presentation is about to begin.

CHAPTER SEVEN

RECOMMENDATIONS

Angelique Dousis, Massachusetts Institute of Technology (MIT)

You're smart. Your test scores are stellar. And, your résumé is impressive enough to blow virtually anyone away! But what is that extra something that will set you apart from the vast numbers of talented students applying to the same university or for the same scholarship as you? This "extra something" is your recommendation letters. In fact, recommendations are one of the most important aspects of your application.

Admissions officers care about who you are. They like to hear about *you* from people who know you well. Your recommendations (along with your essays) make you more than just a test score or GPA. Recommendations give your file personality. Anecdotes written by teachers help colleges quickly identify qualities that they are looking for in a student. Colleges want students who have initiative, who possess leadership skills, and who get along well with their peers.

Each recommendation form asks questions about the student's leadership, interaction with teachers and peers, personality, and social skills. For instance, the MIT evaluation form asks teachers to "comment on the student's originality of thought … and willingness to take risk and go beyond the normal classroom experience." It even goes so far as to ask the teacher to rate the student against everyone else. *Yowza*! So, you are probably thinking: "This is all very sweet. Colleges care about me as a person. But how the heck am I supposed to get good recommendations?" Well, that is where we are headed now. It's time to get dirty—let's get down to the nitty-gritty details.

Note: For younger students reading this book, download some sample recommendation forms to see what qualities colleges ask teachers to rate. Then, try to start displaying these qualities. I mean, why not—they are good qualities, in any case.

Step 1: Figuring Out Who Writes Good Recommendations

First things first: You need to decide who will write the best recommendation for you. Most colleges ask for academic recommendations (that is, from teachers as well as one from your guidance counselor). Some also ask for a nonacademic recommendation; coaches, religious leaders, music teachers, and bosses are good sources for these. The following is a breakdown of several fundamental rules to remember when considering whom to ask to write your recommendations.

Do Your Homework

To get a straightforward answer to the question of who writes good recommendations, talk to friends, older siblings, and others who went to your school and have already graduated. Find out which teachers they think write good recommendations and which teachers don't. You can also ask your fellow classmates what they have heard. For instance, at my school, there was a teacher who wrote such good recommendations that her students would take out the recommendations for years afterward whenever they didn't feel so great, read them, and feel instantly better. If you ask around a little, you might be surprised what information you uncover that can help you make your decision about whom to ask.

Consider Which of Your Teachers Writes the Best

As a rule of thumb, English teachers tend to write well; science and math teachers often have more problems. Of course, if you are applying for an engineering scholarship to Harvey Mudd or another tech school, math and science teachers are definitely the way to go. The following are five things to keep in mind when considering which teachers can write best for you:

1. Go for Diversity. Despite the last piece of advice, don't get two recommendations from English teachers. Colleges like diverse students. If they can see that you kick butt in both French Literature and Physics, that is a *huge* plus.

2. Make Sure You Did Really Well or Worked Superhard in the Recommender's Class. Usually, it's a good idea to choose a teacher whose class you rocked. But what about Mr. Schmitzer, the physics teacher in whose class you worked superhard all year? While that first test you struggled with ended up lowering your grade, you improved over the course of the semester, and gosh darn it, Mr. Schmitzer really likes you. Fine. The main point is that Mr. Schmitzer likes you.

3. How Do I Know If a Teacher Likes Me? As bad as this may sound, think of the teacher who lets you get by with the most. You know, Mr. Gullible who lets you go off campus during his class to buy donuts for everyone. Or Mrs. Trustworthy, who lent you her car so that you could pick up toys for the kids in China that your class was sponsoring. She wouldn't trust just anyone with her new sports utility vehicle. She likes you and will probably write you a great recommendation.

4. Choose Teachers Who Remember You Well. Be cautious about asking for a recommendation from Mr. Ramirez, who taught you Algebra I in ninth grade. He may have loved you, but he might not remember you that well. Plus, colleges want to know what you've been up to recently. Unless a teacher you had earlier can write something really spectacular or unique, go for one of your teachers from junior or senior year.

5. Choose Teachers Who Know You Well. This is perhaps the most crucial piece of advice. If a teacher barely knows you, the recommendation will stink, regardless of how brilliant the teacher is. Plus, admissions officers like to see stuff that you wrote about in the rest of your application reinforced by the teacher recommendations. For example, if you wrote your essay about a research trip to Costa Rica that you took with a school group, it would probably be good to have Mr. Barnes, your faculty sponsor for the trip, write you a recommendation. If the college admissions officers receive the recommendation from Mr. Barnes, they can hear from someone (besides yourself) what an important role you had in organizing the trip. If you haven't gone on any trips to Costa Rica with a teacher (like most applicants), that's fine. Ask Mrs. Stewart, your algebra teacher and the sponsor of the Math/Science team, to write that recommendation for Cal Tech or UCLA. Or ask Mrs. Critzer, your awesome AP English teacher. You go to her office all the time to discuss the latest books you've read, so chances are that she'll write a good recommendation.

Nonacademic Recommendations

What if the college I am applying to requires nonacademic recommendations? If so, look at it as another opportunity to show admissions officers just

---

Uh-oh!

Okay, so you have spent your entire high school career trying *not* to be around your teachers any more than absolutely necessary. You never talk about books with Mrs. Critzer, you spend most of math making fun of Mrs. Stewart, and you elected not to go to Costa Rica with Mr. Barnes because you don't like environmental science (or Mr. Barnes for that matter). Don't worry! Even if you are reading this at the beginning of your senior year, there is still time. Hurry—go, go, go! Drop this book, hop in the car, and hightail it to Mrs. Critzer's office. You must have read a book lately, right?

In all seriousness, the clock is ticking and you need to get to know a couple of your teachers better. It shouldn't be too unbearable, you'll end up with a great recommendation, and you might even learn some cool stuff from your teacher in the process. A word of caution: Don't harass your teachers, just try to become more active. Start by attending meetings of clubs in which (s)he is a sponsor or by dropping by before or after class to engage in a little small talk. Potentially, you could learn something new about the world and even about yourself. Make sure you are genuinely interested in the club you join or the conversations you engage in with your teacher. Teachers are smart and can see through any charade you might be putting on. If they think what you are doing is for the wrong reasons, your efforts will hurt you more than help you.

---

how awesome you are outside of class. Be sure to ask someone who writes well, and who will tell about what a *leader* you have been, whether on the field, in the workplace, or in your place of worship. I cannot emphasize this enough. The nonacademic recommendation must show that you have leadership potential, because colleges want students who can be leaders outside of the classroom and contribute to the campus's nonacademic life. The following section discusses procedures for getting academic recommendations. These procedures also apply to nonacademic recommendations.

An Important Note for Those Still in Fear

What if my school really stinks, you ask? If you come from a not-so-amazing high school where teachers don't have a lot of experience writing college recommendations or are so understaffed that they don't have time to write quality recommendations, admissions officers will understand. You are the type of student they want—the type that succeeds despite obstacles. Be sure to mention something (in a not-too-condescending manner) about the quality of your school somewhere else in your application. Then, get a recommendation from a coach, a pastor, a boss, or whomever who can speak about your academic qualities as well as your leadership potential. If you are hesitant about doing so, don't be. But here's another word of warning: Do not try this tactic if you go to a great, mediocre, or even slightly lousy high school but just haven't taken the time to know your teachers. Admissions officers are smart (most of them attended those selective colleges that you are trying to get in to), and they will be able to tell a lot about your school from the profile that guidance counselors send them.

Step 2: Asking for the Recommendation

Part I: Give Your Teacher Plenty of time to Write Your Recommendation

True/False: Mrs. Slatsky is too old and boring to have a life. If I give her my recommendation form a week in advance, she'll have plenty of time.

False: Mrs. Slatsky might not have a life, but that doesn't mean she'll be pumped about writing your recommendation instead of watching Home and Garden Television. Puh-leeeease, give her *plenty* of time.

While this might seem obvious, make sure you give your recommender a minimum of two weeks' time to write the material. A month's time is best. After all, you do want a good recommendation. Some teachers will tell you how much time they need to write a recommendation. If possible, try to give each teacher a month (maybe even two months) before the school's application deadline to write you a wonderful recommendation. As the MIT application states: "Give them [your teachers] the forms early so that they have time to fully consider the best way to present your accomplishments." Another thing to consider is that the better recommendation writers are going to be bombarded by requests as deadlines approach. Identify your preferred recommenders during the beginning of your senior year and go ahead and ask! Your organization and forethought will impress them and make them happier to write you a glowing letter. So start thinking about who you are going to ask now.

Part II: No Time!

Oh, no! You didn't start working on that "oh-so-important application" until less than two weeks before it was due, or perhaps you simply waited until the last minute to ask your teachers for recommendations. The bottom line is that you only have a little time to get those recommendations done. If you've already gotten a recommendation from a teacher for another school, ask whether (s)he can fill out the recommendation form for this latest school as well. It won't be hard at all to complete the form and reprint your recommendation. Now, if this is the first recommendation, get ready to beg. Sit down with your teacher of choice, and explain your situation. Teachers are very understanding—most of the time. They really care for you, and want to see you go to the best college you can. In the end, the recommendation probably won't be as good, but at least it'll get done.

Part III: Politely Ask Your Preferred Teacher to Write Your Recommendation

So you've narrowed it down to a teacher who "knows you best," and you are about to give him or her the recommendation form several weeks before it is due. It is at this point that you need to sit down and spend some time talking with your teacher of choice. As trivial as it may seem, you need to actually ask your teacher to write you a recommendation. Don't be a pompous jerk and just assume that he or she will write you one. Be considerate of your teacher! You may be surprised to know that "old," "boring" Mrs. Jones is über-busy. Most likely, Mrs. Jones will gladly write you a recommendation, but if she can't, you should have plenty of time to find another teacher to write it for you.

When you ask, make sure to gauge your teacher's receptiveness. Get clarification on whether (s)he will write you a "strong letter of support." If your potential recommender is at all hesitant or tries to make any sort of excuse, run far away and don't look back. The worst thing you can do is to get a half-hearted recommendation or one that just tells colleges what grade you made and nothing else. Your teacher should be happy to write you a letter, so settle for nothing less than a glowing recommendation.

When you get a "sure, I would love to write a recommendation for you," make sure you ask whether (s)he would prefer to submit the recommendation in hardcopy or online. If your teacher does an online recommendation, you will also need his or her email address (and sometimes phone number and mailing address) to complete the online registration for your recommender. If a college accepts online recommendations, it is all right to submit both online and paper recommendations. In other words, one teacher can submit online while your counselor and other recommender can submit paper forms.

Part IV: The Stuff

So, Mrs. Jones has decided to write your recommendation. Are you done? Hardly! With a big smile, give her a few things to start out with.

1. Your marvelous résumé
2. A stamped and addressed envelope
3. The evaluation sheet (filled out with your personal information and signed)

Then, ask Mrs. Jones if she needs anything else. If she asks for orange juice in a clear cup on Tuesday at 7:00 A.M., then that is exactly what you will give her. She is doing you a big favor.

If you have to mail in the recommendation with your application, skip the stamp on the envelope. The recommendation will usually need to be sealed, signed, and dated across the flap. Be sure to remind Mrs. Jones about this.

On the recommendation form, you may be asked to waive your rights to see the completed recommendation. I would go ahead and waive them. That way, admissions officers will know that your recommender didn't write something nice just because they knew you would eventually read the letter.

Step 3: Following Up

Okay, so now you're basically good to go. You've typed up the envelope and the evaluation sheet with all the information you can fill in. You've printed out a copy of your résumé and put all the relevant materials in a folder so your teacher won't lose anything. On top of all this, you've given him or her a month to write it up. As you wait, you can work on other aspects of the application, relax a little, and do some schoolwork. One week passes, another week passes, and now there are only two weeks until the due date. This is a good time to stop by your teacher's classroom and ask (in a nonpressuring way) how things are going with your recommendation. Ask whether (s)he needs anything else, and remind him or her that everything is due in two weeks. Remember, the point of this visit is to show that you are responsible and care about your application, not to nag your teacher.

Step 4: One Last Important Thing . . .

Now, here is an important thing you have to do for Mr. Khan now that he has written your recommendation(s). You need to write him a wonderful thank-you card. You can even give him a little gift with his thank-you card. Bake him some killer peanut butter cookies (use ready-made dough, if baking isn't exactly your thing). This is a common courtesy, and who knows, you might want Mr. Khan to do something else for you someday.

Applying to More Than One College: I Need Recommendations for Other Things Too!

Applying to seventeen colleges? (Gosh, please don't. You'll go insane.) The specific questions that different colleges ask are very similar to one another, so it isn't too difficult for a teacher to fill out more than one recommendation. While you might not ask Mr. Schmidt to provide recommendations for all seventeen colleges that you are applying to, he probably won't mind filling out a handful or two (if you are sure to give him sufficient time). The maximum number of recommendations one teacher can manage without hating you is probably three to four, if the forms ask for similar things.

Plot out which teachers you are going to ask for which schools. Make sure you have a diverse group of recommenders for each of the schools. (You shouldn't, for example, have two different English teachers submit recommendations for the same college.) Then, remember which teachers you have asked. When you are completing scholarship applications later on, you can ask these teachers for recommendations for scholarships since they already have a letter written for you. (They would just need to update the letter with any recent news.)

In addition, some teachers will automatically give you a copy of your recommendation letter. If you feel comfortable, you can even ask for a copy of your recommendation, but first make sure your teacher doesn't mind. Why? You can use the recommendation for many different things in the future, including scholarships, job applications, or both. Plus, it is always nice to be able to read about how wonderful you are when you need a little pick-me-up.

Secondary School Report (SSR)

Ouch! Just the words Secondary School Report sound scary. In everyday-speak, it's just the form that a guidance counselor or "adult" at your high school fills out about you, your academics, and so forth. Your counselor should be a pro at filling these out. Colleges use the SSR for many different reasons. For one, they use it to find out more about the school you attend (large versus small, what percent of the students go on to college, etc.) and therefore orient their perceptions of what you've achieved in the context of what kind of school you attend. The SSR also serves as a recommendation from your counselor. The counselor is asked how well (s)he knows you. The advice that goes for recommendations goes for the SSR as well. Give your counselor plenty of time, a résumé, a stamped envelope, and, afterwards, a thank-you note. And don't forget to remind him or her a week or two before the deadline.

If you go to a large public school and don't know your counselor very well, don't worry about not getting a good SSR. Counselors will wax eloquent about your achievements, and colleges will recalibrate their comments to take into account the size of your school. If you want to get to know your counselors better so they can write something more personal in the SSR, do this during meetings in which you design your course schedule. (See Chapter 1 for more information on meeting with your guidance counselor.)

Recap

- Start early. Think about which of your teachers write well and know you well. Consult friends and family who have attended your school. Do your research on teachers!
- Give your teacher plenty of time (this means at least a month).
- Give your teacher a résumé, a stamped and addressed envelope, and a recommendation form. Ask your teacher if any other materials are necessary.
- Remind your teacher one to two weeks before the deadline.
- Write your teacher a thank-you note.

Follow these steps, and you'll be sure to get stellar recommendations!

ADMISSIONS AND SCHOLARSHIP INTERVIEWS

Alicia Tam, Yale

Your paperwork has been submitted. You've gotten notification that your application has been received. So, are you done? Not yet!

The dreaded admissions interview still looms ahead. College admissions officers use the interview to add depth to that big packet of stuff that you send to them. Whether or not the interview is required varies from school to school, but most of the more selective schools do have interviews. If you are competing for a scholarship from the school, there will also likely be an interview. Despite the horror that they sometimes conjure, admissions interviews are only there to help you get into the school of your dreams and to win scholarships that will pay for your education!

This is your chance to show how compelling and intelligent a student you are to either an admissions officer or a local alum of the college to which you are applying. It helps put a face and a personality behind your statistics and lists of activities. Your teachers send in letters of recommendation, but this is a chance for a representative from the college you're interested in to see just what an awesome person you are! And, it is an opportunity for you to learn more information about the college that might ultimately help you decide which college to attend.

The Three Types of Interviews

There are three main types of interviews: those with admissions officers, those with alumni, and those for scholarships. They differ significantly, so we will examine each type separately.

Interviews with Admissions Officers

Interviews with admissions officers are often required for smaller liberal arts colleges. If you are required to set up an interview with an admissions officer, it's probably very important, so plan accordingly. If you are unable to visit University XYZ, it is usually possible to arrange a phone interview. On the other hand, some universities (for example, Cornell), opt not to have "interviews" but rather have "information sessions" in which admissions officers talk to one or more students to answer any questions they might have. These sessions tend to be more for you to glean information than for the admissions office to evaluate you, but it certainly can't hurt to make a good impression. Each school will have its own policy regarding interviews. If you are planning to have an interview while visiting a campus, be sure to call at least one month in advance (and more than a month, if you are visiting during busy seasons in March, October, or late summer).

Alumni Interviews

Alumni interviews can take place anywhere from your interviewer's high-rise office to the local coffee shop over a double cappuccino. These sessions tend to be more informal and far less important than interviews with admissions officers. After all, alumni vary widely, so comparing their recommendations can be difficult. A member of the College Matters team was talking with the alumni coordinator of interviews in a large metropolitan area for a certain unnamed university (let's just say it is located in Cambridge, Massachusetts, and starts with an H). After receiving the list of admitted students, the coordinator called the admissions office in a fury, upset that absolutely none of her recommendations had been taken seriously. Not one single student she had strongly praised had been admitted, and none of the admitted students had stood out (at least to interviewers in her area). So, what I am trying to say is don't be too nervous about the alumni interview. It is as much an opportunity for you to learn about University XYZ as for the university to evaluate you.

However, heed this word of caution: The importance of the alumni interview varies slightly from one college to another, and in these days of hypercompetitive admissions, it certainly can't hurt and will probably even help to prepare for the interview. Here is a list of sad but true things said at alumni interviews that have jeopardized candidates' chances for admissions:

1. The interviewer asks why you want to go to Harvard. You respond, "Because I heard New Haven was a nice town." (Yes, someone really did say this. It might seem obvious, but be careful not to confuse schools.)

2. You make any type of racial slur.

3. You use foul language. Just don't.

If you have a choice between either an interview on campus or an alumni interview, make sure the college has no preference. If not, go for either one. Your choice.

The Scholarship Interview— $$$ cha-ching! $$$

These interviews are the scary ones—the ones where there might be ten rich old men sitting around a table. The ones where you might be asked about the best way to democratize Iraq, or what the ethos of your community is. (Don't panic; one of our *College Matters* authors didn't know what *ethos* meant but still won the scholarship.) The important thing about these interviews is to know everything in your application backwards and forwards. Be ready to talk more in depth about what you wrote in your essays. If you say you want to be a lawyer, have an idea of why you aspire to that goal. If you wrote on your application that you want to work in international relations, be sure to be able to answer the above-mentioned question about democratizing Iraq. Also, read up on current events in the week before the interview, especially any that relate to something you wrote on your application. So, in summation, know your application and think broadly about subjects that might be related. As long as you didn't lie on your application, you should be in good shape.

Arranging the Interview

It's Never Too Early to Make a Good First Impression

I know you might not think much of it, but I'm sure you remember the first time you called that certain special someone you had a crush on in English class. Make sure you don't sound like a bumbling idiot again—your interviewer may not be as forgiving! Here are some tips for setting up the interview over the phone.

This may be common sense for you, but just in case you've been living under a rock for the past century, here are a few phone etiquette pointers:

1. Be polite.

2. Speak clearly and at a moderate speed.

3. Think before picking up the phone about what you're going to say if an answering machine picks up. No one wants to hear you say "Ummmm" or "Uhhhhhh" a billion times.

4. Don't call too early. Don't assume that your interviewer is a "morning person" (that is, up before 7:00) but keep in mind that most people are at work by 9:00 A.M. Also, remember that most admissions offices are open from 9:00 to 5:00, according to their respective time zones. (In other words, arranging an interview for Dartmouth might be difficult if you live in Hong Kong or even California.)

5. Don't call too late. *You* may be up at 1:00 A.M. doing the homework you should've done yesterday, but I doubt your interviewer is! I'd say anything past 9:00 P.M. is risky.

6. Work around their schedules. The easier you make it for your interviewer to meet you, the better. Have your planner in front of you and *write down* the details of your appointment! Ask for directions at this time, if you need them.

Preinterview Preparation

So you've picked a time, date, and location and marked your calendar. So you're good to go! Right? Well, there are actually a number of things that you should do ahead of time.

Get to Know the School before Your Interview

Make sure that you know more than just the name of University XYZ. There must be a reason why you want to go there! You're probably semifamiliar with every school you're applying to, but they can all start to blend together after a while. Sometimes, students apply to a college just because of its name, or because their parents went there, or because someone they knew went there. In the interview, the question may come up about why you want to go. It's a good thing to know. Try reading through those colorful brochures the college sent you, or look up information on the school's Web site. Talk to students who attend the school, or dig up your notes from a campus visit. Does the college have a special program in which you're interested? Do you especially like the location? Interviewers want to know that you're really interested in their school; researching and learning about it beforehand shows that you are.

So Who Is Your Interviewer Anyway?

Try and find out a bit about your interviewer before the interview, so you can figure out how to approach the meeting. Of course, being the sly student that you are, you are *not* going to dig for factual information like some telemarketing survey! If you're curious about his age, try asking when he graduated from University XYZ. Things like profession and graduation year can tell you a lot about your interviewer. Perhaps your interviewer has an email address that indicates what company she works for; you could look up that company on the Internet to learn more. Some colleges will try to match you up with a person who works in the field that you're interested in studying, but more often than not, it's all about the luck of the draw!

Do not, though, find out everything your interviewer has ever done. All that information is not useful, and besides, knowing it might make you more nervous than you ordinarily would have been. After all, your interviewer may have accomplished some pretty amazing things. And please, do not try to impress your interviewer by reciting facts about him or her during interviews. It's just plain weird. After all, how would you feel if some random person you'd never met started telling you stuff about yourself?

Who Are You, Anyway?

What have been your biggest accomplishments? What obstacles have you had to overcome? What are your goals for the future? With what activities do you want to be involved in college? Do you want to try something new? Why do you want to stay in-state? Or why do you want to attend a college that is so far away from your home? Be sure to review everything in your application, as anything you wrote about is fair game for discussion. Interviewers have a knack for wanting in-depth information about the smallest, most obscure thing that you wrote about. This tendency is especially true with interviewers in scholarship committees.

Dress for Success

Yeah, it's a cliché, but there's definitely some truth to that saying that you need to dress for success! Finding an outfit that shows your personality but also gives your interviewer an awesome impression requires a delicate balance. Here are a few key points to keep in mind:

1. *Think conservative.* It's always better to be safe. This means no loud colors, no short skirts, and no obnoxious or controversial outfits in general. And for goodness sake, try to keep the body piercing, body hair, and body odor to a minimum.

2. *Location, location, location!* How you dress will change depending on where you're meeting. An interviewer's home or the local coffee house will usually be more casual than, say, a corporate high-rise, but I advise you to never be dressed less than "business casual."

3. *What "business casual" means for guys.* A *suit*, or a *dress shirt* and *slacks* with a tie is always safe. That is, as long as your suit isn't neon yellow or anything. And make sure your clothes are not wrinkled—this goes for girls too.

4. *What "business casual" means for gals.* It's more complicated.

    A. *Skirts.* You may love 'em or you may hate 'em, but there's one thing for sure: Older interviewers (that is, your parents' age and up) tend to feel more comfortable with you in 'em. Only recently have pants become appropriate business attire for women. Not only that, but the older your interviewer is, the *longer* your skirt should be! When you're trying outfits on, remember that you're not just going to be standing in it: Try sitting down and moving around. You don't want to be flashing your interviewers and giving them the wrong idea! Also, make sure to wear your skirt with some pantyhose and dress shoes.

    B. *Trends.* Trends are not always trendy with interviewers. Weird makeup and nail polish can be distracting. Remember that your interviewer will probably be a person at least ten years older than you. His or her fashion sense might still be stuck in the nineties—*shudder*.

    C. *Skin.* You shouldn't be showing too much skin either. Be wary of low-cut tops or very clingy outfits. You're here to impress your interviewer, not to pick him up!

D. *Hair.* Pull your hair back, either with clips or in a ponytail. Avoid twirling your hair around your finger and obsessively tucking it behind your ears.

E. *Makeup.* If you want to wear makeup, only wear enough to complement your features. A good rule of thumb about makeup is that nobody except you and your mother should know that you have any makeup on at all.

5. *Cover any piercing and tattoos.* If you have more holes or marks than you were born with (exception: earrings on gals, or if it's a cultural thing), your interviewer won't be impressed and might be grossed out. Take out your visible piercings and cover up your tattoos. It's only for about an hour—you'll live!

6. *Choose good colors.* Black, navy, or dark gray are safest for suits, jackets, or skirts.

7. *Use the personal touch.* Above all, your outfit should accurately reflect who you are; a favorite tie or something. I personally design a lot of my own jewelry, so I wore a necklace I made to my interviews. It made for a good conversation piece.

8. *Double-check with Mom (or your fashion-conscious Dad) before you leave the house.* This time when they say, "Don't you dare leave the house with *that* on!" take their advice. Please.

Résumé and Portfolios

It's a good idea to bring a copy of your résumé that you can leave with your interviewer. It gives a roadmap as to what you do, and what you can talk about. Since you aren't the only brilliant student being interviewed for University or Scholarship XYZ, it's something with which your interviewer can remember you when (s)he writes that great recommendation letter, makes admissions decisions, or decides who the scholarship bucks are going to.

Sometimes your résumé also helps the interviewer become familiar with some basic vital statistics like your class rank, GPA, and standardized test scores. Don't get freaked out if the first question that your interviewer asks is about your test scores or ranking. Some schools require that information from the beginning, so your interviewer is not intentionally trying to make you nervous.

If you're especially talented at something like visual arts or writing, bring your portfolio or a sample of your work with you so you can show your interviewer. I brought a portfolio of some of my artwork to my interviews and also a copy of an essay that won an award. If possible, bring copies they can keep, and make color copies of your artwork. I even had an interviewer ask me to send her a videotape of one of my violin performances, so you never know! Also, remember that if your application describes what an awesome pianist, dancer, or other performer you are, you should be prepared to give a little demonstration, particularly if the interview is in a home. (It's been known to happen!)

Where the Heck Is This Office?

If you've never been to the location you're meeting at, remember to *get driving and parking directions* from your interviewer. You can also look up directions online at places like www.mapquest.com, so that when the calendar date arrives, you'll know exactly where to go.

I made the mistake of going to the wrong building and showed up late for my MIT interview. If something like this happens, apologize profusely upon arrival. If it is too late to meet with your interviewer, ask whether you can reschedule. Then apologize again.

What's Her Name Again?

Right before you go in to meet your interviewer, make sure you know her or his name! It may sound silly, but trust me, when you've got four or five of these interview babies lined up, sometimes names get lost or mixed up. (Recall the Harvard in New Haven example from earlier; avoid bumbling on easy stuff like this.)

Ack! The Interview!

Your life is flashing before your eyes: You're about to go into your interview. Come to a safe and legal stop, park, and breathe deeply.

Be on Time!

There's nothing like being late to start an interview off on the wrong foot, so make sure that *nothing*—neither traffic nor your Great Aunt Flo—makes you late! Pretend like the interview is going to start twenty minutes before it really does to allow yourself plenty of time to get there. If you're afraid of being early, bring a book. I'm sure you've got some reading for school you haven't finished!

Have Confidence in Yourself!

The whole point of the interview is for the school to get to know who you are, and they can't do that unless *you* know who you are. So, stand up straight! Chin up! Shoulders back! Make sure you aren't overconfident, though. No one likes someone who is arrogant or condescending. As *Saturday Night Live's* Al Franken would say, "You're good enough, smart enough, and gosh darn it, people like you!"

First Impression

This may sound silly, but think about the way you're going to walk into that room. Your *handshake* should be firm but not crippling, and no cold or sweaty palms please! *Smile* naturally and warmly. Maintain *eye contact* as much as possible; this lets your interviewer know that you're totally engaged in the conversation. Most importantly, it'll cover up the fact that you're a nervous wreck.

Body Language

What you do with your body can work both for and against you.

Posture Sitting up straight, and leaning slightly forward toward your interviewer shows that you're being attentive and alert in the conversation. Please do not fold your arms. This indicates that you aren't listening or are disinterested in the discussion. Ladies, keep your legs close together (particularly if you are wearing a skirt). Gentlemen, keeping your feet firmly planted on the floor is generally a good thing to do.

Watch your Mannerisms Do you gesture a lot with your hands when you talk? Do you clench your fists when you're nervous? Have a nervous tic? Try not to do anything distracting that takes away from what you're saying. Pen twirling, knee shaking, foot tapping, and so on are all really annoying in a closed situation like the interview. Watch that nervous tendency to play with your hair!

Speaking Make sure you enunciate your words very clearly. Don't mumble. At the same time, don't be overbearing or sound like you're arguing. Nervousness often makes you stutter or talk faster than you usually would; just try to stay calm and speak in a relaxed manner. One tip is to listen to National Public Radio the week of your interview. You'll suddenly find yourself using large vocabulary words (correctly, of course), and speaking in sophisticated sentence constructions. Plus, if your interviewer asks you about current events, you'll be golden.

Ummm, Like, Uhhh ...

Um, *like*, and *uh* are three highly overused sounds in a nervous conversation; try to stay away from them. If you're not sure about what you want to say, small interludes of silence are fine. It's OK to show that deep, pensive side of yourself.

What Interviewers Like to See

Speak with enthusiasm! Show that you are excited about attending college—specifically, about attending the college for which you are interviewing. *Do* discuss your accomplishments and show that you are knowledgeable about the college, but *don't* show off. How do you manage this? For one thing, you can tell anecdotes about your leadership experiences. You can show that you are knowledgeable about the college in question by mentioning that you have spoken with current students or by asking insightful questions that aren't answered on the college's Web site.

Tough Situations: How to Deal with Them

Of course, there's always a chance that something strange will happen during your interview, but here are some questions and situations that you can plan ahead for.

The "Tell Me about Yourself" Question

Interviewers *love* this question because its completely open-ended, and it often catches the nonexperienced interviewee off guard. Think about what you want to communicate to the interviewer about yourself, and start there.

Try to avoid anything too philosophical or abstract. For example, don't just say "I am hardworking." Talk about how you got up every morning at 6:30 to practice cross-country during the summer. Don't just say, "I am a leader." Talk about how you spearheaded a campaign to raise money for cerebal palsy in your community. Also, there's always the autobiographical tactic; start out with your family background and how you became the superstar that you are.

The "What's Your Greatest Weakness?" Question

Hey, it's a great way to judge students' perceptions of themselves. Think about this question ahead of time; pick something that is negative in a positive way, like being overzealous in your activities, being superdriven, or having extremely diverse interests. Being a "perfectionist" is a very common answer, so only say so if you truly are. Try not to mention conflicts with teachers or authority (for example, don't tell them about that night you spent in county jail). Another variation of this question is: What's your biggest failure? Obviously, you don't want to say anything too catastrophic, but maybe it could be something that you've always regretted not learning about or picking up, like proficiency in computers, or a musical instrument, or a foreign language. You should then counter with something to the effect of wanting to correct that deficiency later.

Avoid Saying Anything Strongly Negative

Even if you're applying to a top-notch school and you're talking to someone who went there, don't be quick to disparage smaller, lesser-known schools. Who knows? Maybe your interviewer has family members who went there. In other words, just be careful of what you say. Remember, the world is a happy, feel-good place when you interview.

If It's Getting Off Track ...

Sometimes you and your interviewer may go off on a tangent that isn't particularly important to you, or isn't something about which you want to talk. If this sidetracking happens, don't be afraid to say something to set the conversation back on track. For example: "Something interesting that I'd like you to know about me is …"

I Don't Know...

Sometimes you simply won't know the answer to a question asked. Rather than bumbling like an idiot, it's okay to have one or two "I don't knows" in an interview. However, even if you don't know an answer to a question, you should let your interviewer know how you would go about answering it. For example, the following is an I-don't-know scenario from a scholarship interview with a local club: "I don't know enough about the new energy bill to judge how it will impact the environment. However, in assessing its impact, I would evaluate it based on the following three things: X, Y, and Z." Remember that a few "I don't knows" are fine, but more than that will make you look uninformed.

Do YOU Have Any Questions?

At the end of your interview, most interviewers will ask if you have any questions about the college. Come to the interview with questions prepared (and nothing too obvious). You might express your concern about campus safety, or ask about a particular academic program. One suave maneuver is to ask alumni interviewers what their favorite memories were of their college experience, to put them in a good mood. Alternatively, you can ask them whether there are any drawbacks about going, just to show that you're trying to get some good information from them. You should have at least two questions, because it will look *really* bad if you don't. (Interviewers may think that you don't care enough about their school to inquire about it.)

If the questions you prepared were answered during the interview, you can default to asking about your interviewer's experience at the school, what (s)he liked/disliked about it, and how (s)he chose the college in the first place.

Anything Else?

Sometimes interviewers will close the interview by asking whether there is one last thing that you want them to convey to the admissions committee. You can take this opportunity to express how passionate you are about XYZ College or that this college is your first choice. Just be sure to give it some thought before heading in there.

Following Up

After your *wonderful* interview, be sure to send a thank-you card or email to thank your interviewer for his or her time. Don't take too long to do this, either. Email the day of the interview, and snail mail the card within a few days of the interview. These thank-you notes are just a courtesy, and they reflect what a great person you are! Be sure to ask for a business card at the conclusion of the interview so that you'll know your interviewer's address.

Practice! Practice! Practice!

I can't tell you how much this helps. Ask your family, friends, teachers, or neighbors to go through a practice interview with you. What's great about this is that they'll give you feedback about what you should pay attention to. You'd be surprised! I learned that I talk *really really* fast without realizing it, so when I interview, I watch my pace of speech.

If you have a video camera, get it out and videotape yourself answering the "tell me about yourself" question. Then play back the tape and critique yourself. Doing so is incredibly helpful, and believe me, you will definitely see many things to improve!

At the same time, in your real interview, there is some drawback to sounding *too* polished and practiced, so make sure you sound like you're thinking seriously about the question and not just popping out a formulated answer. Of course, people usually prefer to look more polished as opposed to less.

Here are some good sample questions:

1. What can you tell me about yourself?
2. Why do you want to go to School XYZ?
3. Why do you think you're an ideal candidate for School XYZ?
4. What makes you unique from everyone else who's applying?
5. What do you like to do in your spare time?
6. Tell me about Activity X (something from your résumé).
7. What's most important to you in a school?
8. How would your friends describe you?

9. What are your greatest strengths?

10. What are your greatest weaknesses?

11. What makes you tick?

12. Who are your role models?

13. What three words would you use to describe yourself?

14. What was the last book that you read? Who is your favorite author?

15. What would you like to tell me about that hasn't come up so far?

So remember: Dress appropriately, sit up straight, have confidence in yourself, and practice! By following these easy tips, you'll be poised to blow your interviewer away.

CHAPTER NINE

COLLEGE VISITS

Kelly Perry, Harvard

College brochures are like personal ads: You should not commit to one until you've seen it in person. In fact, committing to attend a college without visiting it first is akin to marrying that nice person from the chat room without ever having met face to face. Sure, a school might look great on paper, but what's it like to eat, sleep, party, chill, and study there for four years?

You should resist the temptation to base your decision solely on the *U.S. News and World Report*'s rankings because they tell you little about how happy *you* will be at a certain college. Instead, you need to get a feel for whether you will enjoy being at a particular campus for four years. Read on to learn how to make the most of your college visits. You can then go about finding a college that will bring out the best in you!

College Visit Logistics
How Old Should I Be and Why Does it Matter?

There is no one right or wrong age to visit colleges, but your age when you visit will determine what your visit will be like and what you'll want to look for. Visiting colleges as a sophomore or younger is a great way to get inspired to do well in school. You'll suddenly realize that there is an entire world beyond high school, and it doesn't include gym class, curfews, or SATs. An autumn walk through Dartmouth's campus may be all the motivation you need to push yourself a little harder when high school work becomes difficult. The first college visits I made were in the spring of my freshman year, when I tagged along with my dad on his business trip to Boston. Touring colleges made a huge impression on me; after that, getting in to a great school became one of my top priorities. Since it isn't essential to visit colleges this early in the game, you needn't plan a separate trip. However, you might join your parent on a business trip, if he or she will be near a college of particular interest to you. Family vacations are another good opportunity for visiting colleges. Just schedule a bit of extra time in your itinerary (a day or at least an afternoon) for the visit.

College visits at this stage should be about surveying what's out there. Leave your list of questions for the admissions officer at home. Instead, take this time to enjoy the scenery and experience the atmospheres different colleges have to offer. Stroll through the campus and the surrounding town. Peek inside the student center to check out the facilities. Observe what students are doing. Are they carrying books or cell phones? Do they smile at others or walk with their chins tucked into their scarves? Do they look happy? Observe the bulletin boards; what kinds of events do they advertise? Are there events that interest you? Consider the weather. Do you see yourself as a flip-flop or a snowshoe person? Take pictures if you like, but try to focus on the vibe you pick up as you explore each college rather than on the specific details.

Juniors can take a more systematic approach to visiting colleges. By this time, you will have some idea of what caliber college is within your reach by assessing your grades, activities, and test scores. You also will have thought more about what aspects of college life are most important to you. Below are several factors that may be important in deciding which colleges to apply to or attend. (For more information on these topics, see Chapters 3 and 10.) If you are unsure about any of them, be sure to discuss them with students or admissions officers during your campus visit. Questions pertaining to each of these factors are discussed at length in the section of this chapter entitled "Factors to Consider When Visiting."

- Location
- Distance from home
- Weather
- Size
- Majors
- Student body profile/ diversity
- Costs and financial aid

- Student-faculty ratio
- Social scene
- Clubs and activities
- Research and fellowship opportunities
- Varsity sports teams
- Club sports teams
- Career services (advising, graduate school applications, job searching)
- Percentage of students living in university housing
- Percentage of international students
- Study abroad programs
- Safety

It's often hard to know exactly what you want until you've seen it, which is why visiting colleges is so helpful. For example, I liked the idea of living in a small town until I spent an entire (uneventful) day visiting Swarthmore, a small town school. Don't get me wrong, I have nothing against Swarthmore, but it just wasn't for me. You may discover after attending the introductory economics course at Harvard, a class which has more than 700 students, that you enjoy the anonymity of a large class. Or, maybe you'll discover that you don't like how you may never get to know or speak one on one with the professor. The more time you spend on a campus, the more you'll learn about the school and what you like and don't like about it.

Visits during senior year are the most important ones, because you'll be making a decision soon. Perhaps you are visiting the campus for an interview or scholarship competition or in hopes that it will inspire you to decide which college is right for you. In any case, college visits during senior year are more focused and more stressful than earlier visits. You may already know which schools have accepted you. At the very least, you'll know the ones to which you are applying. This is the time to arrange for an overnight visit, if you haven't done so already.

Some colleges have something called Admit Weekend, Prefrosh Weekend, or a variety of other names. This event—here referred to as Admit Weekend, for the sake of clarity—offers a chance for all students who have been admitted to visit the school. This is a great time to meet potential future classmates and make some new friends. I know a lot of people who met (and even hooked up) during Admit Weekend. This weekend is guaranteed to boast a full calendar of activities that the college and current students have organized, like concerts, parties, information sessions, and even fashion shows! Admit Weekend is usually described in the acceptance packet that you receive. But if you want to know ahead of time when it is, just call the admissions office and ask whether there are set dates in the spring for admitted students to visit.

You may also decide not to visit during the prearranged Admit Weekend. This way, you can see the college as it usually is, not when it is trying to sell itself to you. Staying with a current student, regardless of when you visit, is key to understanding what life is like. Ask your high school guidance counselor for names of people who graduated from your school and are now students at your college of interest. Parents, older siblings, friends, and relatives may attend or know someone who attends the college. The college itself may even arrange for you to stay with a student, if you do not know anyone there. To do this, call the admissions office, and ask whether they have a student host program.

If student host opportunities are available, take advantage of them! You will see an entirely different side of the school after talking and spending time with real students in their living quarters. You will see what students do at 2:00 A.M., whether it's playing Scrabble, choreographing impromptu music videos, or studying. When you stay with a student host, remember to recalibrate your view of the school depending on what kind of student you are staying with (shy/quiet?, loud/rambunctious?).

Timing

Okay, so now you're pretty clear on how your age will affect your college visit, but when specifically during the year should you go? The best time to visit a school is, of course, when it is in session, so that you can observe students on a normal day and attend classes. Try to visit for at least part of the weekend and part of the school week, to get a taste of both the social and the academic aspects of the college. For example, you could arrive Saturday afternoon and stay through Monday evening, or come Thursday morning and stay through Saturday afternoon. You should devote one full day per college for day visits, and two to three days for overnight visits.

If you have an intended major (notice that I said "if"—no worries if you have no idea), check the online course catalog, call the departments for class schedules, or both. Be sure to sit in on a basic class as well as an advanced one in your area of interest. The timing of these class meetings may help you plan the dates for your visit.

Finally, avoid holidays and be sure to avoid finals period, when students will be superstressed and unenthusiastic about hosting a guest. Plus, you will be bored because everyone will be studying for their final exams. Check the academic calendar on the college Web site for exams and finals period dates.

Arranging a Visit

If you have already been admitted or have applied to the college you are planning to visit, call at least a couple of months in advance to arrange to stay overnight with a student host. (Note that some schools only allow host stays for admitted students.) If you are visiting any time before senior year, it will probably not be possible for the admissions office to arrange for you to stay with a student host, but you should still call them to find out when tours and information sessions are given. Plan to be able to attend these. If you know of students already attending the college, arrange to meet with them as well.

The week before you leave, call the admissions office to confirm that your host stay is still on or that the tours and information sessions are still at the same times. If you are staying with a student host, be sure to set up a time and place to meet. Remember to be considerate—students are busy, so call if you are going to be late.

On Campus

The first place you should go once you arrive on campus is the admissions office. If you get lost, ask students on campus where the admissions office is, as they are usually friendly and helpful. Once you arrive, confirm when tours and information sessions are offered. If you are staying with a student host, the admissions office will often let him or her know that you have arrived. Be sure to ask if free meal passes to the dining hall(s) are available. You'll save money and get the student dining experience this way. Furthermore, don't forget to register; some schools like to see that you've visited because it demonstrates interest in the school. Finally, financial aid offices are often located in the same building as the admissions office, so consider consulting a representative at this time with any questions that you or your parents may have.

What to Pack

Most importantly, bring a notebook with the questions that you want to ask written in it. (See the section "Factors to Consider When Visiting" for some good questions.) That way, you won't realize when you get home that you forgot to ask that all-important question or make that supercritical observation. Leave space in the notebook to take notes while you are on campus or soon after you leave. It's amazing how fast details from different colleges can get muddled.

Secondly, be sure to pack appropriate clothing. It can get bitterly cold in northern parts of the United States. And it can get smolderingly hot in the South. Check www.weather.com before you leave, so that you'll pack appropriately. Next, don't forget to bring the phone number and address of and directions to the admissions office, as well as the phone number(s) of your student host, if you are staying with one. Also, you should budget $20 to $50 for each day you are visiting, not including hotel if you aren't staying with a student. And finally, bring other things that you will need, such as toiletries, an umbrella, and a cell phone, if you or your parents have one. One last note: Pack lightly, especially if you are staying with a student. College dorm rooms are not big, and you don't want to clutter your host's room with all your stuff.

While on campus, please follow all rules. Campuses are often strict about parking violations, so follow the law to the letter to avoid getting a hefty ticket. Do not do anything else that is illegal either. Most notably, this includes drinking (for the majority of you who are underage). If you must drink, do so in moderation to avoid a potentially disastrous incident. Colleges have been known to rescind offers of admission to students who violate campus alcohol policies. They have also rescinded admission for other displays of inappropriate behavior, so don't get carried away partying. Most importantly, be respectful of your student host(s). They are doing you a favor to host you, so act like it.

While on campus, there are all sorts of things that you will want to pay attention to and ask about. The following section will help you know what to look for.

Factors to Consider When Visiting

When you visit, you will want to shadow your student host to see what a normal day is like. Go to class, eat in the dining hall, watch a musical performance, and party! Try to experience everything a student at that college would. Feel free to ask students pointed questions, as they are usually more than happy to brag about or bemoan student life. They have been in your position and they know how tough it is—for the most part they're glad to help! Also, be sure to talk to lots of students, not just your host. One student might be having a bad experience or might hate the school, but the other 99 percent of the student body might love it. Don't let one lousy host ruin your impression of the school! The following are some specific factors to consider, along with questions that you might ask.

Location

Whether it's in a rural town or city, the location of your college will influence your social life. When you visit colleges, pay attention to the kinds of environments in which you feel most comfortable. Hanging out at the local Wal-Mart might sound quirky and interesting when you live in New York City and are talking on the phone to students about what they do in their free time, but once you're actually there hangin' out with them . . . you might find that shopping blue-light specials just isn't your thing.

Distance from Home

How far away you are from Mom and Dad will affect a few things in your life, like how homesick you feel and how often your mom pops into your room. If you are superhomesick during your college visit, consider whether you will be able to handle being away for the majority of the year. Even if you feel ecstatic to escape from your annoying brother during the visit, ask whether he will seem so annoying once you haven't seen him for three months. On the other hand, if you are really annoyed when your mom tags along on your visit to In-State U. and thus decide to go for that university in Mongolia, keep in mind that Mom won't be around all the time, even if you stay close to home.

All this is not intended to discourage you from attending a college that's far away. I attend college on the other side of the country from where my parents live, and while I miss seeing them all the time, my college experi-

157

ence has been awesome. As with everything, talk to students about how they feel about being close to or far away from home, as their thoughts can be useful to you.

Weather

Weather makes a difference in how you feel and how those around you feel. In extreme cases, bad weather can even make for seasonal depression. Pay careful attention to students' reactions to the weather when you're visiting. Are they running around playing flag football in shorts when it's 30 degrees Fahrenheit, raving about how warm it is (a bad sign if you don't like the cold)? Or, are they shivering in sweaters because it's 70 degrees and a cold front has just come through?

Size

A larger school will expose you to a greater variety of people, but it might not provide individualized attention in the classroom or in student services. For example, during your visit to Yale, you are probably more likely to spend time with spelling bee champions, Cuban refugees, actors, junior CEOs, and even royalty than with your potential organic chemistry professor. On the other hand, a small school offers a tightly knit student body but may or may not have as much name recognition when you begin applying for jobs.

Ask students about how much interaction they have with professors and how tight-knit the student body is. Also pay attention to how the size of the school affects your visit. Were your feet screaming during that walk all the way across campus with your host to her calculus class at 8:00 A.M.? Or did you get really claustrophobic because the college is smaller than your high school?

Majors

Finances and politics determine the strength of educational departments; be sure to check out the departmental resources of your major of interest while on campus. The more resources devoted to the subject you're interested in, the richer your educational experience will be. If your student host discourages you from pursuing a certain major, ask why. And be sure to get second opinions. One student may hate the college's biology department because he flunked his bio lab, but that doesn't necessarily mean that the department can't be fantastic for those willing to work hard.

Student Body Profile/Diversity

Are there about as many men as there are women? This will affect your dating life! Is there a mixture of ethnicities? Are the students mostly from upper middle class backgrounds, or are there both wealthy and underprivileged students? Is it even possible to tell? (For example, at my college, Harvard, it is not immediately obvious. As a result, there is not much segregation by social class.) Do the students come from the local area, or are there a lot of out-of-state (or out-of-country) students? Pay attention to whether students from different backgrounds hang out, and observe if the campus seems segregated by gender, race, or socioeconomic class.

Cost and Financial Aid

How much financial aid does each college offer? The amount varies from college to college, so it's something to which you'll need to pay attention on your visit. Ask students if people graduating from the university have a lot of debt. Find out if cushy work-study jobs are available. Can you get paid for sitting in the library and basically doing your homework? Also, consider stopping by the financial aid office to ask any specific questions that you may have. Ask what the average financial aid package looks like, both in total dollars and broken down into grants (which you don't have to pay back) versus loans (which you do pay back).

Student-Faculty Ratio

A 25-to-1 student-to-faculty ratio might not have seemed like a big deal on paper, but do you really like sitting in the back of a thousand person lecture hall where you can barely hear the professor over the person next to you who is talking on her cell phone? Or perhaps your college guide said that the school has a 7-to-1 ratio, but all the senior faculty are on sabbatical doing research instead of teaching, so you'll still be sitting in the back of a large lecture hall. Ask students how large their classes tend to be and how they feel class size affects the quality of their education. Also ask how many

159

of their classes are taught by TAs (teaching assistants), who are grad students, and how good these classes are.

Social Scene

What do students do for fun? Are they heavy studiers? Are the parties wild and crazy? What's the dating scene like? When you visit and compare colleges, you will get a feel for how much time students devote to studying and fun. Your best bet is to go where students have the same priorities as you do. Think about whether you believe homework is a good excuse not to go out. At some colleges this is the typical excuse given for not partying (for example, at Harvard), whereas at other colleges it is inconceivable to even think of using such a lame excuse (for example, at Duke).

Dating

Is the dating culture "ring" or "fling" or something that resembles normal dating? In other words, does dating exist? Or is it polarized into the two extremes of almost-married or completely-single-and-hooking-up? Are there places in the surrounding community to go on a date (theatres, sporting events, cinemas, restaurants, and so on)?

Clubs and Activities

If you already know what club(s) you'd like to join, check to make sure that the school offers them. Otherwise, make sure the school has at least a handful of different clubs that sound interesting to you. Such groups will contribute to a large portion of your social life. Ask students how easy it is to start up your own organization too, if you're so inclined. Also keep in mind that your interests might change substantially during college, so make sure that there are a wide variety of activities available.

Research Opportunities

If you're interested in doing research with a faculty member, find out if the college offers grants for such work. Some schools strongly encourage students to work with professors and provide funding for student research initiatives, whether for a senior thesis or another academic endeavor. For example, people on the College Matters team have received research funding for projects as diverse as obtaining wage data from China to researching how College Matters can better reach underserved students.

Varsity Sports Teams

If you're an athlete and want to play for the school, find out before you visit whether they have your sport and, if so, how strong the program is. Prior to arriving on campus, email the coach to arrange a time to meet and discuss the program and the potential for your participation. If possible, arrange to stay with a member of the team during your visit. Sometimes you can get one impression from a coach and different impressions from the team members, so even if you can't be hosted by a team member, arrange to speak with people on the team. See Chapter 13 for more information.

Club Sports Teams or Intramurals

Fencing anyone? Or maybe crew? Club sports teams are a great way to make friends and try something completely new. You don't have to have any experience to join, so ask whether your college has a few that you might want to try.

Career Services

As fun as college is, its ultimate function is to lead you to a successful career of your choosing. The office of career services can either make this pursuit relatively easy or leave you floundering. Find out from students how helpful the staff is and what kind of programs and services they offer to help you get the job of your dreams. One way to gauge the quality of career services is to ask students about the job recruiting process. What kinds of companies come to recruit on campus? Is it easy to apply to these companies? Is there a wide array of industries and job positions to choose from? Furthermore, ask students about the quality of premed, prelaw, and fellowship advising.

You may also want to ask how easy it is to access the alumni network, as this may be a good resource for you to explore a career path, get a job, or both. Also ask if the career services office has information on what alumni are doing five, ten, fifteen, or twenty-five years after graduating from the college. Don't be placated by a few outstanding examples. Instead, ask to see general statistics on the professions of alumni.

Percentage of Students Living in University Housing

At a commuter school, most students live away from campus and are only around for classes. This situation is sometimes undesirable because it makes hanging out difficult. Ask students whether people living off campus tend to take away from the social scene. Sometimes, large numbers of students live off campus in fraternity or sorority houses. Try to get a sense of how important Greek life is on campus, and determine whether that's your scene. Finally, be sure to find out if you are guaranteed university housing. Some schools will only guarantee housing for your first year, which could lead to hassles involving commuting, transportation, and utility costs.

Percentage of International Students

Your college experience will be enormously enhanced by meeting international students. Not only will you learn about other cultures, but you might also get a chance to visit international friends in their own country. If you arrive and your host is speaking in Norwegian with her parents on the phone while her roommate is talking with her boyfriend in Chinese, this is probably a good sign. Find out if there are a lot of international students on campus and observe whether they interact with American students or tend to be cliquish.

Study-Abroad Programs

Got the urge to study culinary art in Italy, literature in Spain, Hinduism in India, or sunbathing in Brazil? The world can be your playground—that is, if the college you chose to attend has good study-abroad programs. Studying abroad is an exhilarating experience, but not all colleges encourage it. If studying abroad is important to you, find out what programs, if any, are available at each college in which you're interested. A college's glossy brochure might rave about programs, but only students can tell you how much of a hassle it is to actually get approval and enroll. Also, be sure to ask if financial aid will extend to studying abroad.

Safety

And last, but certainly not least, you do not want safety concerns to hinder having fun and studying once you are at college. In what kind of neighborhood is the campus? Are there emergency phones throughout campus? Is there a campus escort service for students who are returning to their rooms late at night? What crime is most common on campus? What are the crime statistics? Investigate these issues now, to ensure that you will be safe later.

Financing Your Visit

For many, visiting out-of-state colleges is not feasible, for financial reasons. However, there are many creative options that could earn you a free trip. Some colleges have scholarship competitions which provide all-expense-paid trips to the campus for finalists. As a bonus, you could win cash for college. An athlete can visit up to five different colleges for free during senior year if these schools want to recruit him or her. Check out Chapter 13 for more information. After you have been accepted to a few different colleges, you could use this information as leverage to get the admissions office to fly you in for Admit Weekend. If you are trying to decide between Harvard and Princeton, for example, and simply cannot afford to visit both, explain this fact to each admissions office and they may just pay for you to come visit. Princeton made such an offer to one member of the College Matters team.

If you manage to save some money from a summer job, you are much better off using this money to visit colleges than using it to buy a fancy prom dress or new rims for your car. Deciding which college to attend is probably the most important decision you have ever had to make. You can earn more money later. If you do your research properly and find the school that fits you best, these next four years could be the best of your life. It is in your best interest to do whatever you can to visit at least your top two colleges.

Some companies such as Amtrak offer discount tickets to students visiting colleges. Be sure to ask about student discounts before you book a trip. Also, if someone in your family has frequent-flier miles to spare (25,000 for a domestic round-trip ticket); he or she could give you an early birthday present and get a ticket for you with miles. Alas, if there are no frequent-flier miles to be had, there are still good airfare discounts for students. Check with a local STA Travel (an agency that specializes in student travel, www.statravel.com) or with www.studentuniverse.com.

Finally, if for whatever reason it is absolutely impossible for you to visit colleges before you send your letter of intent to enroll, there are still some things you can do to get more detailed information about a college. You can email or call students, and perhaps arrange for a phone call with an admissions officer. You are always welcome to email a current College Matters team member who might have friends at schools of interest to you; check www.collegematters.org for email contacts of current College Matters students. These conversations will give you a better idea of what a school is all about than the school's brochures and Web site will.

Conclusion

Visiting colleges is a critical component of the admissions process. It will bring clarity in moments of indecision, and will even teach you a few things about your likes and dislikes. Take notes and pictures to jog your memory later on, but also remember to take in all the sights, sounds, and smells. Remember what kind of feeling you get at each campus. Picture what it will be like to live there for four years. And don't let one bad host ruin your impression of a school. Talk to lots of people and get lots of opinions. Not only will you be able to make a more informed decision after visiting, but you will also be more confident about your choice.

CHOOSING THE BEST COLLEGE FOR YOU

"I've made the Decision... That I'm Undecided!"

Erin Sprague, Harvard

You've aced your SATs. You can take an AP calculus test in your sleep. Your essay makes Twain and Hemingway look like mere amateurs. Now that you've also discovered a small country and cured world hunger in your compilation of the *ultimate* college application, you're done—right? Ha! Not even close! You may have sprinted to the all-night post office at midnight before your college applications were due, but that postmark only means that you've entered a new domain in the alternate universe of college admissions. Cue the music: You have officially entered the Twilight Zone.

At this point in the college application process, everyone falls into one of three categories, which I like to divide into (1) big envelope, (2) small envelope, and (3) all of the above. Of course, in this age of email, iBooks, and Personal Digital Assistants (PDAs), many of you will be receiving big, long emails, or small, short emails revealing the status of your application. For the sake of this analogy, I'm going to stick with the more traditional envelope and letter. In a perfect world, it's April—December if you're one of those overachievers who's applied for the Early Decision/Action—and you have opened your mailbox to find the big envelope from your top-choice school. Congratulations. Now stop reading this section and proceed immediately to Chapter 12 to learn about winning scholarships to finance your dream.

But what happens if you fall into the small-envelope category? Perhaps you only got into your safety school, or nowhere at all. Life is not over. Proceed to the section titled "Life Outside the Gate" at the end of this chapter.

These two scenarios are extreme. The majority of you are probably dealing with a combination of big envelopes and small envelopes, meaning that you've been both accepted and rejected for admission to a number of good schools. How will you ever decide? Read on, my friends. This chapter is for you.

What Is College?

A classic shot of John Belushi's character from the National Lampoon's movie *Animal House* adorns my friend's dorm room wall. While this movie doesn't necessarily represent a collegiate reality, the poster shows Belushi wearing a sweater labeled "COLLEGE" along with a confused and somewhat stupefied expression. You probably have an idea in your head of what college is like, based on movies, friends, stereotypes, and campus tours. But like Belushi, you really have no idea. To make an effective decision about college, you need to know exactly what you're getting yourself into. What is college? An endless string of parties from fall fiesta to spring fling? Caffeine-induced late nights staring at a pile of books and a blank computer screen? A long-awaited chance to say *hasta la vista* to your parents and hometown? In actuality, college is a little bit of all these things.

Yes, you will party. Yes, you will spend inhumane amounts of time in the library. And yes, for better or worse, you will be on your own, perhaps far away from home. But why are you going to college?

You are going for an education. Duh. You don't need this book to tell you that. But you do need this book to tell you that "education" encompasses several different factors. The primary factor is obviously your academics: the classes you take, the teachers you have, the hours you study, and the grades you receive. College is not high school, so don't expect your professors to care that your computer crashed late last night or that your dog ate your homework. They will care long enough to write a big red F on your transcript, and then they will return to their own busy schedules. On a more positive note, you can look forward to not having nightly homework assignments. Instead, expect to have to finish an entire book between class meetings and write a ten-page analytical essay on it a mere three days later.

Beyond academics, college is where you will be living for the next four years. A large part of your education will happen outside of the classroom: the bad roommates you endure, the trek across campus through three feet of snow in February, and 4:00 A.M. conversations over cold pizza with the kid down the hall. Flexible class schedules and around-the-clock interaction with peers make your four years at college enjoyable—some even say the best time of your life. However, do not forget that college is ultimately a means to an end for graduate school and job placement. Therefore, the importance of choosing the right college cannot be stressed enough. All right. Now that I've put even more pressure on you, let's make a decision.

What, Where, and Why

I have a present for you: a formula that will tell you what envelope to pick to ensure the best school for you. It's the *What, Where, and Why formula*. As you consider your decision, be sure to pull out the notes you may have made earlier when determining your college criteria and visiting schools. (See Chapter 3 and Chapter 9 for more information.) Now pause and ask yourself, are the same factors still important to me or have they changed?

Academics, Location, and Extracurricular Life (That Is, the What, Where, and Why)

In a survey conducted by College Matters that asked current college students the three most important factors they considered when they were choosing a school, academics, location, and extracurricular options won hands down. Let's take a closer look.

Academics Whatever you plan to study, whether it's nuclear physics or the art of basket weaving, academics should be your starting point when you evaluate schools. Which school has the best academic program for the discipline you want to study? Which school has the best laboratories, hospitals, or libraries for your research? Are there nearby graduate or professional schools? (This consideration is most important if you need access to research facilities, such as those a medical school might provide. Having a law or business school nearby is largely irrelevant, as there will be little there that you will be able to access.) Does the school have funding for undergraduate research, both in the sciences and humanities?

You should also be looking for top-caliber professors with experience in teaching, researching, and publishing academic papers. Of course, these professors should also be committed to their undergraduate students. Will the professors give you the time of day? Will they hold regular office hours? One good indicator of the professors' accessibility is the college's student-teacher ratio. But the best way to find out is by asking students who go to that college.

When looking at specific academic programs, think about whether you want a liberal arts curriculum or something with more of a preprofessional focus. What's the difference? you may be wondering. Liberal arts schools emphasize a broad education in all disciplines: philosophy, history, literature, quantitative and scientific analysis, and so on. These schools will probably have a required "core" curriculum of mandatory classes in different disciplines. On the other hand, at a school with a preprofessional focus, you will spend the majority of your time studying in the School of Management, the School of Nursing, or even in a Communications track. Education experts often highlight the value of a broad education in liberal arts, especially since most of your professional skills will be learned while on the job. Furthermore, most college students change their majors several times. A liberal arts school might expose you to a new intellectual passion. But, if you are confident in your career decision, a preprofessional track will give you a very marketable résumé.

Location When you consider a college's location you have to think about three subfactors: (1) how far from home you will be, (2) whether you want an urban or rural setting, and (3) whether this setting is relevant to your academic program. Some of my friends from school are a few subway stops away from home, and some are a couple of oceans away. Gauge your own independence honestly, but understand that although Mom and Pop may drive you crazy during senior spring of high school, you'll shed a few tears when they drop you off at college and you watch them drive away. Are you going to want to go home during those occasional free weekends? Most colleges don't give very much time off. The breaks when you will have enough time to go home—especially if home is two airport connections away— are Thanksgiving, Christmas/winter holidays, spring break, and summer break. Breaks aside, don't forget that travel costs going back and forth from an out-of-state school can add up.

Beyond mere distance from home, whether the school offers a picturesque country campus or is squeezed within a few downtown city blocks may affect how happy you are. Are you into urban chic, looking for a trendy café to inspire your term papers? Or would you prefer to go hiking in the mountains that tower over your dorm? Think about places where you might feel bored or claustrophobic after two or three months, and then avoid going to college in those areas.

Location can also affect your academic program. For example, if you want to major in history or biology, you can probably be less selective about the specifics of your school, as long as it has a good program and research facilities. However, if you want to major in something like journalism or international relations, going to a school in New York City or a similar metropolitan area might make more sense than going to one in rural Idaho, because it will offer access to internships in those areas. Moreover, the best professors will often teach at urban schools in order to be close to the organizations important for their work, whether it's the Associated Press, the United Nations, or the White House.

Extracurricular Life What you do on campus, in student organizations, or on Saturday night will also be an essential aspect of your college experience. Furthermore, extracurricular activities relate back to academics as a way to gain practical experience in some fields, especially at a liberal arts school. Most schools have a plethora of extracurricular organizations, from the campus newspaper, to a capella singing groups, to the tae kwon do club. However, some schools might have a nationally ranked debate team, a particularly focused community service program that works with nearby underserved communities, or stellar college publications with lots of opportunities for involvement. Follow your passions. Don't forget that you can always form your own club, and be open to trying new activities. Interests change, and you'll change during college. Make sure all the colleges you are considering have lots of activities, even ones you may not be interested in now.

Even premed students take breaks from their marathon study of organic chemistry to relax occasionally. What kinds of social outlets do you enjoy? In most cases, you will find more restaurants, art, culture, and social options in or near a major city. Even if a major city is nearby, make sure that it is easily accessible by public transportation if you won't have a car. You should also find out about campus events that are held at your schools of interest. For example, are there formals, barbecues, carnivals, and cultural performances? Do students attend sporting events, and do they have a lot of school spirit? How much do fraternities and sororities dominate the social life of the schools you are considering? Understand that alcohol is a reality on most college campuses, but its effect on a school's social options varies from school to school. The best way to get an honest opinion about the diversity of a school's social options is to talk to current students.

Notice the overlap among the what, where, and why factors. This is not a coincidence. Your best option will be to select the school with the best combination of these three factors.

To Be (Ivy League) or Not to Be?

To be Ivy League, or not to be? that is the question, and here is your politically incorrect answer. There is a difference between Ivy League, private, and public schools. The ugly truth is that a school's "reputation" matters when it comes to internships, scholarships, jobs, international careers, graduate school, and even casual dinner conversation. Certainly, there are some excellent public schools such as the University of California–Berkeley, the University of California–Los Angeles (UCLA), the State University of New York (SUNY)–Binghamton, the University of Texas, the University of Virginia, and many others whose academic quality rival top private and Ivy League schools. You will get a great education at these schools and save a lot of money. However, in general, Ivy League and private schools are "better" in the sense that they have more money to fund research and facilities. They can also use their reputations to attract top professors.

The Ivy League was originally formed as an athletic union and consists of eight colleges—Brown, Columbia, Cornell, Dartmouth, Harvard, the University of Pennsylvania, Princeton, and Yale—that today represent some of the top academic institutions in the world. There are also many private schools that are not technically Ivy League, such as Stanford, Williams, Massachusetts Institute of Technology (MIT), Northwestern, the California Institute of Technology (Caltech), Amherst, and Swarthmore, that rival the schools in the Ivy League in terms of name recognition and prestige.

The *U.S. News and World Report* publishes a list of college rankings every year. Although you shouldn't use this magazine as the ultimate authority on college rankings, its research is comprehensive and its top-twenty schools usually do represent the best in the United States overall academically. Public schools and technical schools are also ranked effectively by category.

It will be very hard to turn down an invitation to attend an Ivy League or top-twenty college. If you are deciding between these types of schools, you really can't make a bad decision, although the strength of particular programs, social scenes, and other factors do differ. The first step is to weigh your what, where, and why factors carefully; the next step is to consider finances.

Show Me the Money

With college costs approaching $40,000 a year, even the rich are talking to financial aid officers. Before you freak out, take a deep breath and understand that in most cases you (or more likely your parents) will not be writing a $40,000 check each year to a school. Colleges recognize the huge financial burden of obtaining an education and are committing more of their budgets and endowments toward financial aid to attract top students like you!

In the previous section I explained the difference between Ivy League, public, and private institutions but left out the most important variant: *el dinero*. Although I have heralded the benefits of private and Ivy League schools, many of you will pick a school based on your financial need.

If you applied for financial aid (see Chapter 12 for details), the college will mail you a financial aid package along with your acceptance letter, or shortly thereafter. Compare financial aid packages between schools. Do not be afraid to pit one school against the other! Talk with your parents about the maximum amount of debt that you are willing to take on. Remember, too, that at some schools student loans aren't included as part of the financial aid package because need is fully met by grants (for example, Princeton), and other schools cap student loans at $2000 to $3000 per year (which can be reduced by cushy work-study jobs), mere pebbles in comparison to loans you might take out for graduate school. Also, if you feel that a school has not given you enough, have your parents call the financial aid office and speak to an officer. If you have earned a merit-based scholarship for athletics, music, or whatever, think carefully about how much you will be required to devote yourself to this activity while in college. If you quit that particular activity, you may lose your scholarship. Look at your options, and ask yourself where you are getting the most for your money. Financial aid, in the form of scholarships, low-interest student loans, and work-study programs, can make an expensive school a reality.

Be wary of deciding on a school exclusively for financial reasons. In a survey conducted by College Matters, a majority of students chose more expensive schools because of their better reputations. Most students recommended going to the best school you get into, unless working all the time to pay for a private school that doesn't give you a lot of financial aid will compromise your happiness and academic success. The bottom line: Some of you are going to have to make a decision based on finances. Try to pick the best school you can afford. Go to Chapter 12 to learn how to apply for every outside scholarship that you qualify for!

But I Still Don't Know!

How do you ever survive in restaurants with extensive menus? Okay. If you still really can't decide after looking at academics, location, extracurricular activities, reputation, and finances, we can break this down even more. The following two sections talk about things that shouldn't be major factors in your decision and extras you might consider.

Things You Should Scratch from Your Decision Criteria

Some factors just shouldn't enter into your decision. Often, factors that shouldn't substantially affect which college you choose form the greatest obstacle to discovering which school is best for you. Therefore, I will describe these factors first before outlining other finer points that may help you make your decision.

Where Your Boyfriend or Girlfriend Is Going. I have heard so many times: "Oh, I should go to College X because my boyfriend John is going there." You know what? The plain and simple truth is that most high school couples break up soon after college starts. This means that you should not choose a school based on where your significant other is going. "Ah," you say, "but we're for real." If that's true, than your love will last no matter where you are.

I have seen many couples break up after going to (the same) college. I have also seen cross-continental relationships last four years (for instance, Duke and Stanford). If, by chance, the college that your significant other is going to is also the best college for you based on your personalized set of criteria, then great. But do not bias your attitude toward the college where your significant other will be. It won't be pretty when you and John have broken up *and* you're at a school that's not right for you.

Where Your Parents Went. Some students are pressured into choosing a school because their parents went there. If your parents are dangling the money carrot in front of you by telling you that they'll pay for you to attend their alma mater but no other school, that's just wrong. Your parents should support you in whatever decision you make. Talk to them. Once they understand the thought process that leads to your decision, they will likely be open to your choice. After all, parents just want their kids to be happy (or so my parents tell me). Have your parents refer to Chapter 11 for more information on how they can support you.

Where Your Parents Have Always Dreamed You'll Go to College. Again, this should not be one of your decision criteria. College is about *you*, not your parents. Both parents and kids have to remember that the parent is not the one going to college. You and your dreams come first. Don't be afraid to "disappoint" your parents. If they are pressuring you to attend a particular college, chances are it's because they think you'll be happiest there. Sit down and explain your decision-making criteria. Listen to your parents' advice, but ultimately it's you who must make the decision.

The School with the Cheapest Price Tag. Would you buy pants that didn't fit just because they were the cheapest ones in the store? No. So, why choose a college solely because it has the cheapest price tag? You can find ways to bring down the price of more expensive colleges through grants and scholarships. You can also try good, old-fashioned bargaining: "That store down the street is selling similar pants for a little less—can you try to meet or beat that price?" If neither of these tactics work, you can always ask for creative payment options such as loans or individualized payment dates. More likely than not, once a college accepts you, it will work with you to get you there financially, especially if you show that you really want to attend but that finances are getting in the way. Finally, be sure to make education a priority. I know a lot of people who attended a college they hated because it had the cheapest price tag. In the long run, the extra money they saved and spent on nice cars and expensive spring break trips could not make up for a miserable college experience. Don't forget, your education is more important and a better investment than any material good you can buy.

The School with the Best Coach (for Student-Athletes). Are you likely to go pro? Are you headed for the Olympics or World Championships? Can you make a living off your athletic prowess? If you answered no to any of these questions, then you should not choose a college solely because it has the best coach. As a student-athlete (a distance runner) myself, I know this can be very tough because your sport is such a huge part of your life and a defining part of your identity, and you want to excel to the greatest extent possible. However, while sports may be one of the defining aspects of your life now, this won't always be the case. Several members of the College Matters team went for schools with top academics, despite weaker athletic programs, and none of them regret it.

Factors That Might Tip the Scale in One School's Favor

Additional factors might tip the scale in one school's favor when you make the difficult decision of which college to attend. Many of these are the same factors you thought about when designing your college criteria a year or two ago. However, these criteria may take on new meaning now that it's time to decide.

Size. I hinted at this factor in the section on location. The size of a school definitely influences how comfortable you will feel on campus. Large universities are often more impersonal. However, they also usually have more money to build better facilities and can offer more diverse extracurricular options. Think about your high school class. Is it too small, too big, or just right? Do you want to know everybody in your college class or constantly meet new people? Most college populations will be bigger than your high school class. The question is, How much bigger do you want to get?

Student-Teacher Ratio. In general, the lower the student-teacher ratio, the better. Unlike the situation in high school, in college many of your instructors will not know who you are unless you take the initiative to introduce yourself or take small, intimate classes. Be sure to speak with an admissions officer or current students to get an accurate representation of this ratio. Check that the ratio reflects professors who are actually teaching, and not those who are just researching or on sabbatical. Of course, if you're looking forward to large lecture hall classes where you can fall asleep in the back unnoticed, you might want to move on to a different factor.

Diversity. Whether cultural, economic, social, racial, gendered, or religious, you will encounter "diversity" as a college student. You will meet people whose backgrounds and experiences are different from yours, and you will benefit from this exposure. Some schools specifically emphasize this factor and recruit the most diverse student body possible. At the local college in your hometown, you are likely to find students from your high school who are similar to you. At a larger university, you will encounter students from different backgrounds and all corners of the world.

Safety. You may not be giving this as much thought as your parents are just yet, but once you are on campus living on your own, feeling safe will be a priority. Will you feel safe in an urban setting? What kinds of neighborhoods house your potential schools? What is the police presence on campus? Are there safety phones spread throughout campus where you might call for help during an emergency? Is there an escort service to walk you home late at night? How are dorms and campus buildings secured? Is there some kind of key or swipe card access system limited to students? What is the most common crime on campus? Do female students feel safe? What do the statistics say? Consider these questions before selecting a school. You do not want safety issues to distract you from work and fun once you arrive at college.

Study-Abroad Opportunities. Many students describe studying abroad as one of the best experiences of college and even their lives. Programs vary from school to school. Do you want to work an internship abroad or study for credit? Will your school of interest accept these credits? What language skills will you need? Does the school have a "sister school" (that is, did it establish a program in another country like "Princeton in Beijing"), or will you have to design your own program? Call your prospective schools and ask to speak to a representative in their office of career services or study abroad office for more specific information.

Housing. Where you live and with whom you live will be a major daily influence on your life. Housing options can really set schools apart. Is housing guaranteed all four years at your school? Do most students live in dorms or off campus? Are you going to want the atmosphere of a dorm or of an apartment? How close are the dorms or apartments to buildings where you will be taking classes? Will you have your own bedroom or will you live in a suite with ten other girls? If you don't like your roommate, can you transfer rooms? (As a brief aside, most schools send some sort of survey asking you what you are looking for in a roommate. Be honest about yourself and what you expect in others. If your dirty underwear is going to reside on the floor, you want a roommate who's going to be able to tolerate this habit.) Will a resident advisor or proctor live nearby? Would living off campus significantly lower or raise costs? Are many students at the school local commuters living at home? Would really bad or good housing supersede academic concerns for you? These are all questions for you to keep in mind when you consider the housing factor.

Food. In college, you might be able to go a few days without sleeping but definitely not without eating. Different schools have different meal plans. Check each one out, and decide which works for you. Does your school offer a diversity of options and account for any special needs you might have (for example, kosher, diabetic, vegan, or vegetarian)? If you will live off campus, are there restaurants or supermarkets nearby? Ask students for honest opinions, and visit the campus to try the food yourself. If you're not going to be able to digest that mystery meat or escape to a nearby fast-food joint, you're going to have a difficult time surviving, let alone thriving.

Technology. Internet and email have changed college campuses forever. You will watch lectures online, research library collections from your computer, turn in assignments via email, and communicate with your friends and teachers with the click of a mouse. Make sure every dorm room has enough Internet jacks for all of the inhabitants. Most schools now offer wireless access all over campus. If you will not be bringing a personal computer to campus, make sure that the computer labs are nearby, plentiful, and conducive to paper writing and research. If you are pursuing computer science, engineering, or any sort of "technical" studies, a school's technological reputation will be particularly relevant.

Life Outside the Gate

So the unthinkable has happened. You're staring at a pile of small envelopes because you did not get into your ideal school, or perhaps you didn't get into a school at all. Before you resign from life and join a nomadic tribe in remote regions of rural Nepal, listen up. It is not the end of the world, and you still have plenty of viable options. Taking time off before college can lead to valuable personal insights. Use your connections to set up internships in potential fields of interest, whether that means campaigning for a local politician, volunteering at a hospital, researching at a laboratory or think-tank, or working at a bank. Getting any kind of job will help finance your future education and give you practical experience in the big, bad real world. Studying or traveling abroad can expand your language abilities and cultural appreciation. Take some classes at a local community college, and do well in them. Retake standardized tests if you feel that you can study hard and perform better. Start working on your college applications again. If you were accepted only by one of your "safety schools," think about going. You'd be surprised how much you might like it. Plus, don't forget about the possibility of transferring after one year. Transfer applications are even more competitive than regular admissions, but I know many people who have transferred and been very happy. You know the motto: If at first you don't succeed . . . Learn from your past mistakes, work hard, and try, try again!

Sports. Whether you play sports, watch sports, or don't know a tennis racket from a baseball bat, athletics are a source of pride to a school and an important part of many undergraduate campuses. Budget cuts have forced some schools to eliminate sports programs in recent years. Larger schools will offer a wider array of athletic options, often on varsity, junior varsity, club, and intramural levels. But not every school will have a crew, squash, alpine skiing, and ultimate Frisbee team. Whatever the sports offerings, you should follow your interests. You should also consider the school's athletic facilities. Will you have access to a campus gym, track, or swimming pool? How about workout facilities?

Politics. In general, the student bodies of many college campuses are labeled as liberal. However, conservative movements are gaining momentum at many colleges, including the University of California–Berkeley, the former bastion of collegiate liberalism. You will encounter individuals at school who vary across the political spectrum from radical to reactionary and everything in between. This gamut is intentional, and you will benefit from an exposure to a diversity of opinions and backgrounds. Keep in mind that the politics of the town you live in can create biased and stereotypical perceptions of colleges that might not be true. Don't eliminate a school just because there are more young Democrats than young Republicans, and you worked for Bush's reelection campaign. However, a college's political environment can affect attitudes toward alternative lifestyles such as sexual orientation. You should consider a school's politics seriously if there is a chance that it might infringe upon deeply held personal beliefs or ways of living.

Weather. The Northeastern United States boasts many of the nation's most established colleges—and the nation's most miserable winters. College campuses don't have hallways like high school where you can walk from class to class in a cozy, enclosed space. Instead, be prepared to trek through three feet of unplowed snow some days and, no, they will not cancel class. Unless you are truly hydrophobic, weather should not be the most significant factor in your decision. It is, however, something to keep in the back of your mind if you can't decide between Dartmouth and Rice. Just think: you can bond with your classmates over the miserable weather and have an excuse to buy lots of new jackets and warm accessories! Your first snowball fight at school could end up being one of your favorite college memories. And here's one final tip: The trays in the dining hall are great makeshift sleds.

When You Finally Have to Make the Decision . . . Listen to that Little Voice

The best advice isn't going to come from me, your guidance counselor, or even your parents. Whether you call it your gut, intuition, conscience, or imaginary friend, that little voice inside your head knows what it's talking about. Usually we tell this voice to shut up when it gets in the way of us having a good time, but in this instance you might want to listen closely. You're going to know which school is "the one" if you follow carefully your own goals and priorities. Use this chapter to help yourself define these goals and priorities. Weigh the factors I have described, and you will be able to decide where you can have the best experience both inside and outside the classroom. And if all else fails . . . well, there's always that no-madic tribe in Nepal.

Good luck with your decision and four wonderful years of college.

P.S.: After You've Made the Decision . . . Chat with Your Future Classmates!

Many colleges now give you the option of logging onto an online chat room and speaking with your potential future classmates. It's a cool little feature for students who have already decided where they are going. In these chat sessions or bulletin boards, parents and students can vent their college worries and ask questions of other parents and students. (You don't feel nearly as dumb doing this in a chat room as you do calling the admissions office and asking live.) If you become friends with someone on these online forums, you can trade emails and then skip the chat scene altogether.

CHAPTER ELEVEN

ADVICE FOR PARENTS

Katherine Jane Bacuyag, Brown

While the other chapters in this book let students know what they need to do to pursue their dream schools and scholarships, this chapter is written specifically to address the concerns (and there are many) of *parents* who have children who are about to embark on the admissions process. I would encourage students to read this chapter as well, to get a better idea of what their parents might be going through, but if you are a student pressed for time and want to read about concerns directly relevant to you, please flip ahead to Chapter 12. Now, parents, let's discuss the roles you can play to make your child's admission process as painless and successful as possible.

Well, it's about that time. You've started noticing TV shows and newspaper articles about college admissions, especially those that show parents in the background, waving goodbye to their kids. Meanwhile, money concerns make you fear the necessity of pawning off your valuable possessions so that you can make that first college tuition payment.

Yes, your baby's all grown up and going off to college. In a short time, acceptance letters will stream in, you'll cram your child's belongings into boxes that barely fit in the family car, and then you'll help your child move into his or her dorm room. Before you know it, your child will embark on his or her biggest independent endeavor yet.

But before you get to that pivotal moment, you have some role playing (and studying) to do. This rundown will help to clarify, or possibly even teach, the special roles you will play as a parent of a soon-to-be college student.

What Roles Should Parents Play?

According to parents, the following are the three biggest fears that they face about their child's application process: (1) their child will choose to attend a school that (s)he will not be happy at, (2) their child will not be accepted to a good school (or any school at all), and (3) they will not be able to afford the tuition of the school their child wishes to attend. Fortunately, you can confront these challenges head on by playing two important roles:

Acting as your child's strongest advocate (providing moral support and trusting your child's best judgments, intervening only when necessary).

Being your child's financial advisor (gaining knowledge and proactively completing financial aid applications).

Role 1: Being Your Child's Advocate

Before we talk about specific steps you can take to support your child in the admissions process (see the "Where to Start?" section for a list of tips), let's define the advocate role that most students want their parents to play. We'll do this by first defining what a strong advocate is *not*. Then, the rest of this chapter will move on to a discussion of just exactly what a strong advocate is and what parents can do to support their children in the admissions process.

Overall, try your hardest not to become a "pushy parent." Avoid tugging too hard in the direction *you* think your child should be heading. Living vicariously through your child is okay, but making him or her do what you've always wanted to do is a big no-no.

When I was applying to college, my father became more cognizant of accurately timing his tugs, while I grew more aware of the importance of communicating my needs. My father wanted the best for me and thereby expected the most from me. Many times, we felt as though we'd been to the pits of despair and back. He urged me to apply to twenty schools (an insane number—please do not encourage your child to do this). He had a hard time understanding that the college application procedures are both different from when he applied to colleges and not the same across schools. Before he took a gander at the mountain of college applications, he thought I could simply copy my responses from Rice's essay section and paste them to Brown's essay. Sure, it's true that *parts* of essays can be recycled, but it's important that each essay gets the attention it deserves. Each school is unique and will likely ask why your child thinks (s)he fits in that particular school. Carving out a thoughtful response to these particularized questions takes time.

My father believed that the greater number of schools I applied to, the greater chance I'd have of getting in. Now, he admits that his logic was flawed for two reasons. First, he didn't understand the importance of finding a college that was right for me. He had *his* heart set on my getting accepted to the best college as defined by the college rankings in *U.S. News and World Report*. My father latched on to these national rankings and was blinded by the fact that each college attracts different students and offers a unique curriculum. Thankfully, we hashed out the college specifics such as large versus small, public versus private, urban versus rural, liberal versus conservative, and so on. From our list of college criteria, we managed to pick several schools that seemed to match my needs. (For more information, see Chapter 3.)

If you've been hearing, "Puh-leeeeeease, Mom, puh-leeeeeease Dad, leave me alone!" a lot, it may behoove you to step back and think, What kind of support would I have liked during this process? You might have a burning desire for your child to stay close to home or to apply to your alma mater. Your reasons may be sensible and even convincing. However, when it comes down to it, your child will likely be most successful when his or her motivations come from within. You don't want to have your child regret (like my classmate, Sara, did) taking ownership of a new set of wheels and a ticket to the nearby state school rather than attending a more expensive, out-of-state college that better matched her abilities. Here are some additional *things to avoid*:

1. *Relentlessly calling admissions officers.* Too much parental contact with schools to which your child is applying may lead admission officers to speculate that the child is not actually interested.

2. *Enrolling in get-into-college lessons.* Hardly anyone I know at the most selective schools used an educational consultant (by educational consultant, I mean one of those people that charges high fees to meet with your child on a frequent basis from a young age to coach him or her on getting into a selective school); it's just not necessary. Plus, it puts too much pressure on your child, which could lead to burnout or even rebellion. Instead, enroll your children in lessons (for example, cello, ballet, or drawing) that have a better chance of sparking a lifelong interest (thereby strengthening your child's college application). Above all, let your kid be a kid!

3. *Giving money to the school to get your child in.* Schools have such huge endowments that the only way your contribution is going to make a difference is if it is literally millions of dollars.

4. *Advertising to your workplace and neighborhood community to which schools your child is applying (and to which ones (s)he is accepted).* Most high schoolers put enough pressure on themselves. In cases where parents try to live vicariously through their children, or brag too much about them, students end up feeling controlled and intensely pressured.

This is not to say that you, as a nonpushy parent, shouldn't be involved in the process. At the other end of the spectrum, and equally detrimental, was the experience of my friend Beth, who did not get any help from her parents while completing applications. She now recommends "sitting down at the end of junior year to organize ideas and plans. It would have made me feel better knowing that my parents cared about more than just opening my acceptance and denial letters for me."

College students-to-be want their parents to be involved but in a way that gives the students more responsibility and independence. So, instead of expecting to get tuned out, find something that will make your child's ears perk up! Surprise your child by ferreting out scholarship opportunities. (Try looking at your workplace, on community information boards, and so on.) My mom brought home a newspaper clipping of a scholarship that she stumbled upon during her lunch hour. Thanks to her vigilance, that single scholarship will continue to cover my expenses through graduate school!

Role 2: Financial Advisor

All this talk of scholarships brings us to your second role—that of financial advisor. Getting in is one worry, but being able to pay for college is another. Fortunately, public library and bookstore shelves are stocked with guides containing information on how to pay for college. Furthermore, for free advice, take a look at these Web sites: www.collegeboard.com/pay, www.usnews.com, and www.review.com. And last but certainly not least, be sure to check out Chapter 12 of this book on scholarships.

During my college application experience, my family found, much to our pleasant surprise, that attending an Ivy League school was cheaper than attending a state school would have been, because of our family's financial need (see Table 11.1). This will often be the case for lower and middle class families. For more information on need-based financial aid, see Chapter 12 of this book.

	Brown University	University of Texas–Austin
TABLE 11.1 COMPARISON OF COSTS FOR IVY LEAGUE VERSUS STATE SCHOOLS		
Total cost	$40,480	$15,948
Expected family contribution (EFC)	$10,000	$10,000
Dollars I am qualified to receive (Total cost – EFC)	$30,480	$5,948
Percent need met[1]	X 100%	X 63%
Amount I would receive	$30,480	$3,737
Amount I would pay	$10,000	$12,211

When to Start?

It's never too early to start thinking about going to college. At the same time, it's never too late. From the time your child starts school, make it clear that college is one of the best ways to improve your child's life. While thirty years ago a high school diploma was sufficient for a wide range of jobs, now a college degree is a prerequisite for most professional positions. Nevertheless, it is important to keep in mind that your expectations for your child's future shouldn't be forced down his or her throat. Start by asking your child basic questions such as these: Why do you want to go to college? What are your most important needs and goals? What kind of college will best serve you? Your approach will probably work best if these questions come at spaced intervals, so that your child will be receptive to actually giving you thoughtful responses.

It doesn't hurt to remind him or her as early as freshman year that the high school transcript (that is, grades, course selection, class rank) is one of

---

[1] Some schools can meet all the demonstrated need of your family (that is, the amount beyond what your family can pay without taking out large loans). Others can only meet a percentage of this need. See Chapter 12 for more information.

the primary factors that colleges use in admissions decisions. However, this doesn't mean that you need to pressure your child to be a straight-A student, especially considering that Advanced Placement and honors classes are more challenging. Colleges will also look at extracurricular involvement (including community service), standardized test scores, personal essays, and interviews.

If you're reading this book before your child is ready to start filling out applications, you'll want to pay attention to what your child loves to do. This is an ideal time to offer suggestions for how (s)he can apply that curiosity to things outside of the classroom. For example, my friend Amber's mom acted on her daughter's glowing love for books and young children. Thanks to her mom's encouragement, each summer for seven years, Amber enjoyed inspiring young children as a volunteer in her local library.

Regardless of where your son or daughter is in the college application process, you can help by becoming familiar with the "calendar of events" for aspiring college applicants. These calendars are available online (check out www.collegeboard.com) and maybe even in your child's guidance counselor's office. Once you have the calendar in hand, remember that the information given consists of only *suggested* dates. If you find that you're a few months, or even a year off the given schedule, don't get too anxious. Remember, earlier is easier, but it's never too late to start.

Where to Start?

The following are some specific suggestions of what you can do to make your child's application process as painless and productive as possible:

1. Collect application deadlines, notification dates, and testing dates, and then placed them on a calendar with other important events.

2. You could go a step further by starting a filing system that organizes college mailings, application packets from colleges, and scholarship application materials. This means creating the files, but please allow your child to file his or her own mail and do other work on his or her own.

3. Compile information about yourself. Gather your social security number, job title, official company name, university(ies) attended, month(s) and year(s) of graduation, and your major(s)/degree(s) so that your child has this information on hand when filling out the application. You

could even offer to fill in these basic facts yourself so that your child can focus on the meat of the application.

4. Ask around for contacts at the schools to which your child is applying. See if any of your friends or coworkers have children attending your child's colleges of interest. Your child can write to these students, ask questions, and possibly stay with them during college visits.

5. In addition, try surprising your child with a bag of pertinent office supplies (for example, white paper, red pens, manila envelopes, paperclips, stamps, and toner cartridges for the printer).

6. To prevent heart attacks when the computer crashes and obliterates everything on it, buy a box of floppy disks or a USB disk so that your child can back up his or her work (especially the essays!) after every productive session of working on the applications. Or, if you are really computer-savvy, set up an Internet site for file backups.

7. Help your child fill out financial aid forms (the FAFSA and CSS Profile; see Chapter 12 for further instructions). Most of the information that these forms require relates to parents' financial status, so your child will particularly need your help.

8. Finally, and most importantly, give your child moral support. Let him or her know that you think (s)he is applying to the right colleges and that things will work out. Also, don't overburden your child with money worries. Save those conversations for later in the year when you know what sort of financial aid you will be receiving. There is nothing worse for a child than to feel guilty that his or her educational aspirations will put parents through financial hardship.

These suggestions delineate a helpful and active role for you in your child's precollege preparation. None of them imply that you should become your child's servant. They simply reflect the fact that the application process is stressful—especially when you are seventeen or eighteen years old—and every little thing you can do to facilitate it will help!

The College Visit

The college visit is one of the most important aspects of the admissions process. It will help your child decide to which colleges to apply and ultimately which one to attend. (See Chapter 9 for more details on college visits.) Although financing college visits can be difficult, be sure to make such visits a priority. After all, you wouldn't want your child to marry someone (s)he had never met. Nor should (s)he choose to attend a college sight unseen.

When my parents and I set out on my college visits, I remember being pleasantly surprised when they stayed out of the way and let me ask all my questions. For the schools that we did not visit together, they let me visit on my own. I was able to get a real feel for each university—an invaluable experience that played a significant role in my decision of which school to attend. C. Darryl Uy, the Assistant Director of Admission at Brown University, has this to say about college visits:

> When families visit colleges or attend college fairs, parents should not do all the talking while the applicant stands off to the side, quietly, unengaged. Parents also should refrain from saying "when we were filling out the application ..." or "'we are hoping to study biology in college ...". While I understand that applying to college is a process for the parents as well (especially if they are footing the bill or some of it), college-bound students need to start taking the initiative and be more active in their college search. They must realize that by the time they get to college, their parents aren't going to be around to do everything for them. The students should be the ones to schedule interviews, make college visit reservations, make sure that their applications are complete, etc. Parents need to be supportive without being pushy. For parents, the college process represents the beginning stages of letting go.

In the end...

The college application process has a way of testing the parent-child relationship, but if you keep this advice in mind, difficulties will be ameliorated. Before, during, and after this process, continuously congratulate your child and yourself for your efforts. Tell your child that you love him or her no matter what happens. Don't be too surprised if you discover an entirely new dimension of your relationship with your child. Consider it a golden opportunity to get to know your child as (s)he prepares for the most independent adventure yet.

SCHOLARSHIPS AND FINANCIAL AID

Evelyn Huang, Stanford

Imagine what a relief it will be to have all those college applications finished and an acceptance letter in your hand. No more pressure, right? Not so fast. What about money? Take a look at the price of tuition. Stanford's bills total over $40,000 a year. You're not going to find much variance when looking at Amherst, MIT, Duke, or Columbia.

These figures may seem daunting at first. I doubt they fit comfortably in your wallet (not to mention your parents' checkbook). Don't be discouraged. There are things you can do to make sure you have enough money to pay for college. For some, it may mean reconnecting with rich relatives. For others, it may mean choosing a college in a lower price range. For me, it was applying for financial aid and being awarded over $110,000 in privately sponsored scholarships.

Financial Aid versus Scholarships

What is the difference between financial aid and scholarships? First, financial aid is typically funded by the government or through university coffers. Financial aid comes in two forms. The first is need-based grants (usually awarded by universities or the government). These do not need to be repaid. The second consists of government and private loans that do need to be repaid. I'm sure we've all heard stories about people in their forties who are still paying off their college debt—that is all from loans. On the other hand, scholarships are usually privately funded, and winning them is often based on merit rather than financial need. Best of all, they don't have to be repaid in the future.

A Look into Financial Aid

Since financial aid is readily available for your education, it only makes sense to look at this resource before diving into the world of scholarships. Most top colleges meet 100 percent of need (that is, all students will feasibly be able to attend Duke, Princeton, or any other school that meets 100 percent of need, regardless of their financial circumstances).

Though scholarships may initially seem more appealing than financial aid, most of the money offered to college students from financial assistance does *not* come from private-sector funds. Rather, college, federal, and state funds make up the vast majority of financial assistance. Need-based grants make high-cost, private universities a viable possibility for students who would otherwise have to attend state universities with lower sticker prices. Thus, it is absolutely crucial to apply for university and federally funded need-based financial aid, even if your family's income is in the six-figure range.

Surprisingly enough, nearly all students who applied for financial aid from Harvard (in 2001) whose parents earned between $100,000 and $120,000 received some form of need-based financial aid. If you come from a typical middle class family (that is, combined family income of $40,000 to $60,000 a year, before taxes), a private university could cost less than an in-state public university. It will almost certainly cost less if your combined family income is less than $40,000 per year, except when your family has huge amounts of investments and assets. In fact, Harvard recently did away with the parental contribution for families with a combined income of less than $40,000 per year; it also reduced the family contribution for families with between $40,000 and $60,000 of income per year. Furthermore, note that other factors, like how many siblings you have attending college or large family medical expenses, could also reduce the contribution that your family is expected to make. See the section entitled "Role 2: The Financial Advisor" in Chapter 11 for an example of how, through financial aid, an Ivy League school can cost less than an in-state university with a much cheaper price tag.

The amount your family will be expected to contribute is referred to as the *expected family contribution*, or *EFC*. You can estimate your EFC for free online at www.collegeboard.com/pay or www.act.org/fane (same calculator). Keep in mind that the EFC is a ballpark figure of what your family will be expected to contribute. The actual amount your family will pay will vary based on how much money the school has available for financial aid. Schools with large endowments (usually private schools) tend to have much more money for financial aid than schools with smaller endowments (usually public universities). Nearly all of the most selective private schools meet 100 percent of demonstrated need, meaning that if you get in, your family will be able to pay!

Because financial aid has grown substantially at private colleges within the past decade, more and more students are finding these schools to be an option, thus getting rid of much of the elitism in American higher education. While private schools are becoming more affordable, a huge concern in recent years has been soaring tuition costs at public universities as a result of state budget crises. (Often, it is education funding that gets cut first.) For example, between the 2001–2002 and 2003–2004 school years, the University of California–Berkeley hiked tuition by 35 percent!

Bottom-line costs for public university tuition are still going to be cheaper than private university tuition. However, because public universities tend to have less money for financial aid, it is becoming increasingly common for students from middle or lower class backgrounds to find it cheaper to attend private schools. This trend is a shame, because for many students, it is public universities that provide the best match. If you want to attend a public university but find the soaring tuition rates to be daunting, turn to the section entitled "The Truth about Scholarships" in this chapter and then write a letter to your state representative to express your dismay about the situation (in hopes of inspiring legislative change). You could even organize a youth movement to reverse this trend in your state, strengthening the Activities section of your application and making a tremendously important impact socially!

Regardless of where you want to attend college, the moral of the story is this: *apply, apply, apply* for financial aid! The worst that colleges can say is no, and you just might be surprised at what you'll get. Since most colleges have need-blind admissions policies (those making admissions decisions don't know how much money your family makes), applying for financial aid won't affect your chances of getting in either. And remember, the cost of a college is what your family pays (the full amount of tuition minus grants), not the full tuition amount.

Financial aid packages, including both grants and loans, are typically awarded after acceptance but before enrollment at a university. In many cases, the application process for grants and loans are one and the same, and require submission of official government *financial aid forms*, but check with individual schools to make sure. Now let's take a closer look at grants and loans.

Grants

In recent years, there has been a growing trend to steer students away from loans, when possible. In fact, Princeton no longer awards loans as part of financial aid packages. Most selective colleges cap *loans plus work study* at $3000. What does this mean for you? If you have more than $3000 worth of "need," you're bound to qualify for some type of need-based grant. Usually grants are funded by a combination of federal funds (for example, Pell Grants) and the school's endowment.

Loans

Loans are a bit more complicated and diverse than grants. The following sections give a breakdown of the types of loans available to you and your parents.

Student Loans. These are provided by either a private institution that is guaranteed by the government or by the government itself. Student loans have low interest rates and do not require collateral. Student loans also usually have some form of deferment clause, whereby you won't have to pay until you're out of school and working. All you need to do is apply. In college, you'll find student loans in two forms: Stafford Loans and Perkins Loans:

- *Stafford Loans.* This federal loan is either subsidized (the government pays for accumulating interest during your college career) or unsubsidized (interest must be paid by you, though payments can be delayed until after graduation). In order to qualify for subsidized loans, you must display financial need. However, all students qualify for unsubsidized Stafford Loans. Think about it from the government's perspective: They earn money off of your education! During your freshman year, you can borrow up to $2625 in Stafford Loans. Sophomore year offers $3500, and each following year, you are eligible for $5500. Interest rates vary from year to year, but the ceiling rests at 8.25 percent (at printing).

- *Perkins Loans*. This loan is only available to students who have a large amount of financial need. Perkins Loans are offered through your school, so cut-offs will vary from college to college. However, all Perkins Loans are subsidized: The government pays the interest while you are in school. Perkins Loans award up to $4000 per year, with a cumulative $20,000 cap on undergraduate studies. Perkins Loans offer a flat 5 percent interest rate, and you have ten years to repay the loan. So, no, you won't end up in debt at the age of forty. You'll only be paying off the loan until around the age of thirty.

Parent Loans. The federal government offers the Parent Loan for Undergraduate Students (PLUS). These funds are either offered through a private institution backed by the government or by the government itself. Interest rates are variable, and payment begins sixty days after the loan agreement is reached. Again, payment lasts for up to ten years. But, in this case, you aren't burdened with repayment—your parents are.

Commercial loans. Commercial loans may be used to compensate for the difference between what the government offers you in financial aid and how much aid you actually need. These loans are offered completely through private lenders, which means banks. Not surprisingly, interest rates are high.

Work-Study Programs

In addition, most schools offer work-study programs. This just means that you'll have a job at school that doesn't really pay you. Okay, you're paid for working, but your earnings go toward payment for your education. (Note that your education fees include your personal expenses while in school. So instead of directly sending your paycheck to the school, you might use it to buy exciting things like shampoo, your airplane tickets home, printing budget, and so on.) While you may never see any of the money or otherwise spend it on boring things, these jobs are often very cushy. One of the writers of this book, who shall remain nameless, gets paid to sit in her dorm's study room, do her homework, and basically make sure that nobody steals the multimillion-dollar portrait collection that hangs on the wall.

Reserve Officer Training Core (ROTC)

Finally, look into other services that offer forms of financial aid, such as the Reserved Officer Training Core, or ROTC. The ROTC has scholarships for students who participate in their military training program and commit to enlisting after graduation for four years of active duty and two years of reserve duty in the U.S. military. ROTC scholarships pay the full costs of tuition, books, college fees, and even provide a small stipend for pocket money. To qualify for ROTC scholarships, students must be at least seventeen years old, high school graduates, and U.S. citizens. Furthermore, ROTC scholarships are based on merit. Students must score well on standardized tests, show leadership ability in extracurricular and school activities, and do well in personal interviews.

Important Ways to Maximize Your Need-Based Financial Aid

Rule 1: Never Lie. Your information will be checked against your family's tax returns. Lying on financial aid forms is equivalent to lying on your taxes, and an angry financial aid officer isn't any prettier than an angry Internal Revenue Service auditor. Just don't.

Rule 2: Never Put Money in a Child's Name. While it might be useful for tax purposes, putting large amounts of money in a child's name will be harmful for financial aid. Colleges will typically consider 5 percent of parents' assets as viable contribution sources, but 50 percent of student's assets are typically marked as sources. If $100 is in Mom's name, Yale will take $5 of it. If it is in your name, Yale will take $50. Get the point? However, if money is already in your (the student's) name, be sure to have your parents consult an attorney before transferring it, especially if it is in the form of a trust fund, because removing money from these often has legal implications. If it is simply in a bank account, moving it should be easy. Note that some money (less than $2000) in a student's name is fine and in fact expected, since students need to pay personal expenses while in school; colleges won't touch this money. It is things like inheritances from deceased or wealthy relatives that will cause problems!

Rule 3: Look Poor on Your Forms. This statement might seem obvious, but you want to look *poor* on your financial aid applications, so fill them out when investments such as stocks are low.

Rule 4: If a Relative Wants to Pay, Have Them Reimburse Bills. If relatives first write out a check to you or your parents, your family will have more assets and therefore qualify for less financial aid. It's best to have Grandma write a check to Mom and Dad right after (or right before) they pay the bill.

There are many other special circumstances, like owning a farm or business, which I won't go into here. For detailed advice about your special circumstances, visit the reference section of your local library and check out a book about financial aid. And remember that what's good for taxes does not necessarily fly for financial aid. Although Uncle Bob the accountant might suggest that your parents put money in your name for tax purposes, remember that this transfer could jeopardize your chances for need-based financial aid.

Filling Out the Forms

In order to apply for aid from universities, you must fill out the Free Application for Federal Student Aid (FAFSA). Oftentimes, you'll also be required to complete the CSS PROFILE, which is like the FAFSA except that it is not free; there is a fixed processing fee plus a variable fee per school applied. (Ouch!) It is easiest to fill out the FAFSA online at www.fafsa.ed.gov. If you would prefer to fill out a hard copy, call 1-800-4-FEDAID, or pick up the form at your public library. The PROFILE is also easier (and cheaper) to fill out online; go to www.collegeboard.com/pay. Consult your guidance counselor if you do not have Internet access or would prefer to file a hard copy.

What's the difference between the FAFSA and the PROFILE? The FAFSA deals with general household tax information, whereas the PROFILE asks college-specific questions in addition to general household tax information. Most selective schools require both the FAFSA and the PROFILE.

Filling out the FAFSA and PROFILE is kind of like filling out tax forms, except even more annoying. Both are pretty dense. Be prepared to submit the following information:

- Your driver's license and social security card numbers.

- Your income tax returns, W-2 forms, and 1099 forms for the previous year. If you are married (already?), you will also need these documents for your spouse.

- Your parents' income tax returns, W-2 forms, and 1099 forms from the previous year.

- Current bank statements and mortgage information.

- Records relating to stocks, bonds, mutual funds, and other investments.

- Documentation of nontaxable income, such as social security income, AFDC, and veterans' benefits.

- Business and farm records.

- Records relating to any unusual family financial circumstances, such as medical and dental expenses not covered by health insurance, tuition expenses at elementary or secondary schools, unusually high child care costs, death, divorce, and loss of employment.

Most colleges require you to file the FAFSA and PROFILE by March 1. Consult individual schools for specific details. If you apply for Early Decision, you will need to file the PROFILE by November 1.

Important Notes:

- Remember, you must reapply for financial aid each year. (I am still filling out those stupid forms.) Even if you did not qualify for need-based aid your first year, reapply if your financial circumstances have changed significantly.

- Pay attention to deadlines! They usually aren't as well publicized as needed. And unlike your English teacher, financial aid offices won't grant extensions.

- Finally, photocopy all your financial aid forms and place them in a file. Doing so will save you time the next year, when you can copy a lot of the information.

I Have My Award Offer, Now What?

It might be tempting and seem to be easy to just compare awards, but think twice about it. A $6000 award from the University of Virginia (UVA) for a Virginia resident might be worth more than a $20,000 award from Duke, because tuition at UVA costs so much less. The important thing is to calculate how much you and your family will have to contribute. This calculation of out-of-pocket contribution is more important than how much grant money you receive. This amount should be clear from the award letter that financial aid offices send, but if it is not, call the financial aid office or go to www.collegeboard.com/pay to use a fancy calculator to compare costs. Some schools are notorious for the complexity of financial award statements; if you are confused, don't hesitate to have your parent call the financial aid office and ask questions.

If you are not satisfied with your award, don't be afraid to bargain with schools. Personally, I didn't have too much success doing so, but I've heard great stories. For example, Yale offered to match Harvard's offer of financial aid in an effort to attract a top student. The following are a few tips:

- Make sure you are comparing apples to apples. Don't ask for more money from Cornell because Ohio State gave you an athletic scholarship. Do call Cornell, however, if Columbia's package was significantly different from Cornell's.

- Never use words like *bargain* or *negotiate*. Simply have your parent explain in a professional manner that (s)he is wondering why there is such a large difference in aid packages offered by comparable schools.

- Parents should call. Students should not. Why? Financial aid officers will take parents more seriously.

Got all this? Good, now on to scholarships.

The Truth about Scholarships

While there might not be billions of dollars out there in unclaimed scholarships, money is definitely available for intelligent, innovative, and resourceful students. The consensus seems to be that about $1.25 billion is awarded to undergraduates every year, excluding employee tuition benefits and college-controlled financial aid. But only 4 percent of eligible students get these scholarships, so be willing to put some time into the search and application process. Merit-based scholarships are, after all, highly competitive in terms of artistic, athletic, or academic talent (but you guys are reading this book, so you must be talented and resourceful). Some private scholarships are awarded based on need as well as merit.

You will find that scholarship awards range anywhere from $100 to $40,000 or more. On average, scholarships offer between $1000 and $3000. Though winning a $40,000 scholarship certainly is advantageous, I advise you to look for smaller, lesser-known scholarships. As Mark Kantrowitz, author of the Financial Aid Information Page (www.finaid.com), advises: "There are no guarantees that you will win a scholarship, but if you don't apply, you certainly won't receive any money. Look for local scholarships, since these are often the least competitive."

In general, scholarship applicants have a high school diploma (or will have one soon), are U.S. citizens or permanent residents in the process of becoming citizens, and have a social security number. You'll find scholarships awarding anything from children of veterans from Oklahoma to only those applicants over 6 foot, 1 inch. Sometimes scholarships require applicants to be of a particular ethnic group (for example, African American, Native American, or Hispanic). More commonly, scholarships look for academic achievement, leadership potential, community service, special talents, or a combination of these attributes. And no, you don't have to be valedictorian, varsity swim team captain, and winner of the Miss Chinatown pageant while spending 100 hours a week at your local Red Cross center in order to receive a scholarship. Here's the best advice I can give you: *Apply*! If you don't try, you know you won't win anything.

Where Should I Look?

I've gone on and on about the money that's out there for your taking and what qualifications you need to get it, but how do you get started? First things first: Find some scholarships to apply for! Here is where to look:

- *The Internet.* The Internet is by far the best place to look for scholarships. FastWeb (www.fastweb.com) is a free Internet scholarship search that matches you with scholarships based on your profile of financial need, achievements, interests, area of study, and affiliation. So if, for example, you are a child of a postal worker from Kentucky, the Internet can track down that scholarship for you. Look for other scholarships on the FinAid Information page (www.finaid.com) and on the College Board site (www.collegeboard.com/pay).

197

- *The local library or bookstore.* Take a trip to the library or bookstore and check out some scholarship books. One word of warning: You might find a huge volume claiming to list all the scholarships given in the past five years; *avoid it.* The majority of scholarships listed are so specific (for example, children of Vietnamese chefs from Montana) that it will take you countless hours to flip through 300 pages of 8-point font to finally spot one that fits your profile.

- *Advertisements in popular magazines.* In addition, you may find advertisements for scholarships in magazines such as *Time, Newsweek,* and even *Glamour.*

- *Your school.* Ask your guidance counselors if they have a list of scholarships, and check out bulletin boards at your school or other schools that you might happen to visit. Be on the lookout for information about both local and national scholarships.

- *Social networks.* Take advantage of the social networks that you have already established. Ask friends and families about scholarship opportunities through their employers or other affiliations. This is a great way to find out about local scholarships.

Word of Warning

Do *not* participate in so-called guaranteed scholarship search services. Usually, these search services claim that either you will win a scholarship or they will refund the required processing fee. In most cases, they will disappear and leave you hanging without a dime. Most legitimate scholarships can be found through free resources on the Web or through the sources listed above. *Free* is the operative word here.

What to Do Now?

Now that you have a list of scholarships, what's the next step? In some cases, you will need more information about the scholarship, such as the deadline, your eligibility, and the required documents. Most scholarship resources, such as those listed above, will give you an address, email, or Web page to find more information, and even download the application. If the Web site doesn't provide all that you need, email the appropriate contact person and ask for information, an application, or both. Expect to put some time and effort into the search for scholarships. You might spend quite a bit of money sending out letters; postage can add up. In addition, don't expect to receive replies from all the scholarships to which you wrote. I have to admit that this was one of the most frustrating parts of the scholarship search. I wrote about 150 letters (literally) and received about ten responses, five of which informed me that the deadline had passed, that the scholarship was no longer being offered, or that I was ineligible. But the other five responses (plus a few others whose applications I already had) proved to be a gold mine.

Organize, Organize, Organize

Once you receive all the relevant information from scholarships, make a simple chart outlining what you need to know about each scholarship (see Table 12.1).

TABLE 12.1 SAMPLE SCHOLARSHIP CHART

Deadline	Scholarship Name	Letters of Rec?	Additional Requirements or Documentation	Completed
10/31	Coca-Cola		Interview December 3	X
11/15	Tylenol	Mr. Advil Mrs. Excedrin Dr. Motrin	2004 W-2 forms	
12/15	Soroptimist			X

- Keep a file system of your scholarships. You can organize these files in any way most convenient for yourself: alphabetized, by deadline, or randomly.

- Include a file with copies of your SAT, SAT II, ACT, AP, and IB scores. You'll need to refer to them often. Believe me, it is a pain to search through a pile of papers each time you need to remember what month you took that Math IIC test.

- Keep all of your recommendation letters in a file. Doing so will allow you to easily select which teachers to approach for recommendations for specific scholarships.

- If applicable, keep a file with your financial aid applications, which may include tax return forms from both you and your parents. Be sure to keep these documents even after you start college.

The Scholarship Application

Here are some pointers for filling out scholarship applications. Scholarship committees are usually looking for many of the same qualities as admissions committees, so the advice in this book about courses, activities, and essays all applies to scholarships as well.

- *Be honest.* Don't try to conform to a set standard of what you think evaluators are looking for. In most cases, scholarship committees want to see not only a list of your merits and needs, but also to get a sense of your responsibility and potential for growth in the future. After all, we all want returns from our investments. Be genuine, be creative, and show who you are as well as what you have accomplished. That said, it is still a good idea to tailor the aspects of your résumé to the focus of the scholarship. Read the criteria for the scholarship and emphasize personal aspects that make you seem accomplished and a good fit for that particular contest.

- *Be neat and organized.* Type the application, if possible. If not, write neatly in black ink. Forego the flaming pink pen. Although you may think writing in that color is a sign of creativity, the reader will more than likely view it as an attempt to torture. For online applications, double- and triple-check to make sure that you've entered and submitted all the requested information. It would be terrible to be disqualified from a scholarship just because you forgot to send in your transcript.

- *Don't go overboard.* When scholarships ask for supporting documentation, don't think you need to attach everything from your first attempt at cursive handwriting in fourth grade to the letter your boyfriend wrote to ask you to the senior prom. Limit yourself to copies of test scores, awards, recommendations, documents demonstrating financial need, and the like. If people to whom you're applying don't ask for supporting documentation, don't give it.

- *Proofread.* Nothing looks worse than silly spelling and grammatical errors. I found the best way to proofread, especially for an essay, is to read the application out loud. If you feel silly talking to yourself around other people in the room, lock yourself in the bathroom and read. Yes, *out loud.* Secondly, have plenty of people proofread the application for you: teachers, friends, and family. This means that you shouldn't wait until the last minute!

- *Photocopy your complete application.* Not only is a duplicate proof that you have completed your application, but the best part about photocopying your application is that it becomes a heck of a lot easier to recycle charts, tables, and other elements on future applications. Make it easy on yourself!

- *Make a backup copy.* If you are working on a computer, make sure to save your documents on a floppy, compact disc, or external/USB drive, and save often! You can also upload your files to the Internet. You never know when a virus might strike, but with a backup, you'll be back on top of things in no time.

- *Interviews.* You may be required to have a scholarship interview. Refer to Chapter 8 on interviews for lots of detailed information about the scholarship interview.

Money—$$$Cha-Ching$$$

When you win a scholarship (notice that I said *when*, not if), keep track of how much is rewarded and on what pay schedule. Some scholarships will prefer to pay you a lump sum, whereas others prefer to disburse the money over four (or more) years. Figure out which pay schedule is preferable for you, and try your best to strike an agreement with the scholarship board. Most will be willing to pay you over four years; fewer will be willing to give you a lump sum.

When you get into college, knowing this pay schedule will save you a huge hassle. You'll easily be able to plan out which scholarships should cover which cost, be it tuition, room and board, or books, and you'll easily pick out those scholarships that aren't paying you when they should. Secondly, you'll get to see how much money you've actually won, and that's one heck of a gratifying feeling—for both you and your parents.

So that's basically it. Simple, right? Hardly. It's not an easy process and you won't get immediate results, but in my case, it certainly turned out to be rewarding. I spent much of my junior and senior years of high school chugging out applications on the computer, rushing to the post office five minutes before closing, and staying up until 5:00 A.M. to finish another last-minute application. This flurry of activity was often due to lack of organization and procrastination on my part, and in retrospect, it could have easily been avoided. All in all, I applied for over thirty scholarships, on top of my college applications, interviews, and financial aid applications. I was lucky enough to be selected to receive a few. My total private scholarship winnings: $111,450.

Remember, regardless of how successful you are in scholarship competitions, where you attend college is a large determinant of how happy you'll be, and you can't put a price tag on that. College loans of $2000 to $3000 (on average) per year at top schools will pale in comparison to loans you might one day take out for graduate schools. (Average law school debts, for instance, are $150,000.) Eight thousand dollars after four years isn't so bad in comparison. Best of luck to you in completing those laborious, yet rewarding, scholarship applications!

Word of Warning 1: Avoiding Scams

I was one of the victims of scholarship fraud. A company based in Houston offered a lucrative scholarship that I was graciously awarded as the California recipient. However, by the end of my fall quarter as a freshman at Stanford, I had yet to receive any financial contribution from this company, not even a confirmation of the funds to be distributed. During winter quarter, numerous investigators from across the nation revealed that the scholarship was a scam; its initiator had set up the company on the premise of offering a scholarship to high school seniors in order to solicit funds from outside companies. His underlying motivation was to take this money and run. Thankfully, I had other funds to support my education, but others weren't as lucky. Several students transferred schools, unable to pay for tuition.

Why am I telling you this? It's simple. I don't want this to happen to you after all the effort you will put into scholarship applications. So how do you avoid being scammed? Take the following pointers, and take them seriously. The Federal Trade Commission has publicized scholarship scams to educational facilities around America. The following are a few of the scholarships to avoid:

- *This scholarship has an entry fee; just give us your credit card number to secure your application."* They may as well be saying: "Give me your credit card so I can make some unauthorized charges and then disappear from the face of the earth before anyone catches me."

- *"This scholarship is guaranteed, or your money back."* Scholarships are usually offered through competitive application processes. In the rare circumstance that you believe the scholarship to be legitimate, get the refund policy in writing—before you pay.

- *"You're already a finalist!"* Watch out when scholarships claim you have been preselected as a winner even when you have never applied or were never nominated for them. Remind you of sweepstakes? And how many of those have you won?

- *"We do all the work."* Yeah, right.

- *"You can't get this information anywhere else."* Once again, all the valid scholarship sources you could possibly want are listed in books, magazines, and on the Internet. You're not going to get any exclusive information. You're going to get scammed.

- *"You've been selected by a 'national foundation' to receive a scholarship."* There really aren't too many unknown national foundations out there that are offering legal scholarships. Make sure you know who and what organization you are dealing with before applying.

In addition, the scholarships you apply for should have a telephone number, email, or address where you can easily reach a knowledgeable contact. This was my first mistake; though the telephone number for the fraudulent scholarship was legitimate, I was always given the run-around. I never took the time to research what kind of company was offering the scholarship. As it turns out, it wasn't even a company, just a name. Finally, I've found that most legitimate scholarships notify you by mail, not by phone, my third mistake. Though winners may be contacted by phone in many local scholarships, statewide and national scholarship winners are usually notified through the mail (or email).

If you suspect a scholarship to be fraudulent, report it. The Federal Trade Commission will investigate your claims, and you will prevent other applicants from becoming victims as well. Call 1-877-FTC-HELP, fill out an online complaint at www.ftc.gov/ftc/complaint.htm, or write:

Consumer Response Center
Federal Trade Commission, Room 200
600 Pennsylvania Avenue, NW
Washington D.C., 20580

Word of Warning 2: Scholarships May Reduce Your Need-Based Financial Aid

The most bothersome thing in regards to financing my education was figuring out how to combine *both* scholarships and financial aid into one package. Many schools, especially Ivy League universities, will reduce your need-based grants if they know you have received scholarships in excess of a certain amount. Now, what's the use of all that hard work if it's all going to the school and not you? Well, scholarships will reduce the loan and work-study components of your financial aid package first (no loans or jobs—*whoopee!*). However, the amount you receive per year from loans and jobs usually does not exceed $3000, so scholarships in excess of this amount will probably reduce the amount of grants you receive from your college. Colleges have varied accounting techniques to combine your external scholarships with your internal financial aid. At one time, Stanford applied 50 percent of your external scholarships toward *decreasing* your financial aid award. For example, if you received a $1000 scholarship from your high school, your financial aid award would decrease by $500—a "net" scholarship of only $500.

There are various ways to find loopholes in the system, with varying degrees of honesty. The most honest tactic is to ask the scholarship committee to defer your payment for a year or two. For example, if you won $12,000 in outside scholarships, you would ideally be able to arrange payments so that you receive $3000 each year. Write the scholarship donor a polite (and appreciative) letter and explain your situation. Most donors want the money they give to actually be helpful to you and your family, and thus many are willing to defer payment.

Sample List of Scholarships

Please note: The following list is not meant to be comprehensive, nor an endorsement of any kind. It's just a means to get started. Available scholarships are subject to change each year. The following scholarships were available at time of printing:

AT&T Engineering Scholarship Program

American Classical League/National Junior Classical League

American Legion National High School Oratorical Contest

America's Junior Miss Program

Arts Recognition and Talent Search

Ayn Rand Institute

Coca-Cola Scholarship

Discover Card Scholarship
(Note: this scholarship is for junior year students only)

Educational Communications, Inc.

Elks National Foundation Most Valuable Student Scholarship

Future Business Leaders of America

Gates Millennium Scholars Program

Guideposts Scholarship

Intel Science Talent Search

J. Edgar Hoover Foundation Scholarships

Jackie Robinson Foundation Scholarships

Key Club International Scholarships

Masonic Scholarships

MENSA Scholarships

NAACP Roy Wilkins Scholarships

National 4-H Awards Programs

National Honors Society Scholarship

National Merit Scholarship

Optimist International Oratorical Contest

Quill and Scroll Society

Robert C. Byrd State Scholarships

Scholarship America

Society of Women Engineers

Soroptimist Foundation Youth Citizenship Awards
TIME Education program Student Writing Contest
Target Scholarship
Tylenol Scholarship
United States Jaycees Scholarship

TIPS FOR COLLEGE

College Matters Editors

Just as we recently went through the admissions process, we recently started college as well. There are a few things that we learned in the process, which we would like to pass on to you for when you start college as well.

Tip 1: Buy Your College Stuff After You Arrive at College, and Pack Lightly

Why buy your college stuff at home and then break your back hauling it off to school? Consider buying these things after you arrive. By college stuff, we mean bed sheets, towels, comforters, cups, shampoo and conditioner, soap—you know, all the bulky and heavy things that are a pain to ship or haul off to college. Better yet, you can order your college stuff online and have it shipped directly to your college dorm or apartment.

Only pack the things you can't buy once you get to college (pictures of your family and friends, your special teddy bear, clothes, and so on). One exception: If you are from a warm climate (for example, Florida, Texas, California, or Hawaii), and you are going to college up north, buy your winter gear once you get there. Take it from three Southerners who went to college in Massachusetts, that "thick" jacket they sell at the outlet store in Texas just won't do for the harsh winter months up north.

Most importantly, pack lightly and don't bring too much junk. All three of us editors agree that one of our most unpleasant college experiences was hauling box after box down four flights of stairs, across campus, and up five flights of stairs again to summer storage in the attic – all during the most stressful part of finals period! It is better to have too little than too much; you can always buy more stuff later.

Tip 2: Bring Stamps and Get Your Information in Order

Pick up a book of stamps at your local post office before you go. Even though the post office may be down the street from your college, it will take you a long time to get there. It's amazing how long it takes you to send that letter if you don't have stamps (yes, even with email you write some letters, and by the way two years is our record). While we are on the topic of stamps, let's talk about two related things: bills and contact information.

You may want to consider setting up online bill payments when you get to college. Many banks offer this free of charge to their customers; others charge a nominal fee ($5 to $10 per month). Believe us, it's worth it. It will save you time spent scrounging for stamps, envelopes, or both for the next four years—and possibly a lifetime.

The other thing you need to get in order is contact information for your friends and family. We would recommend saving your many email addresses, mailing addresses, and so on to a secure online site or in a file backed up by a diskette, CD, or USB memory stick. It beats looking for that torn piece of paper on which you wrote Aunt Jenna's address.

Tip 3: Look Out for Computer Deals and Consider Buying a Laptop

If you are considering buying a computer for college, it may pay to wait until you get to college to buy it. Most colleges get special discounts on computers and other hardware items. So, you may save a lot of money if you buy your computer through your college. (Or you may get ripped off; compare your school's prices ahead of time to see into which category your school falls.) In the months leading up to college, be sure to keep your eyes peeled for sales, and have your parents investigate whether or not their company has an employee purchase plan, which could mean big discounts.

If you are deciding between a desktop and laptop computer, we would recommend getting a laptop. It's a nice feeling to be able to tote your laptop around to write your papers. (It definitely beats staring at the same blank wall in your room the whole day.) Plus, a laptop can be easily stored or carried along for a summer internship or semester abroad.

Tip 4: Inquire about Paying for College with Your Credit Card

Ask if you can pay for college (tuition, room, board, or rent, or a combination of these) with a credit card. If the answer is yes, then get a credit card where you rack up frequent-flier miles for every dollar you spend. Instead of paying your bills with a check, charge your college expenses to that card! Depending on how much you pay for college, you can get a free domestic plane ticket every year or at least once every couple years. You'll then save a few hundred dollars on a ticket you were going to buy anyway.

Tip 5: You Don't Have to be Best Friends with Your Roommate

Sure, in a perfect world you'll be best friends with your randomly assigned roomie, but don't try to force a friendship. Giving each other space during this time of transition can prevent feelings of claustrophobia. It might surprise you how homesick some people are, and if you try to be their best friend right away, it might backfire. Just let things proceed naturally, respect each other's privacy, and hopefully you'll be thankful for the friendly person living with you rather than angry at your new mortal enemy. If it really isn't working out, consult the freshman deans' office for information about switching rooms.

No doubt older siblings and friends will have many more tips. Take advantage of this information. Find out as much as you can about starting college now, to avoid headaches and mishaps later! Finally, check out www.collegematters.org for a list of hilarious student quotes about quirky traditions at the college you will be attending.

CHAPTER THIRTEEN

STUDENT-ATHLETES

Rachelle Seibolt, Brown

So you're interested in playing sports in college. Playing on a college team will give you the opportunity to travel, make new friends, bond with team-mates, and see how good you can become! And, it can give you an edge in the admissions process (if a coach decides to recruit you) and big scholar-ship bucks. But how do you go about getting recruited? And once you are being recruited by colleges, then what? What will give you an advantage in the recruiting process, and what makes you more appealing to coaches? How do you decide which team and coach is the best match? The answer isn't always to go with the most talented, highest-ranked team you can find. Prioritizing time commitments, deciding what level of competition is both desired and realistic, and finding a coach and team that's right for you are all important factors when you are deciding which universities to pursue and ultimately which one to attend. This chapter outlines these factors, as well as tactics for getting coaches to take notice of you!

I know that I personally expected huge advantages to accrue from being a student-athlete. My dad was a highly recruited football player in the early 1970s—number three in the nation, in fact. Growing up, I heard so many of his stories about being recruited and the lengths that the Big Ten, Southeast, and Southwest Conference universities went to in order to have him play for them. He was offered a condo on a lake (worth eighty grand at the time), monthly stipends, free education for everyone in his family, clothes, food, a personal chef, cars, and girls. The girls were a part of the football "booster club." They were charged with escorting the top recruits around campus (anything to help the football program) and making sure the recruit felt "special." At one point, he canceled a month and a half of trips through Florida because, after previous experiences, he found all the drinking, eating, partying, and kissing up to be, in a word, "sickening." At one time, my Dad complimented a coach on his tie, and the coach took it right off and gave it to him!

In the early 1970s, the rules of the National Collegiate Athletic Association (NCAA) were not *nearly* as stringent as they are today. So you can imagine my surprise when I found out that since the seventies there has been a major crackdown, and there would be no entourage waiting for me—no car, no condo, no personal chef, and no stipend. Oh, well. But despite this state of things, being a recruited student-athlete is still an opportunity that can open up lots of doors, allow you to gain a more in-depth knowledge of a school, and even earn you a scholarship or a boost when it comes to admissions. Ultimately, it allows you to pursue something you love at a higher level.

To Play or Not to Play?

When deciding whether or not to continue with athletics at college, consider your level of commitment. You must decide what you are willing to give and to give up. How much time per day you devote to your team will vary according to sport and college, but it will rarely be less than three hours per day. Practices are not the only time commitment. You also have to consider recovery time, as it is both physically and emotionally draining to be training and competing at the college level. Drinking, diet, classes, and social life are tremendously affected as well. You will be devoting four years to a sport and training year round, so you'd better love it.

Playing on a college team may require more time of you now, in high school, as well. In order to be on the level necessary to play NCAA sports, many athletes will need extra coaching outside of high school and during the off season. Find a club in your area with a good coach that meets your needs! Playing with a club is a great opportunity to meet new people and get a glimpse of what college athletics are like, as clubs tend to be more serious and usually approximate NCAA athletics to a greater extent than high school teams do.

DI verses DII versus DIII

Once you have decided to play, you have to evaluate which division best suits your needs. One important difference between Division I (DI), Division II (DII), and Division III (DIII) schools is that DI and DII give merit-based scholarships (that is, you can get a free or subsidized education for your skills), whereas in DIII, there are no athletic scholarships. Be aware, however, of the exceptions: Schools in the Ivy League (DI) do not offer athletic scholarships, and there are not many DII schools, although they are out there (one of the College Matters team members was recruited at a DII school). For more detail on the technical differences between the divisions, visit www.NCAA.org.

Beyond the scholarships factor, your decision will basically come down to this: Do you want to be a student-athlete, or an athlete who takes some classes? DI schools tend to demand a higher time commitment to athletics than DII and DIII schools, especially for certain sports like football. This does not mean that you cannot be serious about school while playing DI sports, especially if you are at a selective school where academics tend to be particularly important. Regardless, though, DI sports teams tend to require more of your time. If you are considering DI, make sure you can balance a significant time commitment with school. The competition in DI also tends to be a lot stiffer than in DII and DIII. Finally, the division(s) in which you can play is dependent on your individual skill level. Most DI teams are harder to get on than DII and DIII teams. The best way to evaluate which divisions may be open to you is to speak with your high school or club coach.

The Recruiting Process

Getting Started

Evaluate seriously which sports you want to play in college. Do research to find out at what level you need to be to play varsity athletics. (Ask the coaches at schools in which you are interested what skill level is necessary.) Be honest with yourself about your potential. Also talk to your current coaches and evaluate whether you are at the point where you need to be in order to participate. And remember, even if you decide not to play varsity sports, club sports are definitely still a fun and feasible option.

When in high school, I had to decide whether to continue with volleyball or track. When it came down to it, I realized that I had more of a chance to be successful in track. Track would also leave me more time for academics, as it involves less traveling on weekdays than volleyball. Be sure to keep your academic goals in mind when you evaluate whether or not to participate in college athletics and in which sports to participate.

Making Contact

Contact college coaches early (at least the summer before senior year), and let them know that you are interested in their program. If possible, before you start applying to schools, attend camps or clinics run by the colleges in which you are interested. This superimportant step allows the coaches to observe your skills and attitude firsthand, and it lets you get to know them and their coaching style.

If you've attended a coach's camp, done very well at a national competition, or won a regional competition in a university's region, a coach may contact you directly. However, oftentimes you'll have to initiate contact. At first, I was too scared to call coaches myself, so I asked my track coach to contact coaches at programs in which I was interested. I know that calling people you don't know, especially people who can make or break your acceptance to a school, can be excruciatingly difficult. So, either have your coach make the first call or suck it up and just do it yourself. (There really is no easy way.) If you decide to call a coach personally, introduce yourself and explain that you are interested in attending and pursuing athletics at the respective university. Discuss your skill level and playing potential. If you have the skills a coach is looking for, she or he will likely ask more questions and arrange to maintain contact.

Another superimportant thing to do is to fill out the athletics information card, which should come with your viewbook or may be available online. When you check the box of your respective sport of interest, coaches will often follow up with an information card specific to their sport. Coaches take these cards seriously and may decide whom to recruit based in part on these cards, especially for sports where performance can be easily and quantitatively measured (for example, swimming, track, crew, and other sports with times and distances).

When you know which schools you are interested in, show an interest in the school when speaking with its coaches. Ask questions about the university, academic support, and financial support. For instance, if you receive scholarships for participation in athletics and you get injured or quit, how does this affect your scholarship? Also ask about team practices: How long are they, what do they include, and what is expected during the off season and preseason?

Making Tapes

If appropriate, make tapes of your performances that you can send to the schools in which you are interested. Tapes are often needed for sports such as basketball, football, and gymnastics. Of course, if you do a sport that's not particularly fascinating to watch (for example, running 5000 meters), a tape might put potential coaches to sleep, as opposed to impressing them with your athletic prowess. If you're not sure whether you need to make a tape, ask the coaches of the programs that interest you.

You needn't send tapes only to those schools that you know you want to attend; mail them off to schools in various divisions, and see who responds. Of course, do not hesitate to follow up on the tape. Taking initiative will show the coach that you are genuinely interested in the school's program. The tapes you make do not have to be professionally done. No amount of cool effects and music will enhance the skills that you demonstrate on the tape. Most of my friends put together home tapes. Though the cinematography wasn't the best, the athletic skills they exemplified were impressive, such as bench pressing 500 pounds. In summary, don't stress about cinematography. If you're talented, it will show!

So How Do Coaches Decide Whom to Recruit?

Coaches usually hunt for recruits by looking at state and national performances; by going through their current athletes, feeder schools, or clubs; and through the information cards that you will fill out and send to them. They also might find out about you from the admissions office if you have been offered a big academic scholarship to their school. Coaches love to get athletes who are mostly on academic scholarship, because that way they don't have to shell out money for athletic scholarships.

Coaches tend to look for three specific qualities in the athletes they are recruiting: athletic performance, potential, and academic standing. They also look for a good work ethic, dedication, and a desire to improve and not just to compete for fun. The best way to show the first three traits is by excelling at your sport and in your studies. As for the character traits, they will come through in conversations that you and possibly your high school or club coach have with the coaches who are doing the recruiting.

The main thing to remember is that if you are interested in a school, *show it!* My coach—let's call her Coach E—once called a recruit. The recruit's mother answered and Coach E asked for the recruit. The mom called to the daughter, and Coach E heard the recruit say, "Tell her I am not here." She may have been about to leave or doing work or just had a bad day, but common courtesy is a must. Needless to say, she was never called again.

The Recruiting Trip

The recruiting trip is the perfect opportunity to get a feel for the campus, the atmosphere, the coach, and your future teammates. Most importantly, come with questions, and don't just be a lump on a log! Ask about the program, the coach, how many hours per week you will be in practice, and all the questions you would ask during a normal college visit. Do athletes like the coach? Keep in mind that most people will usually be hesitant to give a directly negative answer. (If you are talented, they'll be anxious to have you join the team.) So, if you get a vague answer like, "Well, it is the team I love," that could be a bad sign. Try to inquire further. Ask questions like the following:

- Does the coach give athletes individualized attention?
- Are practices tailored to meet individual needs?
- How do athletics in college compare to athletics in high school?
- Have team members improved since high school?
- How long is practice?
- Of what does practice consist?
- How hard is it to balance practice and school?
- Does the coach care about academic commitments?
- Does traveling disrupt academic classwork?
- Can students take a full classload or is it often necessary to stay for a fifth year?
- How often do people get injured?
- How is the training room?

- How good is the trainer?
- What about the facilities?
- Does the weather affect practice?
- How is team camaraderie?
- Is there a divide between the students on scholarship and those who are not on scholarship?
- Will you be able to keep your scholarship if you get injured?
- Do the athletes enjoy being on a team?

The athletes that you stay with will do their best to make sure that you have a good time. However, make sure that you bring some work to do so they don't feel like they have to entertain you all the time. Showing disinterest and a lack of respect is not how you make a good impression. Here is one more commonsense tip: Make sure you are clean and sober. One recruit I had smelled so bad that it took several days to air out my room. The same recruit was also obnoxious and pretentious, so of course I let my coach know. While your hosts are not responsible for recruiting you, coaches listen to their athletes, for another perspective on potential new additions to the team. Another recruit we had handcuffed himself to my friend's bed after he had been to a party. My friend was trying to work and was not amused.

Many schools will take you to parties and show you a good time, which could include alcohol. However, I would not recommend drinking. It does not make a good impression if you drink so much that you pass out and EMS has to be called in (yes, this has happened). Some schools have a policy not to admit recruits caught drinking (and this includes in moderation) while visiting. So, in summary, save yourself the risk and don't drink at all.

While this information might seem like a lot to keep in mind, if you can manage to show interest in the school, make some conversation, shower, not get trashed, and refrain from handcuffing yourself to things, you'll be set.

Academics

Remember that you're going to be at school primarily to learn, not to play sports. You need to make sure that you and your coaches have similar academic goals. I was strongly discouraged from double majoring and writing a thesis because it would interfere too much with practice. My coaches were worried that I would not be able to handle a heavy workload, would do poorly, and thus would have issues with eligibility. There are plenty of student-athletes who do double major, take hard sciences, write a thesis, or a combination of all these. Some coaches even encourage it, but others do not. Keep in mind that many coaches are not concerned with your prospects after graduation but merely with your performance as an athlete during the next four years. Furthermore, at virtually every college it is policy that student-athletes are forbidden to take classes that interfere with practice. Before committing to a team, make sure that participating will not infringe on your academic or extracurricular goals.

Signing and Deciding

If schools are offering you athletic scholarships, you may be asked to sign a Letter of Intent. The Letter of Intent is basically a contract between you and the school. You agree to participate in the specified sport for one year, and the college agrees to provide you with a scholarship. Because a Letter of Intent is binding, be *absolutely sure* you want to attend the university before signing. You may still be waiting on admissions decisions from other schools when a coach demands that you sign immediately or lose a scholarship. If this situation happens, contact the admissions offices of schools where you have outstanding applications. Politely explain the situation, and admissions officers may be able to facilitate the process so that you can know before you sign whether you were admitted to other schools and adjust your decision appropriately.

All this talk about signing brings up *the* critical question: How do you decide which school is right for you? All the factors that would normally go into choosing a college are relevant to student-athletes as well. (See Chapter 10, written by another student-athlete, for more details on these factors.) However, as a student-athlete, you have an important additional concern to take into account: athletics. Unless you have the talent to go pro (that is, you are ranked in the very top echelon nationally of high school students who play your sport), athletics should not be the number-one factor in your decision. Holding to this position is difficult, since athletics may be one of the defining forces in your life and a central part of your identity. Keep in mind, though, that this situation may not always be the same throughout your life.

You need to choose a university that will prepare you, once you've finished with school and NCAA athletics, to succeed for the rest of your life! This means putting academics at the top of your decision criteria.

Nevertheless, several potential schools might have great academics and meet your other decision criteria—so how do you decide which of them has the right athletic program for you? The program should match your skill level and level of commitment. In addition, the coach should be understanding of your academic commitments. Coaching style (that is, the content of practices and the way in which the coach interacts with athletes) should match your needs and preferences. Finally, the coach should have a record of producing greatness. This means that most of the athletes he or she has coached have improved, and some have made it to the top.

If you are ready to commit at the NCAA level, you probably have talent and a good work ethic. At this level, coaching is much more important than it is in high school when it comes to setting athletes apart. Playing a sport requires a massive commitment of time and energy, and you deserve the best coach you can find who matches the academic quality you are looking for in a college. If you're on scholarship, playing athletics in college will be a job, and even if you're not on scholarship, it will take the time that a job would. You will work hard for your coach, so that person had better be worth the work!

Another dimension to consider is finances. Athletic scholarships can be a great opportunity to get cash for college. But unlike academic scholarships and financial aid, if you choose to quit your sport or incur a serious injury, athletic scholarships often get rescinded. Ivy League schools don't have athletic scholarships, although they do have great need-based financial aid. Many argue that this situation improves team camaraderie, because nearly all team members play the sport because they love it, not because they have to play in order to get a scholarship. Also, there is no rift between those on scholarship and walk-ons.

Above all, if a school or team is a bad fit for you, you shouldn't choose to attend just because you have an athletic scholarship, unless there really is no other alternative. Ultimately, you and your family must decide how much money can be shelled out for college. The majority of a group of students surveyed by the College Matters team recommended going for the best-quality academic school that you can afford and using other important factors like athletics to differentiate between schools of similar academic quality.

General Rules (Yes, They're Boring but Important)

Keep in mind the following regulations so as not to jeopardize your eligibility. First, you are required to have a minimum high school GPA of 2.0 in a "core" curriculum and a minimum combined SAT score of 820 pre-March 2005. Post-March 2005 minimum scores will soon be available online at www.NCAA.org. If you can't meet these standards, you won't be able to play for any four-year college or university, let alone a selective one. Second, coaches can't just contact you whenever they want, so don't expect the phone to be ringing off the hook! Depending on the sport, there are different rules that govern contact between coaches and prospective recruits. Football coaches may contact students beginning in May of their junior year. (If you decide to pursue varsity athletics in college, you'll soon learn that football players get lots of special privileges, ranging from privileged weight room use to three freezers full of ice cream bars in their massive locker room.) Women's basketball coaches can call on or after June 21 of the prospect's junior year. For all other sports, coaches are not permitted to make phone calls until July 1 of junior year. All coaches can, however, contact students earlier through letters (after September 1 of the prospective athlete's junior year).

Keep in mind that you may contact the coaches at your own expense whenever you want, except during dead periods, which are times when there is absolutely no contact allowed between athletes and coaches. These times differ, depending on specific sports, relating to signing dates for the National Letter of Intent and championship periods. If you try to contact a coach during a dead period, she or he will just tell you that talking is prohibited at the moment. Coaches can come and watch you up to seven times, to assess your abilities. Remember, you may not know when they are observing, as they cannot always contact you or may be observing during the dead period. Thus, consistent sportsmanship is a must.

Finally, you can only visit a college once with expenses paid on a recruiting trip, and may only go on five official recruiting trips in total. An official recruiting trip is one in which the coach pays for your expenses. This official visit can only be done after the university has a copy of your academic record and standardized test scores. Your hosts can spend no more than $30 per day on your expenses. Not all programs are given that much, so don't expect it. You will not be showered with gifts, no matter how great you are. You are not allowed to receive any tangible items, just food and entertainment, so eat up!

And Finally...

Be honest about what your expectations are for yourself, the school, and the coaches. Find the college that is the best match for you, not necessarily the one with the "best" team. (And who is to say which school is the best, given that rankings change every year and a lot of money is pumped into the reviews?) Don't be afraid to choose a school because of its academic reputation, even if the athletic program is not your favorite. Remember that academics count more in the long run.

The benefits of college sports include an instant social network, the opportunity to continue playing the sport you love, gaining leadership skills, and demonstrating your commitment to future employers. Bear in mind that your actions will determine your future, so be active. Do not passively wait for someone to take an interest in you; make the first move. So go after that scholarship—and eventually that NCAA title! Best of luck!

CHAPTER FOURTEEN

MINORITIES

Otis Gaddis, Harvard

Okay, so you're almost finished with the book! You have read about everything from grades to college visits to financial aid and know just what you need to do to blow admissions and scholarship selection committees away. However, you might still be wondering, "Does my ethnicity, race, gender, or sexual orientation matter in the college admissions process?"

The answer is yes, it just might be important in a variety of ways! So let's dive right in. Read on if you have any of the following concerns:

- What exactly is a minority?
- I am a white male—could I still be considered a minority in certain contexts?
- Why can minority status be important?
- Are there special opportunities available for minorities?
- What special factors might I want to consider as a result of my minority status?

What Is a Minority?

The definition of a minority varies widely from context to context and from school to school. Most people who fall outside the category of middle class straight white male could be considered a minority in one context or another. Even middle class straight white males could be considered minorities, for example, when applying to a historically black college or if they attend a high school that is primarily nonwhite. For more information about such "contextualized" minorities, see the section entitled "So Why Do Universities Care If I'm a Minority?" More traditionally, minority groups in the college admissions context are those groups that are currently underrepresented in U.S. universities: African Americans, Native Americans, Latinos, and women who apply to schools where they are underrepresented (primarily certain engineering and military schools).

Breaking It Down

So now that we have a broad definition of what a minority is, let's narrow it down some. First, there is the distinction of relative representation: There are *underrepresented minorities* and *overrepresented minorities*. Underrepresented minorities are those that have *less* than their share in the general population represented in the student body of their school of choice. (For example, Harvard's African American students make up about 7 percent of the total student body, while African Americans comprise about 12 percent of the national population.) Overrepresented minorities are those that have *more* than their share in the general population represented in the student body of their school of choice. The classic example of an overrepresented minority is East Asian Americans. (At Harvard, Asian Americans make up about 18 percent of the total student body, while they represent only 4 percent of the national population.) This chapter contains advice for both groups.

Second, there is the distinction of race: There are *racial minorities* and *nonracial minorities*. Examples of racial minorities are Native Americans, African Americans, and Hispanics, and an example of a nonracial minority (in certain contexts) is women. Note that one can be Hispanic and also be any other race (for example, white Hispanic or black Hispanic).

Nonracial minorities include those groups that are minorities due to religion, ethnicity, gender, sexual orientation, or nationality. Keep these two distinctions in mind, because they will pop up throughout the chapter.

So Why Do Universities Care If I'm a Minority?

So who cares who is a minority and who is not? I mean, come on, don't we live in a society that claims to believe that race, gender, and nationality are just superficial labels that need to be dispensed with? Why put people in a box? And isn't it unfair to let the group someone belongs to affect something like college admissions?

Looking at the issue from the university's point of view may help to explain the significance of minority status in the admissions process. First, you must ask yourself, what is the college's main priority? It's to educate its students to think critically and to succeed in a diverse world. While the classroom experience is an important educational tool at college, many—if not most—students will tell you that it is in interacting with their classmates outside of the classroom that they learn the most about the world.

An idea may get sparked in class, but it is explored at the lunch table and over pizza at 3:00 A.M. with the guy living across the hall. Thus, it becomes really important who is in the cafeteria as well as in the dorm room next door. A conversation about religion, for example, could benefit from the diverse perspectives of black fundamentalist Republicans, Chinese Muslims, devout liberal lesbian feminist Catholics, and Latino gay evangelical Christians. The fact that some of these descriptions seem either odd or downright improbable only demonstrates the kind of assumptions and categorical rigidities that the university, in admitting a diverse student body, is trying to challenge.

In short, the university has a vested interest in producing graduates that can relate to and understand people who come from different places in life. This interest is so strong that it is even recognized in law in the recent Supreme Court decision on affirmative action (which will be discussed later in the chapter). For the college to succeed in its task, it will need *qualified minorities* of various backgrounds in its applicant pool.

However, universities define minorities not just as people belonging to a certain race or gender but also as *contextualized minorities*. This has more to do with your relative status in your present environment, rather than your status in society as a whole. Are you the only Russian in your senior class? Your entire school? Is there something unusual in your past that makes it more likely that you would view the world from another point of view than other people in your classification? For example, are you a child of gay or lesbian parents, or part of an interracial family in an area of the country where people are still hung up about that? Are you the only black guy in the advanced track of your high school, a devout Jew at a hard-core Catholic high school, or a basketball player paralyzed from the waist down?

Well, these are the kinds of things that colleges are looking for. Why? Not just for the education of the student body, but also because your background may indicate that you are likely to do something great in the world. Great achievement usually requires visionary ability, the capacity to break the rules, and the willingness to see what other people cannot see. The more "unique" your background is, the more likely it is that you are able to look at the world from a different point of view. Of course, when you become famous, people will say, "Oh yeah, and she graduated from University XYZ," and then your school will rise in future esteem. The university of course knows this, so they are looking for people who may gain them glory and honor in the future. They are looking to be part of your legacy.

You may have noticed that many of the contextualized minority examples have more to do with combinations of personal characteristics (like race or gender or sexual orientation) and some sort of political-religious philosophy that is being actively practiced. This is not an accident, since universities are looking for indications that you recognize the uniqueness of your social position and *are already acting on that uniqueness*. For example, a gay Evangelical Latino could be providing mentoring to gay students at a Latino community center while not shying away from his Christian faith; this combination of characteristics is interesting to colleges.

What You Need to Make It Happen

So, if you have read this far, you now know the ways in which you can be considered a "minority" for the purposes of college admission: either as a generally recognizable minority (for example, black or Hispanic) or someone who in a particular context could be viewed as a minority. Now we'll discuss to what degree your status as a minority affects you in the admissions process.

The State of the Law

In the summer of 2003, the Supreme Court of the United States (in *Grutter v. Bollinger*) decided the most important affirmative action case since 1978. In *Bollinger*, the Court held that the university's interest in having a diverse student body is so strong that it is considered a "compelling state interest." Only interests that are "compelling" can meet the constitutional requirement that allows the government to use race in its decision making. So what does this mean in layman's speech? By declaring this ruling, the Court upheld racial affirmative action as constitutional. The court also explained the manner in which an affirmative action program must be implemented in order to be constitutional. Basically, the Court said that point systems that give extra points to an applicant for being in an underrepresented minority group are illegal. However, a system that gives an individualized "plus factor" to underrepresented minority applicants was considered legal.

What does this mean for you? Well it means that affirmative action *may* still be used by public and private universities to achieve a diverse student community. Some states, like California, do not allow affirmative action (private universities are unaffected). However, the overwhelming majority of selective colleges use affirmative action in one way or another.

By definition, racial affirmative action gives applicants who meet the qualification requirements of a college (that is, the college's determined requirements of high school grades and SAT and ACT scores) an additional boost compared to a similarly situated applicant who is not an underrepresented minority. Affirmative action can also be nonracial when taking into account gender, sexual orientation, or other characteristics. However, racial affirmative action is the most common. Just because you, because of gender or sexual orientation, may be considered a nonracial minority, you should not assume that the school to which you are applying has affirmative action for that particular category.

This is where the distinction between the underrepresented minority and the overrepresented minority comes into play. Because affirmative action is meant to increase the number of underrepresented students in a college, affirmative action will have no effect on overrepresented or contextualized minorities.

The Barriers to Academic Achievement: Frequently Asked Questions

Now I will address some of the practical concerns of minorities in regards to the admission process.

Question 1: I feel like my teachers don't believe in me. What can I do?

Answer: Underrepresented minorities face various barriers to academic success. Many of these barriers have to do with the racism present in the structure of organizations like schools, work, and the government. This problem often surfaces in the perceptions of teachers and academic administrators. It is a fact that underrepresented minorities, especially African Americans, are more likely to be channeled into the lower-performing classes in a high school as opposed to the honors classes or gifted track. These assignments happen regardless of whether the student is objectively qualified to participate in the honors classes or gifted track. Moreover, this pattern can still occur even if the teacher or administrator making the decision is of the same minority group as the student.

Structural racism can also be manifested in the advice that school counselors give to minority students who express interest in pursuing a dream that requires higher education. One of my friends, after attending a career fair, told her counselor that she wished to be a lawyer. In response, he said, "Oh, honey, you can't do that, you will have to study for years, and only if you are really smart will you be able to make any money; so you should just do something that someone like you can do."

While statements like this are an outrage, especially coming from a school administrator whose job is to encourage and uplift students, the truth is that it happens all the time. Minority students can get sidelined by the very people who are supposed to be helping them, so start protecting yourself. Dream—and dream big. Then be confident that you are capable of making your dreams come true.

If you feel that you can do honors-level work, fight attempts by teachers and administrators to place you in anything other than the honors track. If you are just figuring out after reading this book that you are already being sidelined, then resolve this right now, and I mean *now*. Ask your teachers what you have to do to raise your grades and get into the honors track. Keep asking until you find someone who is genuinely interested in helping you. Get your parents involved. Be persistent!

Question 2: I heard that underrepresented minorities do not score as high as whites on the SATs. Is this true? If it is, does that mean I am fated to get a lower score?

Answer: The answer to this question is a bit complex. It is true that there is an SAT/ACT testing gap between whites and underrepresented minorities. However, that answer does not really tell you what will happen to you when you take the test, since the testing race gap is a result of preparation and resources, not a result of race. What can you do to close the gap? Here is one suggestion: Take an SAT/ACT prep class or join a free program that specifically prepares minority students for the SAT/ACT. (Consult www.collegematters.org for links to these programs.) This is probably the most important thing you can do. For more information about standardized tests, see Chapter 4.

Question 3: Would I be selling out to my culture and my friends if I studied and worked hard in school? I would feel as if I were.

Answer: The social pressures of your own minority community can sometimes be the greatest barrier to pursuing academic success. For example, I never thought about not attending college and also wanted to go to the best school possible. As a result, many of my black classmates from elementary school through high school accused me of "selling out." In their minds, my desire for academic success was really a desire to be "white," since the only people they ever saw going on to college were white. Of course, this was merely a reflection of the limitations of their environment. In many poor African American communities, college is not an appreciable goal because of the pressure of trying to survive day to day. And—as with any group—the desire to step outside of the norm is often met with ridicule and derision. While my classmates' constant taunting was definitely difficult, I didn't give up my dreams of getting a great college education. I must say it was not easy being one of two black kids in my AP classes or being laughed at because of my mannerisms and speech.

But after I was accepted to top schools, my black classmates began to respect me, as they realized that my focus on my studies had paid off. Now, with a Harvard degree (and a Georgetown law degree on the way), I have a lot to offer the black community—so much more than I would have if I had given into peer pressure from my black classmates to not think outside of the box. Now I can see the pride on their faces and those of other blacks as they see me do well in elite environments that not too long ago were closed to us.

From my conversations with other underrepresented minorities at Harvard and elsewhere, I've discovered that my experience is a fairly common one for many successful minority students. So if you may be experiencing something like this now, know that with success comes respect, and this respect is much more satisfying than the short-term approval provided by high school kids afraid to dream big.

Question 4: Why aren't there as many African Americans, Hispanics, and Native Americans in colleges as there are in the national population? Does it mean the colleges are discriminating against us?

Answer: No. The fact that there are underrepresented minorities does not mean that colleges are trying to avoid admitting minority students. Rather, many African Americans, Hispanics, and Native Americans are less likely to be in a position to get into college for several reasons.

First, African Americans, Hispanics, and Native Americans are more likely to be poor than Caucasians. Poverty can be a very strong barrier to getting a good high school education. It often reduces the amount of resources you have in school, and there may be pressure from the family to get a job right after high school in order to supplement the household income. Furthermore, applying to college can be expensive, and many students do not know that application fee waivers are available. (See Chapter 5 for more information on application fee waivers.)

Second, African Americans, Hispanics, and Native Americans are also less likely than Caucasians to have people in their families who are college educated. Because of the absence of personal role models or relatives who have already been through the process, it is harder for members of these minority groups to see themselves as being able to go to college.

Third, some minorities, especially immigrants, have language barriers as well. If someone doesn't speak English as a first language, the educational process can seem especially daunting. If you are in this category, it means that you will have to work extra hard. Get a list of SAT vocabulary words and study them backward and forward. Read as much as possible, no matter how difficult it is or how slow you have to go. Seek out special programs to improve your English. Whatever you do, don't give up! A fair number of the authors of this book (including two of the editors) and lots of my friends at Harvard did not speak English as a first language. But with lots of work, over time they became completely fluent. You can too!

Question 5: Nobody in my family has gone to college. None of my relatives understand anything about college. I feel completely alone and I do not know where to turn. What can I do?

Answer: First of all, you are not alone. Many people are in your situation. Part of the reason underrepresented minorities exist is because they do not get enough information regarding the college admissions process. But by just picking up this book, you have made a big step forward in getting the information you need to get a good education.

Need some support? Once again, be creative. Do you have friends who have relatives that have gone to college? Do not be afraid to ask them questions. Do you know leaders in your community (like your minister, your principal, or your doctor)? Ask! They are more likely to have gone through the educational system and can give you emotional support and encouragement (perhaps as a mentor). Finally, College Matters can help you with any questions you may have about college. Feel free to contact us at info@collegematters.org, and we will connect you to a student who will answer your questions.

Question 6: To what extent should I emphasize my minority status in my application?

Answer: This is a tough question to answer. As has been emphasized throughout this chapter, admissions officers *are* interested in how your background has given you insight into particular phenomena or experiences. However, you want to avoid giving the impression that you are *just* your background. You are also your academic and extracurricular interests, and that fact should come through. For example, if you are an African American student with a keen interest in mathematics or the classics, feel free to write an essay about how that interest developed and how the college you are applying to fits into that interest (even if you don't end up talking about your background at all).

Question 7: I am biracial. Will I still be considered a minority?

Answer: According to an inside College Matters admissions source, biracial students who have African American, Hispanic, or Native American heritage are usually considered to be part of these groups. If you are biracial, you should check all the boxes that apply on your application. (Usually, to be considered part of a racial group, you should be at least one eighth of that group.) Admissions officers will be interested in your diverse background.

Question 8: I've heard about African American colleges. What are they? Should I go to one?

Answer: Historically African American colleges are a set of private and state schools that were built during the era of legal racial segregation. These schools were meant to be a safe haven for African Americans to get an education in a hostile world. These African American colleges still exist and provide a unique educational experience. At many of these schools, there is a sense of community that you may not encounter elsewhere. You may also find that the invisible and structural racism that can exist in a mostly white environment isn't present at these schools. Many people go to historically African American colleges because they wish to study in an environment where most of the student body is black and where they can feel surrounded by a familiar culture as opposed to the overwhelmingly white student bodies of other schools. Some historically African American schools include Howard, Morehouse, Spelman, and Florida A&M.

As to the question of whether you should attend one, the answer is really up to you. Many historically African American colleges are well respected and have strong and impressive heritages. If you want the unique educational environment they offer, then you should consider them. If you are indifferent to the mostly African American educational experience but you still value being supported by and connecting to black culture while at college, then look into schools that have strong and active Black Student Associations as well.

If you feel a general lack of connection to your racial background, then I suggest the following: You should know that college is a space that is defining for most people who experience it. Many people who go into college without a deep connection to their culture find that connection in college. So seek out colleges that have strong minority communities. (I say minority communities because you'll probably find that when you connect to your own culture, you'll want to experience someone else's cultural heritage as well.)

One important note: Not everyone at a historically African American college is alike; there are still diversities within specific racial groups. I've heard of students who chose to attend a historically African American college because they thought that having race in common would mean everyone would get along—and then they were shocked when this wasn't the case.

Question 9: How do I know if a college has a good minority support system?

Answer: This is a really important question that applies to all the types of minorities that have been mentioned in this chapter: racial minorities, religious minorities, sexual minorities, gender minorities, and people with disabilities. To assess the strength of a minority community at the school in which you are interested, look in the following places.

First, look for student organizations that serve your group. In addition, make sure they are active. By active, I mean that they are putting together programs for the campus and have regular meetings and events. Also, check to see if students from your group participate in the extracurricular activities in which you want to participate (and take the classes you wish to take). You can do this on your college visits or through phone calls with current students.

Second, are you religious? Many schools have religious groups that try to create a space for people to explore their spirituality in the context of their race. (This is especially true for Christians.) Keep in mind that this is not negative self-segregation but rather a place for a particular culture to express itself in a unique way. The stronger your community is on campus, the more likely it is that it will have a unique spiritual space. Now, if you are gay and spiritual, do not just throw in the towel. There is usually at least one student group that is considered to be more accepting of gay and lesbian students. It may take time to find it, but ask. Try the gay student's alliance and ask if anyone is available to talk to who is actively religious. Seek out your options.

Third, are you a woman? What you want to look for are structures that help women deal with the stress of college. Two issues that many women deal with in college to a greater extent than men are sexual assault and eating disorders. (Men also deal with these issues; their numbers are simply underreported.) *Do not discount these issues!* It is a well-known fact that many women will be sexually assaulted in their lifetime, with many incidents occurring while they are in college. Does the college you are thinking about attending have resources for women who are in this situation? Are there blue phones (that is, phones you can use to call for help) around campus? Are campus escort services available—and adequate—for when you are studying late? Are self-defense classes taught? Are there confidential peer counseling services or counseling services for people with eating disorders? What I have said is especially important if you are going to a school that has just recently begun admitting women or has historically admitted women in small numbers.

Question 10: I'm gay. Does that help me get into college?

Answer: Well, no and yes. No, you will not be directly helped by the fact that you are gay, lesbian, or transgendered. However, as I stated above in the section on "So Why Do Universities Care If I'm a Minority?" being a sexual minority can make you more interesting to the college. And the numbers bear this out. Selective colleges are filled with sexual minorities.

Question 11: I'm Muslim. Is 9/11 going to hurt my chances of getting into selective colleges?

Answer: Not at all. In fact, I think colleges will want to have Muslims in their student body for the education of other students, who might benefit from the experience of a Muslim perspective in a post-9/11 world.

Did You Know?

The selectivity of a college has a larger impact on future earnings for African Americans than for any other group.

Aaliyah Williams, Harvard

I am an African-American female from Tulsa, Oklahoma. Given that statement, I believe the two major challenges to my entry into an Ivy League college were region and race. These challenges existed due to external perceptions.

Specifically, as a high school student in Oklahoma, the majority of college-bound students I knew wanted to stay in state for college. Moreover, as a black student, the Ivy League did not seem the natural choice for someone committed to her heritage. I would be viewed as a sellout to put myself in such an environment. Yet I always knew that I wanted to receive the best education possible. Throughout high school I constantly challenged myself by taking the most academically rigorous courses and at the same time devoting myself to the community and extracurricular activities that interested me.

One major hurdle for me was the fact that I came from a lower middle income family that had provided all it could in terms of direction and support, but absolutely could not afford college trips, application fees, and an Ivy League tuition. I have friends who applied to fourteen schools and traveled all over the country to visit all of them. That was simply not an option for me.

I applied to Harvard only because they sent me an application and because my dad urged me to apply. I was certain that I would attend Johns Hopkins (because I did a precollege program there), so I bet my dad that if Harvard accepted me through Early Action, I would go to Harvard. Otherwise I would go to Johns Hopkins—if accepted, of course. Understanding the financial burden that either of these colleges would place on my family, I was very focused on securing scholarships and grants from a variety of sources.

One more thing: If you are African American, definitely apply to the Ron Brown Scholar Program. Visit www.ronbrown.org for more information.

Martha Isabel Casillas, Harvard

I am a child of immigrant parents. Both my mother and father immigrated to the United States in pursuit of the American dream, hoping that their children would have opportunities and benefits that they lacked in Mexico.

Being a first-generation Mexican American, the language barrier was probably the most difficult obstacle. My parents could not engage in my education because they could not talk to my teachers or help me in my homework since their English was minimal. I know that other first-generation children have an extra hurdle to overcome with language. Usually, we take it upon ourselves to learn English and then help our parents translate.

Not only did language create a barrier for my parents in participating in my precollege education, it also impeded their ability to help out with the admissions process, especially when I started applying for scholarships and needed their tax forms and information about their finances. Whereas most American students let their parents fill out the "parent section," I had to do that on my own. It was difficult and frustrating at times, but I know that in the end, it made me more independent and has contributed to my success in college by making me more self-reliant.

Another issue was that my parents didn't know much about the American college system. I had to navigate through colleges on my own. I only applied to one school—Harvard—because it was one of the only schools I knew about.

To others in a similar situation, I would suggest that you research all the colleges that you can. Start looking at colleges that focus on what your interests are. Perhaps also look at schools with a strong minority community. I know that I have benefited from having a strong support system here at Harvard with the Mexican community. It is easier to adjust to change when you go to an educational institution that expresses an interest and concern for you and the issues that affect you.

Conclusion

So, now you've read what I have to say about being a minority and applying to college, and you've also read what others have to say. Let me conclude by drawing out the common themes of this chapter—and, really, of this book.

First, it's not being a minority that will get you into college and get you the scholarship dollars. It's being an interesting and unique person, someone that is shaped positively by his or her background (racial or nonracial). This *uniqueness* will get you in.

Second, whether or not you are a minority, you should work with what you have and make something great of it. It may be that African Americans, Hispanics, and Native Americans are statistically more often in the lower income levels, but guess what? That just gives you an opportunity to overcome any hurdles that you may have in front of you—and thus to shine in your applications!

This brings me to the last common theme, which is to go for it! If you don't try, you will never get in. Don't let others—those people around you or those invisible faces of society—hold you back. Believe in yourself, and set your goals high. Apply to the colleges to which you dream of going, and apply for all the scholarships that you can! Best of luck!

CONCLUSION

We hope this book was helpful in breaking down the college application process and giving you useful tips. If so, spread the word. If not, let us know! Email your comments and suggestions to feedback@collegematters.org so we can make it better the next time around.

If you are a student, we would like to extend a special invitation for you to join College Matters in a year or so when you are in college. As a College Matters team member, you would have the opportunity to help others in your community get an edge in the admissions process and get accepted to great schools. You would interact with students like us, full of aplomb and pizzazz. You could host College Matters seminars in your home community, write for future editions of the book, lead student teams, hold the keys to CM online, and much more. Just fill out the College Matters team application form at the back of this book or go to www.collegematters.org to do it online.

If you are a parent or teacher, thank you for supporting your kids. The college admissions process can be draining, so it is wonderful that you are involved.

Here are our final words of encouragement. Remember that in the end, you are still yourself. You are going to flourish no matter where you go to college, if you have the right attitude. Best of luck!

Jacquelyn, Melissa, and Joanna
College Matters Editors

Sample Application Timeline

Month of July

Goals:_____, _____, _____

	MONDAY	TUESDAY	WEDNESDAY	THURSDAY	FRIDAY	SATURDAY	SUNDAY
POSSIBLE CALENDAR ENTRIES							
Get SAT scores back							
Evaluate what I have against what colleges want							
Call Emory to ask for application							
Poke around online app sites							
Other:							

Month of August

Goals:_____, _____, _____

	MONDAY	TUESDAY	WEDNESDAY	THURSDAY	FRIDAY	SATURDAY	SUNDAY
POSSIBLE CALENDAR ENTRIES							
Brainstorm essay ideas							
Write 3 drafts by this date							
School starts							
Run for President of band							
Check class rank							
Narrow down college list by this date							
Other:							

Month of September

Goals:_____, _____, _____

	MONDAY	TUESDAY	WEDNESDAY	THURSDAY	FRIDAY	SATURDAY	SUNDAY
POSSIBLE CALENDAR ENTRIES							
Collect or print out all hardcopy apps by this date							
Teacher/ counselor recs: drop off and pick up dates							
Go to college info sessions							
Order 2 transcripts							
Other:							

Month of October

Goals:_____, _____, _____

	MONDAY	TUESDAY	WEDNESDAY	THURSDAY	FRIDAY	SATURDAY	SUNDAY
POSSIBLE CALENDAR ENTRIES							
Finish early action/ decision application							
Postmark it by this date							
More Teacher/ counselor recs: drop off and pick up dates							
Go to college info sessions							
Other:							

Month of November

Goals:_____, _____, _____

	MONDAY	TUESDAY	WEDNESDAY	THURSDAY	FRIDAY	SATURDAY	SUNDAY
POSSIBLE CALENDAR ENTRIES							
Homecoming							
Interview for XYZ College							
Set up an interview with ABC College							
Fill out the PROFILE							
Other:							

Month of December

Goals:_____, _____, _____

	MONDAY	TUESDAY	WEDNESDAY	THURSDAY	FRIDAY	SATURDAY	SUNDAY
POSSIBLE CALENDAR ENTRIES							
Final exams							
School ends							
Hear back from early action/ decision college							
Possibly: Finish X, Y, and Z application							
Postmark by this date							
Other:							

Month of January

Goals:_____, _____, _____

	MONDAY	TUESDAY	WEDNESDAY	THURSDAY	FRIDAY	SATURDAY	SUNDAY
POSSIBLE CALENDAR ENTRIES							
School starts							
Get lists of eligible scholarships and due dates for each							
Download or copy scholarship application forms							
File FAFSA							
Other:							

Month of February

Goals:_____, _____, _____

	MONDAY	TUESDAY	WEDNESDAY	THURSDAY	FRIDAY	SATURDAY	SUNDAY
POSSIBLE CALENDAR ENTRIES							
Practice for the SAT							
Interview for scholarship XYZ							
Other:							

Month of March

Goals:_____, _____, _____

	MONDAY	TUESDAY	WEDNESDAY	THURSDAY	FRIDAY	SATURDAY	SUNDAY
POSSIBLE CALENDAR ENTRIES							
Practice for the SAT							
Visit colleges							
Other:							

Month of April

Goals:_____, _____, _____

	MONDAY	TUESDAY	WEDNESDAY	THURSDAY	FRIDAY	SATURDAY	SUNDAY
POSSIBLE CALENDAR ENTRIES							
Take the SAT or ACT (younger readers)							
Last minute college visits							
Decide which college to attend!							
Other:							

Month of May

Goals:_____, _____, _____

	MONDAY	TUESDAY	WEDNESDAY	THURSDAY	FRIDAY	SATURDAY	SUNDAY
POSSIBLE CALENDAR ENTRIES							
Take SAT IIs for classes just completed							
Apply to attend summer programs							
Apply for summer jobs							
Other:							

Month of June

Goals:_____, _____, _____

	MONDAY	TUESDAY	WEDNESDAY	THURSDAY	FRIDAY	SATURDAY	SUNDAY
POSSIBLE CALENDAR ENTRIES							
Study for the PSAT in the fall (younger readers)							
Attend summer programs or work at a summer job							
Bum around and do nothing (if you are a senior)							
Other:							

COLLEGE MATTERS SCHOLARSHIP INFORMATION

What Is College Matters (CM)?

Started in 1999, College Matters is an educational nonprofit run by students. CM student volunteers give nuts-and-bolts one-time seminars across the world about how to apply to college and win scholarships. During our seminars, we share what we wish we would have known when going through the admissions process and what led to our success. CM also has a Web site (www.collegematters.org) and a book (the one in your hands), whose proceeds are financing this scholarship.

Who Is Eligible for the CM Scholarship?

Applicants must be either high school graduates or in their last year of high school and planning to enroll full-time in a four-year college or university the following fall. There are no citizenship requirements. Currently enrolled university students are not eligible.

At What Criteria Does the CM Scholarship Look?

- Potential for academic success
- Leadership ability
- Public service
- Extracurricular involvement
- Financial need

So What Is CM Really Looking for in Applicants?

We are looking for interesting students who have taken advantage of opportunities available to them and who have the potential for future success. Winners will have had a unique and positive impact on their community (broadly defined) and will have achieved academic excellence.

Who Will Be on the Scholarship Committee?

- Four College Matters book writers
- Two university faculty members
- Two at-large members, one of whom will represent Let's Get Ready! nonprofit

Why Is the CM Scholarship Based on Need?

We have a limited number of scholarships to give away and want to help students whose families require assistance in financing their education. There is no cutoff, but demonstrated need is one factor that we will take into account.

How Much Is the CM Scholarship?

We will be awarding scholarships between $1000 to $5000, to be paid in one installment. The number of scholarships awarded is a direct function of royalty proceeds from the book.

My Company or I Would Like to Make a Contribution to the CM Scholarship Fund; Whom Should I Contact?

Wonderful! Please email donate@collegematters.org.

Scholarship Application Instructions

We would prefer that you go to www.collegematters.org to fill out an online application.

For those who do not have Internet access, please fill out the following paper application and send the requested materials to:

College Matters
P.O. Box 380287
Cambridge, MA 02238

Application deadline: March 15 in the year you will be entering college

College Matters Scholarship Form

Name_____

High School _____

Home Address _____

City/State/Zip_____Country _____

Email _____

GPA _____out of _____

SAT (m)_____(v) _____(w) _____ACT _____

Ethnicity/race _____

Father or male guardian's

Name _____

Occupation_____

Highest level of education _____

Mother or female guardian's

Name _____

Occupation_____

Highest level of education _____

Colleges you applied to _____

_____

_____

_____

_____

_____

How did you hear about this scholarship?

____TV or radio   ____CM Book   ____CM Web site
____Guidance counselor ____Friend/family member
____Other (specify)_____

Essay (500 word maximum): Please write a personal statement on a topic of your choice. We realize this is very broad, but we do not want to limit what you tell us.

Short Answers (seventy-five-word maximum per answer):

What are three ways your community is better because you are in it?

What has been the biggest obstacle that you have had to overcome?

What do you see as being your goal in life?

Please attach the following to your application:

- Official high school transcript
- Résumé (two pages max.)
- One academic recommendation letter
- One nonacademic recommendation letter (optional)
- Completed FAFSA filing (Free Application for Federal Student Aid)

International applicants should go to www.collegematters.org or write to the address below for an international student financial aid form.

For more information on filling out this and other scholarship applications, check out the *College Matters* book.

Send your completed application to:

College Matters
P.O. Box 380287
Cambridge, MA 02238

Due March 15 in the year you will be entering college

COLLEGE MATTERS (CM) TEAM INFORMATION

Dear Potential CM Team Members,

So you're interested in joining College Matters and helping students like yourself? Below you will find general information about College Matters. Consult www.collegematters.org if you would like more information, and do not hesitate to email info@collegematters.org, with "CM Team" in the subject line, if you have questions that are not answered on our Web site. If you are reading a paper copy of this application, also note that you can apply to be on the CM team on our Web site.

College Matters has been one of the most rewarding and fun experiences of our college careers, and it can be so for you as well. After learning more about College Matters, we hope that you'll decide to join the team!

Melissa Dell
CM National Director 2004–2005

Jacquelyn Kung
CM Founder, 1999

What Is College Matters (CM)?

Started in 1999, College Matters is an educational nonprofit run by students. CM student volunteers give nuts and bolts one-time seminars across the world about how to apply to college and win scholarships. During our seminars, we share what we wish we would have known when going through the admissions process and what led to our success.

What Opportunities Does College Matters Offer for Getting Involved?

- Giving a CM seminar in your home community
- Maintaining or contributing to the online CM presence
- Starting a CM program at your college or university
- Writing chapters for future editions of the *College Matters* book
- Creating press materials for CM events
- And much, much more

What Are the Requirements for Being a CM Team Member?

To be a CM team member, you must be interested in helping others. If you are a current college student, then you can join right away. If you are a high school student, you can apply now and plan on joining the team once you matriculate at college.

It is not necessary to attend a private college, as we also give seminars about applying to public universities. All seminar leaders must be knowledgeable and articulate about their experiences applying to colleges and for scholarships. International students are also encouraged to apply.

We reach audiences through the book as well as through community seminars. In these seminars, we are able to interact with students and parents and respond to their needs on the spot. These seminars are central to the way CM contributes to the community.

What Responsibilities Does Giving a CM Seminar Involve?

- Preparing and giving a presentation
- Recruiting a 2–5 person panel of students (when geography permits)
- Choosing a time and venue for the seminar
- Publicizing the event through the local media
- Thinking on your feet (to respond to questions)

Some CM seminar leaders have also gotten local businesses to donate food and even local television crews to cover the event (but this is by no means required). The CM leadership team will provide you with all the necessary resources and help to achieve these steps. While the process might seem daunting at first, we promise to walk you step by step through it. It is a richly rewarding experience of helping others and learning new skills for yourself.

How Much of a Time Commitment Does Giving a CM Seminar Involve?

The amount of time spent will vary, depending on whether you have organized seminars in the past and a variety of other circumstances. For our team members who only give seminars, they have reported that College Matters is one of their more minor time commitments. Unless adding a single thing more to your schedule will push you over the edge, worries about time commitment should not keep you from applying to be a CM seminar leader. If you wish to lead the CM program at your university or want to hold a leadership position within the organization, the time commitment will of course be more substantial.

Where Should I Give a CM Seminar?

You could give a seminar to students from your own high school or to an underserved group in your home or college community. We also look for students to give CM seminars abroad or in the cities where they are spending their summer. CM students have done all of these (and have incredible stories to tell about them)!

College Matters (CM)
Team Application Form

Name _____

University_____

(or indicate you are still in high school)

Street Address _____

City/State/Zip_____

Email _____

I am interested in:

_____Giving a CM seminar
_____Joining the CM Web team
_____Starting a CM program on my college campus
_____Other

General Question (200 to 500 words—answer regardless of which position you are applying for)

Tell us about your college/scholarships applications process. You do not need to specify where you were admitted/rejected or what scholarships you won. We are more interested in personal stories: what you know or wished you would have known, what you found particularly frustrating.

Specific Questions (Don't exceed 200 words—these vary depending on which area of CM you are applying for)

For Seminar Leaders:

Where is your proposed seminar location (city/state/country)?

Who would be your target audience?

Do you have any unique ideas for publicizing the seminar?

For Web Team Members:

What Web design experience do you have? (It is also fine to have an interest in learning.)

What are your ideas for improving the CM Web site?

For those interested in starting and/or leading a CM program on their college campus:

How would you recruit students to join your program?

How would you keep students involved with CM throughout the year?

How would you ensure the integrity of the CM name?

All applicants should also include a résumé (please, no more than two pages).

Feel free to email the requested information to info@collegematters.org with "Joining the Team" as the subject line.

Or, send the completed application to:

College Matters
P.O. Box 380287
Cambridge, MA 02238

INDEX

ABOUT THE AUTHORS

Katherine Jane Bacuyag, the only American-born of her family, was taught by her Philippine-immigrant parents to aim high and live the American dream. During her senior year of high school, she was lucky enough to garner helpful tips from one of the first College Matters seminars. Little did she know that one day she would be the CM Seminar Director while a student at Brown (life is funny that way). Humble and sweet, Kathy confesses that she couldn't have juggled high school and sixteen college applications without the love and support of her parents. In Chapter 11, she shares a student's perspective on the role parents can play in the admissions process.

Joanna Chan, a current Stanford medical student and recent Harvard graduate, is a true showstopper on the dance floor as well as an accomplished musician. Although she did not have many of the traditional advantages (Joanna and her parents fled to the United States from Burma), she flourished in high school, taking over 15 AP and IB classes, acing the SATs in tenth grade, and winning high honors, including U.S. Presidential Scholar. Moreover, Joanna graduated first in her class of 1100 with the highest GPA ever recorded in her school district. Oh, and did we mention that she skipped a grade in the meantime? In college, she helped to found College Matters and has led several CM seminars. Joanna shares her wisdom in Chapter 1, which deals with high school courses.

Melissa Dell is an avid runner and Latin American traveler and an impressive test taker. During high school, Melissa was privileged—or cursed—enough to take all the tests that make up the so-called standardized testing alphabet soup: the ACT, the SAT, various SAT IIs, and a dozen AP tests. Drawing from her ample experience, Melissa organized and taught ACT classes to students in Oklahoma and helped her high school start an AP program. Once at Harvard, she taught classes on standardized tests to underprivileged students and later became the Managing Director of College Matters. Her accomplishments were recognized in 2004, when she was selected as a recipient of the Truman Scholarship, one of the nation's most prestigious and selective graduate fellowships. Melissa shares a wealth of testing knowledge in Chapter 4, which discusses standardized tests.

Angelique Dousis hails from the Massachusetts Institute of Technology (MIT), where she was a varsity swimmer and team captain as well as a coach of the MIT Masters Swim Team. She has used her Greek roots (and language skills) to make several trips back to Greece, most recently to be in Athens for the 2004 Olympics. Angelique has been involved with College Matters since the first CM seminar in Arlington, Texas, and over the years she has used her admissions savvy to help scores of students. While in high school, Angelique's keen ability to build relationships with those around her and get great recommendations from teachers landed her admission to several top colleges. She fills Chapter 7 with good, tried-and-true advice about recommendations.

Jane Feng of Stanford is what you would call a well-rounded individual. She was valedictorian of her high school and involved in a host of activities. However, it was her ability to clearly present her accomplishments on paper that gave her the extra edge in the college admissions process. She has continued to use this skill in college, landing a job at a top investment bank during the worst recession since the early 1990s. Besides being smart and funny, Jane is great at noticing the little but important things that others miss, the details that give you a big edge in applying. As author of Chapter 5, Jane shows you how to make your hard-earned achievements look good on paper when applying to schools.

Otis Gaddis is a current Georgetown law student and a gifted gospel singer, budding philosopher, and amazing cook (you name it, Otis makes it). In high school, Otis participated in several activities, including nonprofit fundraising and track. His involvement in his school and community, plus his stellar academics, earned him acceptances to tons of top colleges. He chose to attend Harvard, where he led several initiatives within the Christian Fellowship on diversity and inclusion of racial and sexual minorities. Otis's diverse racial makeup and social viewpoints, supplemented by his knowledge of the law, makes him a great authority on minorities and college admissions. He is able to analyze the college admissions and scholarship process for minorities and guide students in what matters and what doesn't.

Mitch Ginsburgh is one fantastic guy who keeps busy editing schoolbooks by day and dancing Israeli style by night. He even runs his own dance class! Before college, Mitch was the college research guru at his high school. Students would come to him for advice on what schools to select long before they would go to their guidance counselors. Mitch got into every college he applied to, and that included big places like the University of Michigan and small schools like Haverford College. He chose Northwestern, where he majored in social policy, kept playing viola, and kept giving advice—only this time as a resident assistant. Mitch shares the lessons he's learned about researching colleges in Chapter 3.

Kiran Gupta, believe it or not, actually enjoyed writing her college admissions essays. Okay, she did find the writing process to be daunting, but Kiran was able to use the essay as an opportunity to explore who she was and what she was looking for in a college. Through this self-meditation, Kiran discovered that Harvard was the place for her, and because she had a killer essay that really reflected who she was (along with some other impressive credentials such as U.S. Presidential Scholar), Kiran is now at Harvard as a government major on the premed track. She teams up with Manik Suri in Chapter 6 to share how you too can write a successful essay.

Evelyn Huang of Stanford is the College Matters trump card, the one who's so impressive that even the most demanding parents can't believe she's for real. Her scholarship awards alone include the Tylenol Scholarship, Masonic Scholarship, Elks Scholarship, Junior Miss Scholarship, Key Club Scholarship, National Pan-Hellenic Scholarship, Ardis Knox Scholarship, Salute to Youth Scholarship, OC Centennial Scholarship, and CTA Scholarship. Not enough for you? Even when showered in accolades, Evelyn is incredibly sweet and funny—a cool person who does "regular" things like ballroom dancing. With over $110,000 in independent scholarships in her pocket, she writes about scholarships in Chapter 12.

Jacquelyn Kung founded College Matters in the summer of 1999 and is the diva who established and molded the organization. Born in China, Jacquelyn lived in Norway and Iowa before settling in Texas at age eleven.

In high school, she was president, editor, director, and founder of a host of activities (not to mention a one-year stint as Texas's Junior Miss). Even after gaining admission to top colleges, her pace of activities did not slow down. While at Harvard. Jacquelyn spearheaded numerous initiatives, from techie startups to nonprofit organizations. Together with a position at a top consulting firm, these experiences landed her at Harvard Business School. In her spare time, Jacquelyn enjoys hobbies such as knitting, skydiving, and foraging for frequent-flier miles. With a knack for activities, it is fitting that she shares her secrets about activities in Chapter 2.

Kelly Perry has an infectious zest for life, reflected in the diversity of her interests, which range from making stained glass windows and decorating cakes to paragliding and bee-keeping. When it was time for her to think about going to college, she was so eager about the prospect that she began visiting colleges while she was a freshman in high school. As organized as one can be, Kelly personally rated, catalogued, test-drove, and analyzed more than a dozen schools by the time she had to submit her Letter of Intent to the school of her choice (Harvard). Needless to say, Kelly shares her insights about college visits in Chapter 9.

Rachelle Seibolt claims she was accepted to Brown University based on the mere fact that she can throw things really far. Just kidding—she is a fantastic student and a distinguished athlete as well. She throws the hammer and the weight on the track and field team and is a 6-foot, 1-inch blond who loves to wear heels, much to the chagrin of short, insecure males. Rachelle competed at Nationals in shotput while in high school and was captain of two varsity sports. To top it all off, she was selected as a State Finalist for the Wendy's High School Heisman. Rachelle lays out what other aspiring student-athletes need to know in Chapter 13.

Erin Sprague takes multitasking to a whole new level. A state-caliber athlete and captain in cross-country, Nordic skiing, and track while in high school, Erin was also president of her chapter of the National Honor Society, vice president of her class, and recipient of the Principal's National Leadership Award. Not surprisingly, Erin had tons of top colleges vying for her. She chose Harvard, where she has since organized freshman orientation week and edited for the bestselling travel guide *Let's Go*. With her experience advising younger siblings and their friends on their college decisions, she'll be sharing her veteran tips about choosing your college in Chapter 10.

Manik Suri grew up loving to read, but discovered in high school that his true passion and talent lay in writing. During high school, Manik wrote for his high school's literary magazine, *Torch*. In his senior year, one of Manik's essays was awarded the National Council of Teachers of English Writing Award (the most prestigious high school essay award in the country), and he also won first place at the California State Academic Decathlon for an essay on international development. Manik is currently a student at Harvard and, as a writing tutor in the University Writing Center, helps other students improve their papers. Manik will be sharing his know-how about essays in Chapter 6.

Alicia Tam, daughter of a New England Conservatory (NEC) musician and an MIT engineer, combines artistic mastery and logical brilliance. She is also an excellent communicator. During high school, Alicia won the gold medal for Interviewing at the Texas Academic Decathlon. It's no wonder she aced all her college interviews. While at Yale, she directed operations of the *Yale Daily News*, and, along with Ramey Ko, co-founded SPACE, a college admissions organization that merged with College Matters. Alicia is always brimming with great advice, which you'll recognize in the chapter she wrote, Chapter 8, which is packed with tips and a winner's wisdom about interviews.